ADULT LEARNING

IN

VOLUNTARY ORGANISATIONS

volume 3

case studies 16 - 30

K T ELSDON   JOHN REYNOLDS

SUSAN STEWART

Department of Adult Education
University of Nottingham

1993

Published by:

The Department of Adult Education
University of Nottingham
1993

ISBN for complete set of volumes: 1 85041 043 7
ISBN for this volume: 1 85041 046 1

CONTENTS

Notes on the Authors

Konrad Elsdon, Special Professor in the Department of Adult Education at Nottingham University and formerly HMI, has had a lifelong commitment to the education of adults, and practical experience in all its forms, including voluntary organisations. He is the author of a number of well-known books and many articles on the subject.

Dr John Reynolds, a mathematician and former HMI, has been involved for thirty years in teaching, teacher training and in-service training. For the past five years he has worked in voluntary organisations.

Susan Stewart has had twenty-odd years' experience in adult and community education, as an adult education tutor, a warden of a community association, manager of a community education centre and as part of a multi-disciplinary neighbourhood project team.

GENERAL INTRODUCTION

This research project aims to investigate the ways in which members of local voluntary organisations learn, develop and change, how such learning, development and change is passed on to other people, and how these organisations consequently affect the local population and its quality of life.

The importance and effectiveness of voluntary organisations in our society has been fairly generally accepted for a very long time. Considerable and growing reliance is placed upon their contribution by statutory authorities at all levels. There is a good deal of descriptive literature about them, mostly about particular organisations and historically oriented. However, there have been few attempts to research the impact on individuals and society which has been claimed.

It might be argued that strong empirical evidence makes research unnecessary. However, only research will tell us what that impact is, how it is achieved, how great, how and how far transmitted. Such enquiries, by discovering the origins and characteristics of successful experience, should enable people and organisations to learn from, apply and spread good practice.

The project aimed, in the first instance, to carry out intensive studies of a sufficiently large representative sample of local voluntary organisations to reflect the range of their, and their members' objectives, their characteristics, and the wide variety of contexts in which they operate. This third volume completes that sample. It will be followed by one further case study. This will seek to show how voluntary organisations in one single locality interact with each other, with the statutory sector and public services, with business and industry, and with professional services.

When the whole of this new and essential body of evidence has been assembled, a cross-analysis of all the case studies will be attempted. Its purpose will be to interpret the findings as a whole, and to set them in the context of such literature and experience as is germane to the topic.

The process of carrying out the case studies and producing a full final report is taking several years. The case studies will be the main evidence for that report, but as the first such body of information they are judged to be of intrinsic interest as well. The reception of our first two volumes appears to confirm this, and this present volume completes the studies of individual organisations. Publication of the locality study is expected early in 1994, and the final report in 1995.

The aim of the case studies is not so much to describe the organisations and their work - though some of this will be necessary in each instance, if to a varying extent - as to trace their effects on their members, their catchment populations and the social environment. Description of areas (however tempting) and activities (however praiseworthy) will therefore be eschewed and commentary, whether specific or generalising, is to be reserved for the final report. Naturally the effects to be traced will be most obvious and immediate in the case of the members themselves. In many instances, however, they will be communicated more or less directly and deliberately to other individuals, networks, institutions and organisations in the locality and perhaps beyond. The case studies will seek to trace these ripples of influence wherever possible.

Condensed versions of the standard aide-memoire which was used as a foundation for the interview programmes and as a framework for recording them, and of a supplementary individual questionnaire, will be found in the Appendices. Only the most essential references relative to each particular case study will be given at this stage. The final report will include a detailed bibliography. The project's expenses during the pilot year were met by the Nuffield Foundation. A research grant from the Universities Funding Council supported it during 1991-93. We are grateful for the imaginative generosity with which the Paul S. Cadbury Trust has supported our work throughout and is ensuring its completion. It and the Boots Charitable Trust are also supporting our publications programme.

Our work continues to be greatly assisted by the constructively critical support of an advisory group which consists of Professor Chris Duke, Dr. John Field, Harold Marks, Richard Mills, O.B.E., and Dr. Keith Percy. Drs. Mark Dale and Dick Jotham, and Messrs Ian Minion and Dave Roddis have helped and advised over computing and related problems. The case studies would not have

2

been possible at all but for the generous help and co-operation of hundreds of members of voluntary organisations and scores of other informants who have patiently answered questions and generously offered hospitality to members of the research team.

Comments from readers on any aspect of the enquiry would be welcomed and appreciated.

K.T.E., J.R., S.S.
Nottingham University
September 1993

Case Study 16

THE WEST KIRBY FIFTY-PLUS GROUP

THE CONTEXT

When the current year's case studies were being planned a number of major characteristics of local voluntary organisations were as yet unrepresented. Among others they included location in the North West of England, objectives centred mainly on physical activities, and an elderly membership. The West Kirby Fifty Plus Group (50+) accurately met these criteria. In the process of getting to know the area in which the group operates, a number of characteristics emerged which require description because they are likely to exert a significant influence upon the organisation.

The first of these is institutional: almost all 50+ activities take place at The Concourse. This is a substantial and well equipped leisure centre with a good swimming pool and a café-bar which serves snacks and full meals. It also houses a fairly substantial branch library and some other public services. It is located immediately next to the bus and railway stations. Bus and rail passes covering a wide area are available to elderly residents, and there are good parking facilities.

Geographically, The Concourse serves, roughly, that area of West Kirby, Hoylake and surrounding smaller communities on the North West corner of the Wirral peninsula which used to be administered by the Hoylake Urban District Council. Most 50+ members live in West Kirby in particular and, in diminishing numbers, in more distant parts of the district, though a scatter of individuals is drawn from as far away as the large urban area of Birkenhead and the outskirts of Chester.

A number of peculiarities make the district particularly attractive to the elderly. It is a restrained seaside resort area with pleasantly understated facilities. Most but by no means all of the residential areas are flat and therefore comfortable for heart sufferers as well as pram-pushers, and access to a full array of shops is easy. So is access both to fine rolling hill country and flat walking, and North Wales is within easy reach, as are the theatres, concert halls, museums and art galleries of Liverpool, Manchester and several smaller towns. There is no industry of any substance within the area but it is at the distant end of a rapid commuter line to Birkenhead and Liverpool and has excellent road links to the whole of the North West.

West Kirby and its environs therefore also attract relatively well-off families depending on employment in the whole of the Merseyside industrial complex and beyond. Its attractions are, if anything, more compelling for them when they retire from work. Both our own questionnaire findings and information obtained from the Social Services confirm a number of typical patterns. One is of young families moving out of Liverpool or Birkenhead as their material circumstances improve. Another is of young professional and business families moving from other parts of the country straight to the area and using it as a dormitory. In both instances people tend to stay on after retirement. There is also a large number of elderly couples one or both of whom grew up in the area, who return to it on retirement from a lifetime of work elsewhere. Moreover, a surprisingly high proportion among the elderly have lived in the area all their lives. Together these factors produce an unusually stable and elderly population.

The 1981 Census showed 22.7% in the old Hoylake UDC area of pensionable age (8.3% over 75) and 32.6% in West Kirby itself (13.8% over 75). Single person pensioner households were 17.7% of the total for the UDC area, having risen by 26% since 1971, and 28% in West Kirby. All these figures are far above national average, and are known to have risen substantially since 1981, though the precise 1991 figures were not yet to hand at the time of this study. They illustrate the enormous need for provision for the elderly in the area.

The factors which bring people to or retain them in the area cause a social imbalance which expresses itself in a variety of ways both generally and in the 50+ membership in particular. A clergyman who is involved in caring and developmental activities noted the very close mesh of services and activities in the area. It 'is full of dynamic people ... A busy place; people are always involved both in work and now in leisure, whether unemployed or retired.' In his view the rate of participation and level of performance in voluntary activity is high. This general ethos may well affect the 50+ Group, since it attracts 'fairly self-reliant, generally competent' people who want to 'fill the time they've got now and in front of them' by joining in activities and, many of them, by volunteering to help others in a variety of ways. Staff of the Social Services confirmed this. They consider the area to be particularly well served by a variety of community groups. Volunteering is very much a natural tradition among a high proportion of the people living here. Comparing it with another, less favoured, area where there is no such tradition except for a diminishing one within families, they find and welcome 'a dense strong sub-structure and volunteer network'.

A final characteristic which is bound to have affected the 50+ Group throughout its existence is that public provision of general adult education has always been exceptionally weak in this area, and that the little there has ever been has become exiguous as a result of the combined onslaught of reorganisation, cuts and high fees. There seemed to be no evidence of mutual awareness; for the elderly, at least, the 50 Plus Group fills a near-vacuum in public provision.

THE GROUP AND ITS ACTIVITIES

50+ was founded in 1983 at a public meeting called by a retired teacher training lecturer who, together with her husband, had moved to West Kirby on retirement. Positive stimuli were the Sports Council's "50+ And All To Play For" campaign and acquaintance with the work of the University of the Third Age. A negative one was that enquiries with the Pre-Retirement Association locally as to what was happening about post-retirement had drawn a blank. The public meeting produced an enthusiastic response; another former teacher agreed to be co-opted as joint organiser, and the group was launched.

By the time of the present study 50+ had grown to 28 regular

7

activities with average attendances totalling over 1,200 a week and an overall membership in excess of 1,500. Seventeen of the activities and some two thirds of attendances are devoted to various forms of physical exercise. The current programme is reproduced as an appendix. There is an unknown proportion of duplication among the attendances because many members attend more than one activity. The individual membership, however, must represent (on the basis of the 1981 figures) a proportion of almost 20% of the old UDC's pensionable population, or a staggering 66% of West Kirby's.

Owing to the uneven geographical spread of the membership neither percentage can be the true proportion of the target population that is attracted. This must lie somewhere between the two; it represents an extraordinarily high and possibly a unique proportion.

This was confirmed both by the management of The Concourse and by senior officers of the Metropolitan Borough's Leisure Services. According to them the existence of 50+ is responsible for a degree of day time usage of the leisure centre which is unique for the Authority's area and quite possibly elsewhere. They were not aware of any other comparable situation nor of another 50+ or comparable group as large and successful as this. The activities it organises are crucial to the provision made by The Concourse because members' payments represent a very substantial proportion of total, and account for the bulk of day time entrance fees and catering receipts. The centre might well be unable to sustain full and regular weekday opening but for these. Alternatively, if it were to attempt to run the activities itself, the cost of providing paid coaching, leadership and organisation would be prohibitive.

All 50+ activities take place during the day. Of the 28 regular ones 4 are fortnightly and one is monthly; all the rest meet every week on Mondays to Fridays. Only singing, snooker and, of course, rambling take place outside The Concourse. In addition the rambling group arranges two 5-day residential outings every year and a number of members participate either fully or as day students in a 5-day residential 50+ course held annually at Burton Manor College. Many occasional and informal activities are arranged by various groups in addition to the programme. They include concerts by the Singers and the Music Workshop.

The structure and finances of the group represent what is, among

8

our case studies executed so far, an extreme along the spectrum from formal to informal patterns. There is no constitution, no Annual General Meeting, and no committee; there are no elections or appointments, no officers, no formal membership other than the decision, after trying out an activity, to join it and the 50+ Group, which is recognised by the issue of a membership card. 50+ continues to be led by the two founder-organisers, and each activity group is led by one or more individuals who are appointed by them, usually after informal discussion with that group's members. Ideas for new activity groups seem to arise from individual suggestions, to crystallise within existing groups, or may be offered by those who are willing to lead them. Where appropriate (e.g. in swimming or badminton) groups are led by individuals who hold the necessary recognised coaching qualifications; in other instances the same or a sufficient but informal expertise is to be found. At least one of the organisers, and usually both, are on duty during the five days of activities each week.

All leadership, coaching and organisation are undertaken in a voluntary capacity. The group is financed by members paying as they go, usually 60p per attendance (swimming and dancing cost 65p and rambling 20p a time), of which 5p is collected by the activity's leader to pay for equipment and expenses, and 55p goes to The Concourse as a sessional entrance fee. The activity groups hand over any surpluses from their 5p per session to the organisers, who transmit a monthly contribution to the Pestalozzi Village where it helps to maintain two students.

This absence of structure has a number of significant implications; they will be discussed in the context of "political" learning, below. It is important, however, to stress here that what look like authoritarian arrangements are, in reality, extremely informal. Respondents kept describing the atmosphere of 50+ as being like a family, and the leaders as being 'like parents'. There is a sense of group and members being fostered, cherished and cared for, not led. An observation ingrained in the researcher's memory is of the unfamiliar and in his experience unique *sound* of 50+ swimming sessions: neither hectic and high-pitched like a family session, nor a grim hush punctuated by the regular gasp and puff of serious swimmers; it is the warmly satisfied sound of some 80 to 100 people with controlled voices taking sensible exercise among their own

9

companionable chatter, greatly amplified by the pool's acoustics.

THE CASE STUDY
Except for shorter visits and telephone enquiries all the interviews were conducted over an eight day period during the Autumn of 1992. For external evidence 9 interviews were conducted with a total of 11 respondents. These were supplemented by a number of informal conversations with a variety of individuals in the town. For interviews with members of a very large organisation such as 50+ it seemed best to concentrate on certain groups within it, since a reliably representative sample would have had to be uneconomically large. Both group leaders and members opted for group interviews. 9 of these and one individual interview were conducted, covering 27 individuals. These included the 2 organisers, 7 group leaders, 6 ramblers (some of whom lead occasionally or regularly), 6 swimmers and 6 study group members. All leaders also had experience of being group members. The concentration on just one sedentary and two physical activities was due to our sampling requirement. However, the respondents, between them, brought current experience of 12 other activities to the interviews. Both the range of activities and that of personal responses were more than adequately covered.

The researcher is most grateful to the founder-organisers in particular for their advice, their help in organising interviews, and to them and all the members and other respondents and informants for their interest and patience. As in any study such as this it was, and remains, necessary to ask how far the evidence of respondents is coloured by their natural kindness leading to a desire to tell a researcher what they believe he expects to hear. This is even more important where, as in this case, both external and internal evidence are not just consistent but a unanimous paean of praise. Yet unanimity, too, is evidence of validity, and praise stood up to probing questions for specific illustrative instances. This researcher was convinced that respondents' views were soundly based.

CHARACTERISTICS OF THE MEMBERSHIP AND HISTORIES OF PARTICIPATION
The membership breaks down into two thirds women and one third men. Given the incidence of male mortality this is an unexpectedly

10

high proportion of men, which may be due to the prevalent emphasis on physical activities. The interviews were supplemented, as usual, by individual anonymous questionnaires intended to cover the respondents' personal characteristics and histories of participation. 21 (77%) of these were returned. They are not a fully representative sample of such a large membership, but they provide useful supplementary information. They are, however, disappointing in that they produce an age distribution which differs considerably from what observation and informal enquiries would suggest is a correct estimate. The figures clearly overstate the proportion of members in the 61-65 cohort and greatly understate that between 66 and 80:

Age	51-5	56-60	61-5	66-70	71-5	76-80	81-5	86-90+
%age	0	9	43	19	24	0	5	0

The discrepancy between return and estimate is likely to be due to the fact that 90% of the interview respondents were deliberately drawn from among participants in physically active pursuits. If the distribution had been representative of the *overall* range of activities and participation the addition of substantially older sedentary groups would have produced a distribution more akin to that of the following estimate:

Age	51-5	56-60	61-5	66-70	71-5	76-80	81-5	86-90+
%age	1	5	15	29	29	15	5	1

The discrepancy is liable to affect certain other statistics as well, and attention will be drawn to this where appropriate. In other respects the resulting picture appears to be reasonably reliable.

The returns confirm the general impression of the stability of the local population and its reflection in the 50+ membership. Of the total, 62% may be described as belonging to the general area. They break down into 29% who have always lived in the immediate district; 9% of the total grew up here and have returned to it and 24% have moved into it from the adjoining conurbation. The other 38% of the total moved to the catchment area from places other than the Wirral and Merseyside generally. A different breakdown of the figures shows that 33% of the total have been living in the 50+ catchment area since making an early or mid-career move and stayed on when they retired, while 38% moved to it on retirement from both Merseyside and elsewhere, leaving the 29% who have spent all their lives in the catchment area.

Stability also extends to length of membership. 39% of the total have belonged to 50+ since its foundation almost ten years ago or soon after, and 14% are subsequent immigrants who joined immediately on arrival. 19% have been members for between 5 and 8 years and 28% for between 2 and 4.

The predictive link between terminal education age (TEA), last paid job and the number and kind of activities undertaken is well illustrated by the sample. So are the possibilities of "self-improvement" and, in some instances, the comparable effects of marriage in some instances. Thus four (19%) completed their initial education at the then minimum age of 14, of whom just one individual rose to a modest managerial position while the remaining 3 retired from manual and unskilled jobs. One of these, however, scored a participation total (i.e. the total number of present *and* past leisure activities and interests engaged in by the individual concerned) of 12 assorted intellectual, physical and social activities and was engaged in at least one voluntary service activity, while the other three averaged just 3.3 activities. The one individual with a TEA of 15 also seemed to be exceptional, with a participation score of 9 physical and craft activities. Three of the four individuals with a TEA of 16 had occupied clerical jobs and the one other had moved on from this to Further Education teaching. Their participation scores ranged from 6 to 11, averaged 8, and included intellectual as well as physical and craft activities. Three of them were engaged in regular and demanding voluntary work. The three with a TEA of 17 had retired from teaching, the civil service and secretarial work. Their participation scores were 7, 11 and an exceptional 20; their average would have been 9 but for the exceptional respondent's score. Two were involved in voluntary work. The largest group (38% of the total) had TEAs ranging from 20 up and consisted of 6 ex-teachers or lecturers and two others. Their participation scores ranged from 5 to 21 richly mixed activities and averaged 13.5. The returns are not entirely clear but this group appears to be most involved in voluntary service.

With the expected exceptions, these statistics therefore confirm the Trenaman effect by showing a quantitative and qualitative causal relationship between TEA, subsequent occupation and likelihood to engage in constructive leisure pursuits in adult life. They also confirm the observation of social workers and clergy that readiness to engage in voluntary service relates to social class (which, in turn, relates to TEA). However, the returns are unusual in two respects. The least, and less, privileged 50+ members are *very much more likely than expected* to engage in constructive activities, possibly including intellectual and cultural stimuli. They are also very much more likely to become involved in voluntary service to other people. This reinforces the impression of a strong cultural and social impact.

The questionnaires also provide some evidence of the influence of 50+ in introducing people to activities for the first time. 48% of respondents had been thus introduced to one or several activities or interests which were new to them, and in which they are now regularly engaged. However, the actual number of these activities and interests was unexpectedly small, suggesting that joining 50+ linked more often with the resumption or extension of interests and their expansion than with a new start. Owing to the skewed sample most really new activities appeared to be physical, especially swimming and rambling, but a surprising number of respondents had been stimulated to make a habit of visiting art galleries, theatres and concerts.

Membership of 50+ thus appeared to extend and enhance people's interests. It did not noticeably lead to any great concentration upon particular ones or any consequent abandonment of activities previously engaged in. However, it encouraged a minority to move on to additional studies at more demanding levels. A number of respondents had, indeed, given up activities, but for reasons such as their physical condition, transport and the widespread but locally erroneous belief that it is unsafe for the old to go out at night. These histories of participation are similar to those from other "generalist" organisations in respect of the factors described. Differences will, however, emerge from other findings.

Some time after the compilation of this account three additional questionnaires were returned. As they were not fully completed they did not trigger a revision. If they could have been used, they would have reinforced the impression of long-term stability and raised the proportion of members with a low TEA and occupational status compensating for these by a wide range of educational activity undertaken both outside and in 50 Plus.

13

MEDICAL AND PSYCHOLOGICAL EFFECTS OF MEMBERSHIP

This case study sheds interesting light on these effects. Indeed, membership often proceeds from professional referral. Most often this originates from a doctor, but some referrals or recommendations to join do so from general or psychiatric social workers, health visitors and others connected with statutory and voluntary caring services. The reasons may be physical such as a need for regular but controlled exercise, social such as loneliness, psychological such as loss of confidence and depression, bereavement or the stresses caused by the sudden loss of role and status due to unemployment, redundancy and retirement. For these and the many other ills, separately and in combination, to which the elderly are particularly exposed, membership of 50+ is not uncommonly prescribed and administered with notable success. Easily visible in the case of the owners of new hip joints learning to swim and working their way up from the short walking group to the all day ramblers, it is the testimony of those who have been helped to overcome, or live with, more painful suffering that is most moving and at the same time too intimate to recount in print. It must be remembered that in a group of the elderly these are likely to be at least a large proportion.

As far as the Social Services are concerned the most significant role of 50+ is thus prophylactic: it keeps independence alive, with all the benefits to physical and psychological health among the elderly. It 'keeps people off our registers'. Social workers meet members professionally only on the rare occasions when they have severe problems, or when they refer them or recommend them to join. Here again the problems are noticeably class-linked: those who do not join 50+, and the Social Services' clients, are largely the same kind of people: those who have received only a minimal education, have held jobs which entailed little or no responsibility, have never been self-motivated and find it hard to adopt such an attitude for the first time when faced with a penurious retirement or redundancy.

Some of this had been implied in the response of the local clergyman which has been quoted earlier. Perhaps the fullest statement came from a senior member of the local medical group practice. While obviously unable (like the social workers) to comment on individuals, his exposition drew on detailed knowledge and careful observation over a long period. Like the social workers he noted, with regret, the fact that it was mainly the socially and culturally advantaged who are active in retirement pursuits, and therefore benefit accordingly: the inactive 'die very quickly'. Socially it is important for the mental and physical health of the old that they should not become isolated. One of the great benefits of 50+ is that it encourages and enables the retired and the elderly to make new friendships to replace contacts lost from work or due to bereavement. Moreover, 'retirement is a very different thing for *couples* from singles'; it strengthens relationships by creating 'a healthy opportunity to do things together'.

Most important of all, in this doctor's view, is a set of positive attitudes to activity - most easily acquired by finding and pursuing an activity that is driven by personal interest. Such a set of attitudes supports personal health, is self-reinforcing, and this in turn 'keeps them away from the doctors'. 'It's extraordinary how keen people get ... I'm quite sure they're healthier as a result.' Moreover, it is not just engagement in personal activity that is important; the fact that so many 50+ members (and others like them) engage in various forms of voluntary service affects their mental and physical state positively. 'The more you do for other people the healthier you are ... it leads to all-round well-being.' This applies to mental no less than physical engagement; the two kinds of activity are mutually reinforcing and help equally in maintaining or even in improving health.

One conclusion from these observations is that 'I believe very much in the *wholeness* of people. ... Someone taking part in these sorts of activities becomes a much more rounded whole.' 'Taking responsibility (as a volunteer), whatever it's for' is an important aspect of this. Retired people who used to have responsibility before retiring miss it. They need to have it replaced in some other form, because playing a responsible part is healthy. And so is engagement, whatever its costs: 'One thing which impresses me is the elderly who're getting infirm and who still come to meetings. It diverts their attention from their infirmities. It gives them activity and that transforms their quality of life.'

SOCIAL EFFECTS OF MEMBERSHIP
Group leaders among the respondents stressed the high proportion

15

of new recruits to all activities, but most often to swimming and rambling, who are referred to 50+ by doctors, health visitors, the asthma clinic and social workers. However, most other members bear scars, too, and are aware of the normal risks of old age. Many, perhaps most, become physically and socially more timid with age even though some convert this attitude to bravado. Serious illness and death are too frequent to be ignored. 'People care, they're concerned for each other. Of course it's always risky to ring up and ask' but 'If I don't come swimming you can bet your bottom dollar somebody will be on the phone within an hour to ask if I'm alright.'

The walking group (one of its leaders says) is often the starting point for new members, and they then branch out into other activities. They have a high proportion of widows among their members. They and other lonely individuals find others of their own kind here, with whom they are able to share their pain. Here and in other responses there is important evidence of 50+ activities carrying out functions which elsewhere might be specialised into self-help groups. It may be significant that, among so many widows and widowers, arthritics and asthmatics, not a single response referred to what might have been considered appropriate self-help groups, but very many spoke of 50+ as a source of that mutual caring and empathy which, elsewhere, are associated with these organisations. At the same time they saw advantage in and greatly appreciated the variety of company available to them within the groups and the organisation as a whole.

This, then, is the context in which members say they are able to do things together which they would no longer do on their own, or lack the social confidence to engage in. The companionship is thus not just a desirable end in itself but a means to further personal and social development. A member of another group pointed out that he felt less nervous about joining because he knew that everyone else was elderly, too. By their very nature, rambles induce people to move between continually changing sub-groups, and this extends the social experience. Coming from ramblers, this evidence can be paralleled from every other activity. Swimmers, too, perceive theirs as usually a start and a source of considerable social satisfaction and personal learning, but they move on from it to lunching together in the Concourse café, to social activities with individuals and smaller groups in each other's homes and elsewhere, and to joint outings;

they tend to develop a large circle of friends. The relationship that evolves is described as 'deeply caring' (it was significant how often the word was used by respondents) and supportive. Moreover, 'it's fun', and fun becomes possible even after losing one's partner because the members feel they 'learn to be really intimate with each other', to form close friendships within the larger social framework.

Members organise their own systems for providing lifts to the centre and back and this becomes 'a lifeline' for people as travel becomes more difficult or driving impossible. This, and regular visiting, also help to reduce the loneliness of the housebound, both temporarily among current members and on a permanent basis for ex-members and others. In all these ways 50+ has come to be regarded as central to people's lives, and they find it enriches them by such an all-embracing friendliness that the table tennis and bridge groups can co-exist in the same hall because they have to. 'It's an organisation that doesn't feel like an organisation.'

Several respondents described the experience of retiring, or first moving to West Kirby, of knowing nobody and of suddenly being terribly lonely. 'It's like somebody opened the gates of heaven when they started this place. Nobody here need ever be lonely again'. Within the group they find they are able to be more outgoing than in individual relationships, and they themselves and some others they know come for one or more whole days or for several each week, moving from activity to activity. Others stressed the fact that for them the group's context is dynamic: 'We do *new* things together ... we make *new* friends ... this is *most important* as you grow older.' Enjoying company, having people to talk to, sharing activities with a spouse after a working lifetime of being unable to do so, conveying and enjoying (quite possibly for the first time) a sense of belonging, are simple but fundamentally constructive ways of filling time and pursuing the leisure of the elderly, as described by two outside observers.

Some of this evidence suggests an emphasis on quantity of interaction, or superficiality of relationships, and it is right that an organisation such as this should respond to quantitative no less than qualitative needs. However, overtly or not, members showed themselves to be very much aware of the frequency of bereavement, serious illness and hospitalisation among them, their spouses, close relatives and friends. They kept referring to the 'massive support

17

and mutual caring for each other' at these times.

For almost all respondents 50+ has thus become central to their social lives and an important stimulus to continuing, or resumed, social *development*. Those who were widowed were helped to cope with their new status; every ex-school teacher among the respondents claimed to have become less shy among adults, to have learned to cope with the society of their peers. Two women had not joined for social reasons at all because they already had a circle of friends. However, being *in a group* had enabled and stimulated them to do more than they had expected and had made them 'more outgoing, less shy'. Even those who are so deeply involved in work for the organisation that they have to protect a separate social life of their own find their capacity for relationships and their social coping skills enhanced.

EDUCATIONAL AND CULTURAL EFFECTS

The formal range of regular opportunities offered by 50+ emerges from the schedule on p.32. What cannot be shown there are the multifarious ad hoc activities ranging from walking holidays to gallery visits which are organised by various groups and individuals. Such information, as well as the effects upon members, emerges from the interview responses and is reinforced by personal comment, often extended, in the questionnaires.

The evidence is rich and external sources, group leaders and members are so completely at one that it would be pointless to separate them: they confirm each other, even though the outside observers tend to couch their statements in general terms, such as 'doing things they might not have had the chance to do earlier', 'following up and developing earlier activities', 'seeing things they never thought they could do', 'activity itself can be a point of growth'. They support the emphasis on physical activities because fitness is a condition of many of the others. Equally fundamental is an intelligent use of available resources such as the local library, where 50+ members are thought (by staff) to represent a substantial proportion of the elderly readers. They know what they want from the service, produce a high number of requests and home in on non-fiction and high quality fiction rather than pulp. These readers 'are aware of what goes on in their corner of the world of books and want to keep up with it'. As loyal library users they are aware of the shrinkage in the book fund and its consequences, but only complain to local library staff.

Members spoke repeatedly of 'the great emptiness' they had felt following some terrible personal crisis or loss, or quite simply on retiring from work, 'when you're very busy. Now retirement gives you time to get to know more about people and about life.' One feels the need to 'have one's mind turning over', and so one learns new skills and revives and develops old ones. The mere existence of the various groups whets appetite and the Newsletter sharpens it. It also challenges members successfully to contribute to it in both verse and prose. The three from whom these particular comments are drawn have between them taken up *for the first time, since joining 50+*, yoga, keep fit, swimming, short tennis, country dancing, painting, singing and conducting. Yoga teaches one 'how to *use* her (sick) back' and swimming keeps another's spondylitis at bay. Singers who do well are encouraged to move on to better choirs; coaching is available to swimmers, badminton and table tennis players who want to progress. The many physical activities naturally stimulate discussion about health and diet generally. People bring in books and compare notes and results, encourage and learn from each other.

The rambling groups seem to stimulate a particularly varied range of specific learning in addition to their remarkable social impact. The leaders take their responsibility seriously and reconnoitre each walk and whatever features of interest it offers. As a result map reading and local geography and geology, local history and pre-history, birds and flowers all feature consciously and a number of members have joined appropriate specialist societies. The two annual five day residential trips to places which combine interest with good walking reinforce the process. The use of footpaths leads to study, advocacy and maintenance.

Most people declared themselves (or, each other) to be very hesitant and lacking in confidence as they take up activities with 50+. The range of both actual and potential talent is very great and people use each other across that range for mutual support and for tuition if, as so often happens, they are beginners or prefer to think they are. Such mutual help is an addition to the leaders or instructors at each activity. This informal extension of the group's resources is valued and confirmed by providing whatever training

19

can be rustled up to turn experienced members into additional leaders or instructors. In several activities members have thus travelled all the way from being a raw beginner to leading or instructing.

This is especially important in physical activities, where some, at any rate, of the members are keen to raise their standards of skill or performance, and safety is crucial throughout. However, all the leaders who were interviewed felt that they had 'learned enormously' not just about their activity. Tolerance was mentioned above all, but also mixing with people, the skill to teach and organise informally, to organise caringly and without the taint of either authoritarianism or patronage. This learning in its turn had helped them to a knowledge of themselves and to a high degree of personal fulfilment, 'to cope with (their) own handicaps', 'to live after a lifetime (of work) in closed institutions'. These are some approaches to self-knowledge and fulfilment; so are others such as the discovery that one is capable of leadership and responsibility for others. There is also the discovery or re-discovery of physical resources which one had thought lost or never recognised, and which are now being stretched to whatever are their present limits.

Whatever it is people undertake in their groups thus leaves room for additional interest and learning and more often actually stimulates it. This may be closely related to the activity concerned or as remote from it as model railways are from bridge or swimming. Such additional pursuits are mentioned no less frequently by those who engage in the Study Group's intellectual activities. Study Group members (who base their activities on the Open University Arts Foundation Course) not uncommonly undertake extramural courses in addition, read widely in subjects new to them, learn to appreciate other people's opinions and to discuss constructively, to bounce ideas off each other, draw learning experiences from other 50+ activities and from outings to art galleries, museums, theatres and concerts. The learning process is intensified by regular writing (a new experience for some, and a skill to be re-learned by others) which, one of them explains, 'made me think more about what I'm reading'.

The educational and organisational skills which have been illustrated in the preceding paragraphs *seem* to develop in 50+ apparently as a matter of routine. There is no formal talk of self-knowledge, fulfilment or learning from responsibility. This may well be wise. But in the founder-organisers' own experience it had to become, gradually no doubt, a conscious process as they learned to re-deploy their school-based skills into the very different adult and informal organisation they were creating. It involved the discovery in themselves of a new kind of leadership and its development in as many of the members as possible: learning to delegate, not to hug responsibility to themselves in order to protect others, to trust, to take the adult teacher's and organiser's daily leap into the dark which is her or his only safe course. Compared to that, other learnings - to become aware of the desperate and the ordinary needs of people in their locality, to learn to play the necessary diplomacy and politics to obtain space and resources, edit a newsletter, organise - were relatively simple.

That these things were learned and are continuing to be learned enables the 50+ group as a total organisation to cohere and to experience organisational (and not just numerical) growth. More often than not this can only be guessed at, but it becomes overt on occasions such as the annual 50+ study week at the local residential college. Its Principal finds that she is able to turn to West Kirby 50+ not just for the leadership of groups and activities but as a kind of host community which provides 'an assured group who are good at meeting other people and drawing them in'. She uses them as 'a welcoming presence for other students coming singly or in pairs' in the knowledge that they contribute an important element to the educational and social ethos of her courses.

There is one area of real or perhaps only potential concern at present. It is difficult to judge whether standards are as high as practicable or, more importantly perhaps, whether there is a degree of progressiveness in each of the organisation's activities which enables all members to fulfil their potential for learning and personal growth. Some of the activities are led by exceedingly well qualified people and others by those whose skills and experience at any rate satisfy the founder-organisers who have to find and appoint all of them, as well as the members concerned. However, there is awareness of training needs in some instances at least. It is a source of great concern to some members of the Group that the current régime of the education service places prohibitive costs in the way of meeting them. At the very time when a voluntary

21

organisation has to take on the responsibilities of the public service, it has been deprived of any practicable means of discharging them as effectively and safely as it should.

OCCUPATIONAL EFFECTS

Only a small number of the younger 50+ members are still in employment and none, as it happened, were included in the interview sample. Two respondents who held coaching qualifications were using them on a part-time basis to help out The Concourse management. For almost all, however, 'occupation' is solely a matter of their own household and, for a few of them, of parents living with them or nearby. All quite firmly regarded their 50+ commitments as taking priority and planned household tasks to fit in around them where possible and to give way where it is not: 'I never have time to do my tidying up.' Family members who are affected by this régime are said to be taking it in good part or even with pride. One husband has taken on a major share of normal household duties on a regular basis to enable his wife to be a virtually full-time volunteer.

It has not always been easy to maintain the absolute principle that all responsibilities in 50+ are undertaken on a voluntary basis. The example and powers of persuasion of the two founder-organisers, who work almost full-time, are crucial in this respect. There has been only a single failure to observe the principle; it led to the departure of the person concerned. The organisation has managed to arrange for one volunteer leader to be trained to a very high standard for one particularly large activity, and this individual has been able to train others to assist in the work.

POLITICAL EFFECTS

Virtually the whole membership undertook overt political action on a single occasion, when they played a major and successful part in lobbying to prevent The Concourse being turned into local government offices. Those with responsibility of one kind or another have had to learn the difficult art of diplomacy and negotiation, especially with a centre management and staff who do not seem to be fully aware of the crucial importance of the 50+ Group to the life of the Centre and the service it provides for the general population.

22

Mostly, however, the members' sense of "active citizenship" is revealed in more informal ways. Ramblers, of course, are aware of the obvious political issues that affect them, such as bulls, wired-up stiles, blocked footpaths and other points of interest on their route. A number of them have become active in the defence of footpaths and public access areas, and bodies such as the Friends of Ashton Park. In addition to the substantial work entailed in running the whole of 50+ and all its activities, a very high proportion are giving voluntary service to organisations and individuals in the area who need help. Some members of the swimming group described how the mutual awareness that had grown from their group's social life had spilt over into their other activities, and especially their awareness of older and less independent people. It is particularly the passive old, the housebound and the institutionalised who thus benefit from the voluntary services of those who are themselves elderly.

The extraordinarily loose structure of 50+ is of particular interest in the "political" context. The founder-organisers are there because they founded and organised, the group leaders because they have been appointed by them. There are no committees or elections and the former monthly open meetings (discontinued on the orders of the Fire Brigade because they outgrew the largest available space) never had any organisational role or constitutional powers. Indeed, there is no constitution. All the members who were asked to comment welcomed this situation. 'There's always plenty of jobs to do for those who want them'. One can learn a lot from the study group, and become aware of all sorts of issues through meeting 'other people's experience and their views and politics'. Groups such as the gardeners and singers, who have to arrange programmes and engagements, have committees. All members feel strongly about being members and having responsibilities in that respect, and some at least were sure that this sense of membership spills over in many instances into social (i.e. volunteering) and civic responsibilities and activities. 'I'm more interested in these matters because of the people I meet in my 50+ activities and the problems which they have to cope with.' These would seem to be the characteristics which make 50+ a coherent organisation, a group rather than merely a service.

But, says another, 'I feel no need for structure' and a third, 'I don't like being bossed about. That's where the loose structure comes in.' One member pointed out that the loneliness of the retired and the old is central to all these organisational issues: they are aware of their need for, at least, company, and for some organisation or body to belong to, but they want it to be *non-threatening* in a manner which they believe is impracticable for highly specialised organisations.

Indeed, the present system of apparently unstructured ad-hocery works admirably because of the skills of those who make it work without threat, 'like a family'. This enables a strong sense of belonging and responsible membership to develop, which was evident both in groups and the overall organisation. Far from being dictatorial, the organisers have created a set of relationships which is, in effect, as touchingly "parental" as respondents kept observing. There is some dispersal of responsibility in the sense that they have largely let go of control of the individual groups, whose leaders thus have the opportunity to acquire experience of the kind of responsibility which is appropriate to an adult organisation such as this. Nevertheless a structure (the term hardly applies) such as the current one can never be person-proof. Fifty Plus is an organisation whose membership must always experience relatively rapid turnover owing to the most natural of causes. It is surprising that informal arrangements are not in place which might enable members generally to be aware of responsibilities, and some, perhaps of varying ages, to learn by sharing organisational tasks and preparing for eventualities which must arise.

The temptation to discuss here the whole question of structures and the nature and place of responsibility and democracy in voluntary organisations must be resisted. It is certain to be an important topic of our final report, which will be able to draw upon the full array of case studies.

PERSONAL EFFECTS
'We're all learning to be happy. Without (50+) a lot of people would be sitting at home being depressed.' 'I'm 83 but I've got younger because I've got something to live for, something to do for others.' 'I'm easier to get on with, far more tolerant.' I have 'a sense of there being a family here to belong to and contribute to.' 'It's the happiest part of my life.' The verbatim testimonies continue

in the same tone. There are many others which go some way to explain the reasons. 'I spend a lot more time out of doors and meet a lot more people than I'd have done otherwise.' 'I stretch my body to the limit and ... I keep fit', and for this respondent that is the beginning of self-knowledge because 'I didn't know what to do with myself until this. My fears about retirement were unfounded.'

The new sense of physical well-being is important for many. As a result of being fitter there is less pain, more reliable health, and that is a direct cause of being more sociable, more involved, more relaxed. That in turn caused some respondents to develop a broader outlook, be more aware of other people's problems, and the resulting empathy makes their own problems and handicaps seem less disproportionate. Two members who had suffered greatly from depression now feel every morning that there is something exciting to look forward to. For another going out to 50+ is an incentive to keep tidy, clean, and dress properly. There is a general claim of greatly increased confidence resulting from the acceptance of responsibility (for instance for reconnoitring, planning and shepherding a ramble) and from the mutual support of members. This is especially true of the women, but almost all respond in ways which suggest a greater sense of physical, social, intellectual and aesthetic adventurousness. Yet at the same time they also tell of being 'easier, more outgoing' or to be with people 'without keeping your corner or keeping up your status ... not being competitive'. A qualified professional in physical education noted that the absence of competition is important. 'To work for personal satisfaction and personal improvement is essential (but) competitiveness can be dangerous especially in sport for the elderly.'

It is difficult to remember oneself ten years ago, and to be sure what caused the changes one believes one witnesses in oneself. Were they there, waiting for time to germinate? Does 50+ merely reinforce what will happen anyway? Does one become calmer, more tolerant of other people's foibles simply because one is ageing? Is that assumption true, or are the old also capable of greater rage, of more "savage indignation" as powers of action lessen? One or two at least value the experience of 'learning to *be*', of becoming more patient and teaching that virtue acceptably to others, to be more aware of them and their needs. The rambles and especially the living cheek by jowl on the 5-day excursions, teach mutual awareness and tolerance, and 'counteract the impatience of old age'.

What does emerge is that every single one of these respondents gave evidence of having resumed and developed, or started new activities, shouldered new responsibilities *in the context of* 50+ and as a result of stimuli received there. There is not just more time now than before retirement, the greater social awareness that leads them to fill it constructively is new, and comes from the group. Many now are 'more aware of things going on around you'; it widens your horizons, ... broadens your outlook' and that in turn leads many to undertake 'a massive involvement in the community'; 'it makes people more caring who'd never cared before'.

What almost all these reactions reveal in one way or another is not just a growing self-knowledge developed in and as a result of the group. For many this is also coupled with a new and not always uncritical self-consciousness. I 'brought this element of bossiness' to the group, says a former teacher, but 'I think I've dropped it.' He feels he has moved from being in authority over people to becoming a member with certain skills to share with others.

All this leads to a sense of delighted surprise at the discovery of being stretched towards unexpected potential within oneself. 'There's something in a lot of people that wants to do a little bit more.' 'I'm not just old Mum now but can take more of a part ... it lifts you up.' But it has also 'made me more aware of the impact of tragedy on people's lives, and how much help we can give them by being there.' And the quality of that 'being there' depends in turn upon 'being better with people of my own age', upon the access of confidence that comes from the successful experience of creating something new and important to other people.

INDIRECT EFFECTS ON FAMILIES, FRIENDS AND OTHERS
Except for a small number of enthusiasts acting on their own initiative, 50+ seems to engage in no publicity other than the monthly newsletter to members, which is also available to the public at the reception desk, and a very restrained notice board in a corner of The Concourse lobby. It must be assumed that, in its small town and established in a central venue, such an organisation will be as it were self-publicising and self-propagating once it

attains a critical mass and continues to meet real needs effectively. Its size in proportion to the target population, and its continuing growth, seem to lend credibility to the assumption.

Members clearly make a habit of talking about the organisation to their families, friends and neighbours no less enthusiastically than to the researcher, to bring them along on a trial basis, and to make a point of easing new members into their groups. 'It's surprising, the difference after a month or so, they're different people ... gives them an absolutely new outlook on life ... they've got to make a space of their own, and if their husband doesn't want to learn he's just got to accept.' Some, of course, are more co-operative: 'I married a man who wouldn't say boo to a goose. We're retired here now and he's running (one of the groups) and a member of others.'

Nor are families recalcitrant. 'They think I'm mad, but they're interested.' Many become involved. Events and learnings are discussed and enrich conversation in the home and elsewhere. As a result the young are becoming better prepared for retirement than the present generation, and they are often proud of their elders, seeing them as some kind of pioneers. Some, indeed, now follow that example by joining classes and other activities, and giving voluntary service. A few 50+ members have started up groups of their own in other areas. The many informal activities such as coach outings, theatre parties and the like which 50+ members have started outside the organisation's umbrella attract many non-members who come to share the interests, want to read the books, and thus generally prepare for membership or participation in other organisations which do not stipulate chronological attainment as a condition of membership.

Many members are very much aware of the important part 50+ has played in ensuring their happily constructive transition from work to retirement. Some at least share this experience with former colleagues and others who face the same prospect: 'some of my under-50 friends are queuing up to join.' There is a growing awareness among people and institutions of the extent and depth of the organisation's success. They are often approached for advice on retirement and, by the media and organisations and services elsewhere, on how to set up and run groups such as their own. Their newsletter has, by now, a countrywide circulation, and some people are known to have moved to West Kirby because of the existence of 50+. It is impossible to measure the influence they have exerted elsewhere, but it must, by now, be considerable.

When an organisation is so widely and obviously effective it would be valuable if the *depth*, too, of its influence could be traced more effectively than it has in this study. Are 50+ members more tolerant of their family members and people in general, as well as of each other? How conscious are they of the possibility, perhaps the responsibility even, of sharing the principle and the means of their own continuing development and individuation with family, friends, the population in general?

EFFECTS ON THE QUALITY OF LIFE IN THE AREA

It is impossible to ignore the fact that 50+ discharges many though by no means all the functions of a community association, and does so, *as far as it goes*, rather more effectively than some of these. It obviously could not function as it does if it were not for the availability of The Concourse and its admirable location. On the other hand it seems fairly likely that The Concourse as a large scale provider open all day and every day, could not function as it does if it were not for the fact that 50+ fills all the space the management will make available to it during five days a week. It is an instance of symbiosis which only requires more willing and efficient management to reach perfection for both partners. For the public it ensures the continuing availability during the day of a leisure centre with all its services. Without 50+ there would be a real risk of a great many other people losing this facility who can only use it during the day. They do so in comfort and with a feeling of personal safety ever since the large-scale presence of the elderly has disposed of the vandal sieges and invasions which are said, previously, to have been endemic.

It seems to be beyond doubt that 50+ as an organisation is widely known in the immediate area, both for what it does for itself and because of the very substantial part played by its membership in other voluntary organisations, and especially so in those devoted to the welfare of old people who are in one way or another less fortunate than themselves. The Social Services' luncheon club for the elderly, several old people's clubs and swimming for the disabled depend on 50+ members, and many others rely on their assistance. Its membership is skewed in favour of the educationally and socially privileged, as has been shown (p.12). The reason, as with so many other comparable organisations, is not that it is exclusive, but that so many members of our society have been taught by its educational system and its socio-economic patterns to exclude themselves. The exceptions in our sample prove that the way in is open, and by no means uncomfortable. In any case it is clear that, as an organisation, 50+ develops the kind of social conscience in its members which prompts them towards voluntary service to those who choose not to avail themselves of membership. As an organisation it opens up a multiplicity of ways of enriching the quality of individual lives through the discovery and fulfilment of personal potential, and it is not content to do so only within the boundaries of its membership.

All this was confirmed by officers of the public services, an elected member and workers in the voluntary sector. At the same time it should be noted that all the organisation's contributions to the area's quality of life (excepting only that to the availability and finance of The Concourse) benefit the elderly and the disadvantaged. There appear to be no direct contributions to the quality of life of the majority of the population. Given the exceptional size and needs of the minority such a concentrated impact may well be preferable to aimless dilution of effort. In its chosen area of work 50+ makes a very substantial and wide-spread impact. The quality of life available to the elderly in the district is high as a result of its activities and its influence. 'If these people weren't all busying themselves they'd be in all sorts of trouble' themselves, with all sorts of troublesome social and economic consequences for the community. The members' claims about the effect of 50+ on their physical and mental health, and the value of their voluntary work with those who need help, are certainly confirmed by medical and social service evidence. 'Once you find your feet in this kind of group you get the confidence to go beyond it', and this is the source of the volunteer manpower that has been mentioned. The example set by the group and its members is also said to have an interesting side effect: younger people in the area are reported by members to be no longer afraid of retiring.

All these are not just ways of improving the area's quality of life, but aspects, however informal, of active citizenship. If that phrase were to be defined as the acceptance of, and implicit education for, overt social and political responsibility, then the organisation appears to be less active or inventive than many community associations. Except on the one occasion that has been mentioned, when its existence was at stake, 'we are not a crusading organisation', though where specific interests, such as those of footpath users and friends of woodlands are concerned, they take action. From issues such as these which directly concern themselves, some members move on to become more generally aware of community issues and the provision of amenities. Many also see themselves, as one interview group stressed, as part of the general effort to 'put a very broad range of facilities for the elderly into the community', and this links to their large-scale personal involvement in voluntary service.

Active citizenship in the narrower and overt sense of the term is probably not widespread beyond the organisers and some group leaders; indeed, officers of the Directorate of Leisure Services thought that civic consciousness is certainly more advanced in their inner city community centres than in this organisation. It might be said that, being better off and better served (though by their own efforts), 50+ members need it less. Yet some of their complaints about conditions and relationships at The Concourse are not only borne out by observation - they are also the kind of problems which, given the failure of personal negotiation, could be expected to yield to skilled application of political nous. In any case it appears that, to some extent at least, 50+ may be an instance of a generalist organisation which does not vividly illustrate the trend that seems to be discernible in others like it, of developing civic consciousness and skills in its membership, except for the limited but important area of voluntary service. Whether the difference from other such organisations is a consequence of limitation to the particular age group is worthy of consideration.

CONCLUSION
As a society we are becoming increasingly familiar at any rate in theory with both the capacities and needs of the growing number of the "young old". Really massive and highly successful ventures, however, which exploit the one and meet the other across a comprehensive range of human social, physical and intellectual

potential for their own good and that of the community at large, are rare. This Project is by no means omniscient, but it is certainly not aware of any other comparable venture that equals the degree to which the West Kirby 50 Plus Group penetrates and serves its catchment area.

Personalities and personal circumstances have played an important part in this instance and continue to do so. But it should also be remembered that at the crucial stages of innovation the founders were matched by a Concourse management which was then equally innovative and dynamic. Elsewhere the feeling that "Authority", and certainly society at large, undervalue the old continues to be justified more often than otherwise. The tendency continues to patronise, and treat them like passive entities instead of fostering their activity and therefore their health, their independence and therefore their creative contributions to society, their responsibility and therefore their continuing personal development. At a materialistic valuation, a small investment in fostering organisations such as 50+ saves enormous public expenditures, releases undreamed of resources and bolsters the determination not to be defeated.

Moreover, what is at issue is not just what is usually regarded as "the young old years" extending to about 75 - the antechamber of old age, leaving the years beyond as that of the great unmentionable. That assumption is negative, ill informed, supine, and far too common. There may be a growing awareness but too little organisational and practical recognition that the years beyond retirement *and* the years beyond 75 are, like the rest of life, a continuum. They *may* be devoted to *constructive* change and development and even to contributions to the common good not just on the part of rare and exceptional individuals, but by almost all who can be placed in circumstances where mutual support and empathy can be released and a really widespread response mobilised. The West Kirby 50+ Group is more than a source of learning and change for its large membership: it has much to teach society at large.

31

APPENDIX: The programme and approximate attendances, Autumn 1992

Monday a.m. Singing (choir)   60
       Study Group (fortnightly)   15
       Short Tennis   30
    p.m. Chess and Scrabble   10
       Old Time & Ballroom Dancing (fortn.)   70
       Art (fortn.)   20
       Bowls   40
       Playreading (fortn.)   15
Tuesday a.m. Rambling (3 groups)   80
       Swimming   80
    p.m. Gardening (fortn.)   50
       German Conversation   15
Wednesday a.m. Yoga   25
       Badminton   40
    p.m. Bowls   40
       French Conversation   20
       Music Workshop   15
Thursday a.m. Swimming   80
       Keep Fit   50
    p.m. Canvas & Tapestry Work   20
       Country Dancing   50
       Snooker   30
Friday a.m. Swimming   80
       Short Tennis   45
    p.m. Table Tennis   45
       Bridge   80
Various   All day tours (3-4 per month)   150+

Case Study 17

THE BEDE HOUSE ASSOCIATION, BERMONDSEY

.

The Settlement idea implies a synthesis of social service, education (including that of settlement workers and volunteers) and community development. The siting of these organisations in deprived metropolitan neighbourhoods made it obvious that one of them should be included in our sample. Bede House is the second settlement we have studied. We decided not to publish the first of these studies, but comparison of findings between them greatly enriches our understanding of a number of issues. They include the impact of public policy on the character and role of voluntary service organisations, and relationships between paid and voluntary personnel.

As a settlement, Bede House is a very complex multi-purpose venture. It embraces an education centre, a café training project for adults with learning disabilities, a project for under fives and their parents, community development and outreach work, a youth adventure project, work with the elderly and work with volunteers. The case study necessarily concentrated on just a few of its activities, and the choice of respondents reflects this selective approach.

Twenty-nine interviews were carried out, and these involved a total of 34 respondents. 25 of the respondents were "internal" and 9 "observers". A number of informal conversations also took place within and outside the organisation. The Project is much indebted to staff, volunteers and users of Bede House and its sister organisations and to many professionals and others in the area. They have been inexhaustibly helpful and endured questioning with patience, good humour and even enthusiasm. The researcher cannot but express his admiring sympathy for women and men who continue to serve their fellows in accordance with their principles in conditions of severe professional and personal insecurity.

AREA, CONTEXT, HISTORY
Bede House serves Bermondsey in particular but its activities and influence extend to Rotherhithe and throughout the London Borough of Southwark. It shares this task with several other settlements, comparable projects with community development, community work or personal and social service objectives. Two points need to be made at the outset: the area needs all the support and assistance it receives, and more, and the level of co-operation and co-ordination between these service organisations appears to be rising. This is a form of organisational learning and change which seems to owe much to staff at Bede House.

Pre-war Bermondsey was an area of docks with their associated industries, and of densely packed Victorian working class housing. There was tight control over both lettings and jobs in the docks: they went to relations and associates of current or preceding tenants and dockers, respectively. The consequence was a deeply embedded insularity among the immobile and seemingly unchanging population. This and the adverse conditions of work and life contributed to an endemic hostility to those coming from the world outside.

Much of Bermondsey's densely crowded dockland area was "cleared" by the war and most of the rest subsequently by the Local Authority. It has been re-developed on a very large scale, including some tower blocks and a prevalence of medium-high cliffs mostly negotiated by decks. More recently there has been some low-rise infill housing. The docks and their associated industries have gone and left unemployment (30% in Bermondsey in particular) and a high proportion (25%) of old age pensioners. The area is deprived and depressing and those who can afford to do so move out. Because it is regarded as undesirable the gaps tend to be filled by those who needs must: young, not uncommonly lone-parent and frequently unemployed families which cram the schools to bursting, black people, refugees, and those who suffer from combinations of these and other handicaps such as physical frailty, old age, or simply being women. They form an ideal quarry for roving gangs of youngsters. Some of these are said to be organised by the National Front and the British National Party, which are said to concentrate their efforts in the area.

The insularity which has been mentioned centres not just upon the area as a whole but upon particular estates, whose gangs of footloose youngsters may harrass "intruders" who look different, or just vulnerable. This hostility of "natives" against all "foreigners" is played upon by extremist politics. It and the many unemployed or truant youngsters make the area threatening and dangerous for those who are at risk. There is a pervasive feeling of fear, especially after school and in darkness. Southwark Park, which is large and very fine, was found deserted even in broad sunny daylight. Violent incidents reported by the local press make a substantial and distressing dossier.

In addition to the problems already mentioned there is a general tradition of passiveness among the population. It includes a refusal to interfere with inner-tribal activities however nefarious, as well as the better-known expectation of being cared for by a high concentration of public services (even now 98% of all housing in Bermondsey is said to be provided by the Council) and by the surprising number of settlements and related bodies which sprang up to deal with an earlier generation of social problems and general deprivation in dockland as a whole. These expectations are now less fully met because the public services have shrunk and are continuing to do so. The settlements could probably maintain or even expand their work in so far as they are prepared to be diverted into cheap substitution for public services. If they stick to their task and refuse to fall victim to the "contract culture" their work is reduced by prevalent short term and under-funding.

The needs are thus great. However, *if* the area ever had any general tradition of volunteering, of giving one's services for the general good, or of organising to combat problems and overcome obstacles, then it has all but disappeared in the physical, social and economic changes of the last fifty years. Bermondsey lacks the skills and motivation which might have been injected by a

35

significant middle class. There is said to be no local leadership that has any credibility with local people even if it has the support of settlements and public services. This is bound to be an immeasurable handicap to any community. It is exacerbated by the reported fact that the only local leadership said to be acceptable on certain estates is fascist-organised and to rest on the authority of organised gangs.

It has become all the harder to cope with this situation since the Borough has shut down both its Council of Voluntary Services and its Volunteer Bureau. In so far as the attempt continues it depends on occasional and time-limited appointments such as that of the Volunteer Co-ordinator at Bede House, whose Borough-wide brief hardly compensates for the two lost organisations and the closure of the local Social Services office: one time-limited post cannot replace so much permanent staffing and infrastructure. New volunteers require training and, usually, continuing support. These used to be provided by the services which have been wound up. In their absence, and with shrinking staff, Bede House and other organisations can no longer use volunteers who need much support. If they are from ethnic minority communities they usually have to be placed in work outside the Settlement's area in any case. In effect, the degree to which lost professional staff can be replaced by volunteers is severely limited at the very time when Government expects voluntary organisations increasingly to take over from the statutory sector.

It might have been expected that in these dire circumstances the major voluntary organisations and especially the remarkable concentration of settlements serving dockland would have given considerable attention to the task of trying to foster active and responsible citizenship and to develop its competences among the local population. However, possibly because their own earlier social service tradition meshed with the passiveness of local people, they had not so far noticeably engaged in such activities. Instead they tended to sit still and grieve as their staffing and therefore their work was being lopped and shut down branch by branch. Only recently, and under the spur of more and more severe cuts in funding, have these essentially generalist voluntary organisations begun to teach and act and co-operate in a context of civic and political (though naturally non-party) responsibility.

The origins of the Bede House Association differ from most settlements' in that it arose in the 1920s and 30s from local clubs, clinics and related services developed mainly by the Church Army. They included a hostel not, at that time, for temporary helpers from the universities, but for local girls. In 1938, when dilapidation and shortage of funds threatened closure and the loss of the workers, it was the former club members who raised £400 to buy the present building, and thus precipitated the foundation of Bede House.

During the war the newly established settlement devoted itself mainly to relief work. It shared in the efforts of post-war reconstruction. To help in this task it imitated other settlements by establishing young residents to assist, especially with youth work, in which not just the usual students but a long succession of young naval officers from Greenwich became involved. It was some time before it was realised that youth work, particularly in areas such as this, requires degrees of skill and street credibility not always found among young volunteers from very different backgrounds of experience. 'The residents' were not uncommonly resented while the experience some of them garnered was not necessarily as productive as the pain involved might have suggested to those who did not have to share it. The analogy with some present-day forms of adventure training obtrudes itself.

Bede House is governed by a Council which consists of individuals of varied and often considerable seniority. A substantial proportion, including three very senior naval officers, were volunteer workers in the past. The contact with Bede House of the young officers who were encouraged to help there was said to have produced a 'magnetic effect' and to be the cause of continuing support by the naval community. As they and others found themselves occupying posts of great responsibility in Government and elsewhere, the continuing engagement with Bede House and Bermondsey assumed a different though no less important place in their lives. 'It's been very important to me ... a way of paying for my own security.' 'To come and see the realities compared with Whitehall' has been a form of continuing political education. This also extends to the clarification of policy issues. Voluntary work is seen to be not just necessary, but 'it's actually good for society' that it should be happening. Yet its continuance, and the social benefits which flow from it, are 'desperately insecure in a way people in

Whitehall don't appreciate ... it would be a tragedy if the willingness of people to do voluntary work were lost' or frustrated for lack of the relatively tiny support it needs.

The Settlement's headquarters is an exceedingly awkward and hard to maintain wedge-shaped Victorian bakery, a worn-out building with mis-shapen and poky spaces used as offices and classrooms, on a bend in the busy Southwark Park Road. Having given up additional premises in the past, Bede House acquired a 1960s designed youth club building which perches on a wind-swept connecting deck between two blocks and is reached by long concrete ramps. With almost bizarre ignorance of local conditions it was placed within a particular estate instead of neutral ground in the Park. Administration, offices and specifically educational work, and the crowded little kitchen which serves as a general common room, are in the original Bede House building, which therefore also serves as a base for most workers. A café project, work with small children and their parents, the old people's group and youth work are based in the 1960s Bede Centre Building which is only a few minutes' walk away.

STAFF AND VOLUNTEERS
Staffing is determined by the nature of funding. The outstanding fact about this is that there are no capital resources, and that, therefore, there is no core funding whatsoever unless the Borough's present grant of £11,000 is regarded as such despite the fact that it is awarded only on an annual basis, and by no means secure. As a result no staff members - not even the nine who are employed full-time - can regard themselves as being secure for more than a year at a time. The nine include the Settlement's director, the volunteer co-ordinator who also acts as deputy director, two full-time adult basic education (ABE) staff, one youth worker, the head of the Children's and Parents' Project, the two in charge of the Café training project and a recently appointed, time-limited, community development worker. They are assisted part-time by a secretary, two accounts staff, cleaner and caretaker, and up to twenty other individuals employed part-time for varying periods in the ABE, Café training, and Youth Adventure projects.

The principles of settlement work, financial exigencies and personal skill among paid staff have jointly created a pattern of "employment" and of relationships between paid and voluntary workers which are unique among the case studies carried out by our team. We have studied, or know of, other professionally staffed organisations which are good at attracting voluntary service, though few equal Bede House. It is not uncommon elsewhere, especially in ABE, for loyal volunteers to be rewarded with some paid part-time work. What distinguishes Bede House from all others we happen to know is a continual two-way flow (and therefore a sense of equality) between volunteering and paid employment, or sometimes a coexistence of both within the same person.

People volunteer for a wide variety of tasks, are cherished and trained. If they show exceptional potential they may be offered short term paid part-time work and immediate training. A few fail at this stage, and their services have to be diverted or dispensed with, but selection appears to be made with skill and is usually successful. If there is money or a newly financed project, a part-time paid ex-volunteer might graduate to full-time work. Several full-time staff specifically stated that it is Settlement policy, wherever possible, to start out by filling part-time posts with volunteers who have proved both their ability and dedication and their readiness to go on learning. Recruitment is, of course, open, but the experience and training of volunteers seem, reasonably, to favour their chances. The system has proved itself not just in the quality of teaching and other tasks performed, but in what it does to develop the potential of volunteers, and in improving the area's meagre leadership resources. 'Volunteers get an enormous amount out of it ... you can encourage them to do things they wouldn't dare do on their own, or aren't ready for unless you support them. They progress very rapidly.'

On the other hand money all too commonly runs out, a project ceases, and so, consequently, does paid work. But not so employment: it seems to be taken for granted that one may, and does, switch from paid employment to voluntary work just as easily as from volunteering to paid employment. It is not unusual for an individual to be paid for part-time work and to be working voluntarily at the same time at either the same or another task. Nothing that could be described as a firmly uni-directional career path exists here. Most full-time and contract staff, and all part-timers and volunteers, find themselves on a kind of Jacob's ladder, moving between roles, and it is a single ladder, not two separate ones.

Most volunteers seem to be in the same relatively young age group, have come originally for training or help in some form, and stay on to serve while unemployed. If they find a paid job outside the Settlement they necessarily leave. This creates a considerable turnover in the volunteer force. Long term volunteers are those exceptional individuals who have the energy to give service in addition to doing a paid job, and some few who seem unlikely to find paid work. In addition there are, of course, those experienced and often long-established volunteers who serve on the Bede Council of Management. The Settlement could certainly do with a sprinkling of additional experienced long term volunteers to involve in its day-to-day work. They might have to be sought among older people from outside. The emphasis on the gains obtainable by the volunteers is appropriate, but so would be acceptance of the organisation's own needs, especially for a core of continuity in day to day work.

There seem to be several forces at work in creating the pattern of relationships which has been described. It would be simplistic to talk merely about abstractions such as "leadership". Rather, it seems likely that here, at least as much as in some earlier case studies (especially Nos. 2, 3, 4, 14, 15) we are approaching the nub of the complex puzzle of what makes for constructive relationships between staff and volunteer, professionals and lay people, paid and unpaid, leader and member, client or user in voluntary organisations. Certain characteristics which are likely to be significant seemed to emerge strongly at Bede House. One was an absence of any feeling of hierarchy, a genuine egalitarianism which was unaffected by the obvious differences in levels of responsibility borne by different individuals. The volunteers included fully qualified professionals, and paid professional staff were only too aware that their own position might alter. This may have contributed to another characteristic - the absence of distinctions or symbols of status attached to either the type of employment - whether paid, full or part-time - or the actual task undertaken. This absence of status distinctions was, however, a positive, not a negative characteristic: it expressed itself in every person and his or her contribution being *respected*. A third, and perhaps the most important, was linked negatively with the first and positively with the second. It was the pervasive sense that "leadership" was exerted modestly by example in every conceivable respect, rather than aggressively by demands. Council members and senior members of staff not only made do quite naturally and unassumingly without any symbols of rank or status but took their share on equal terms of those menial jobs for which voluntary organisations always rely on volunteering; with equal lack of fuss they added substantial voluntary time and service to what might have been regarded as their "proper" jobs or hours; they engaged in continued learning and inservice training no less than they expected and facilitated it for others. Among all those who were observed and interviewed there was an obvious and at the same time unselfconscious respect for volunteers and their contribution, and a consistent effort to find every one a service which was real, which was appreciated, and which stretched the volunteer's potential, however limited it might be, or however exceptional. This was true both of that majority who lived in the catchment area and the rest. All were far too busy for mere make-work.

Given these circumstances it seems difficult as well as improper to distinguish between staff, volunteers and others interviewed when reporting what learning and change have taken place. Despite the resulting complexities, the evidence will be taken from across the board under each heading, regardless of seniority. The only exception to this will be that of outside observers, which will be taken separately.

SOCIAL EFFECTS

For obvious reasons hard information is missing, but it was clear that people attracted to Bede House are especially those who are most exposed to the hostility of the environment which has been described. A monitoring officer from the Borough finds it 'an excellent supportive environment for vulnerable and handicapped adults. It gives them an opportunity to progress and they thrive.' For black people, refugees, for women generally, and especially those who are unemployed - all those who have reason to feel most insecure - Bede House is a haven and often their first or even their only one. It offers them companionship, friendship, the opportunity to form a social network and a set of relationships within which

41

they can feel safe, accepted and welcome. The general relationships which have been described are crucial in this, but physical factors, too, play a part. The sheer pokiness of the building, and the focal position of the kitchen on the first floor, in a spot everyone must pass, is significant. However tight and uncomfortable, it acts as a perfect common room where casual visitors, students, staff and volunteers mingle in easy sociability. People 'learn to make social contacts, to get on with other people'; they acquire a 'feeling of belonging to a place, to a group of people', an ability to make relationships, to be committed. 'We used to take people away on weekends together and these were climactic in that way.' Unfortunately funds for this purpose have now run out.

A girl trainee in the Café Project, a slow learner from a conservative Turkish Muslim family, illustrates one kind of extreme under this heading, however tongue-tied. 'It makes me feel very happy, I enjoy it and I like it here ... (in other places) people weren't interested.' Even brief observation of her handling of colleagues and customers illustrated the astonishing progress in her social competence, as did her easy confidence in discussing it, and her family background, with this European male stranger. A group of local women aged about 30 who had recently joined a very elementary Information Technology (IT) course 'love(d) coming here' because 'it's friendly'; it has formed a social network among them. They had been nervous of the young, of 'dolled-up birds'. It was a great relief that they found people like themselves and around the same age, 'not like school'. So now it is 'somewhere I look forward to coming. I miss it in the holidays' but they have taken to 'pop in on each other at home'. Social learning can extend into one's own family, too. 'It's made me more confident and in touch ... I can talk computers with my children ... I don't need to change the subject now.'

Volunteers with varying degrees of involvement responded in similar ways but usually in more articulate fashion. One, who used to be shy and try to 'blend in' is now the confident centre of a friendship group and deliberately uses Bede House as the focus of her social life. A very young woman who is both part-time paid and a volunteer in one activity (which she was running with immense aplomb) and a volunteer in another, felt that it was here she had learned to deal with people in all their variety and to

42

cherish their individuality. Another, at present purely a volunteer but formerly a professional member of staff here and in other organisations, clearly felt and spoke as such of both her past and present experience, without making any distinction. It seemed that she was giving not much less than full-time service in a variety of activities at professional and at menial levels. The contacts she had made in the groups with which she worked, both past and current, were part of her own natural social network. The same was true of members of the monthly walking group she leads, whose members are drawn from a variety of sheltered and supportive schemes including the Café Project. Here again people learn to develop social networks with her and with each other, and these are maintained during the intervening weeks. This comes as naturally to her group as giving voluntary help to the Under Fives group comes to the Café trainees, who work next to them.

Two young women from abroad who both started as students and are now very responsible volunteers had to travel farther than some, although both had the advantage of substantial educational backgrounds. For one, from the West Indies, the centre developed both social skills and a social network she badly needed on arrival in a new country and a very different society. For the other, too, (from a Balkan country) 'Bede was the first step', providing essential language teaching and the social and emotional support arising from its friendship. It gave her 'the opportunity to do well' and this in turn gave her 'a boost and enthusiasm to go on from there. If you're giving yourself you'll get a positive response from people.'

For full-time and substantial part-time staff the work itself is exceedingly demanding and therefore stressful, but all appreciate the mutual supportiveness which makes that stress endurable. This included an individual who, though perhaps less aware of the overall aims of the place, was nevertheless respected by colleagues who had all pressed the researcher to interview her.

EDUCATIONAL AND CULTURAL EFFECTS

Almost all formal personal learning at the Settlement derives either from users' need for paid work or from the tasks (paid or unpaid) which people undertake there. Most of what would, in our other case studies, appear under the category of occupational learning therefore finds its way into the present section. ABE teaching at

Bede House includes literacy and numeracy, elementary IT and word processing, English for non-English speaking students, and facilities for taking GCSE in English and Mathematics and some Royal Society of Arts qualifications. During the last year a total of 350 students took part. In these overtly educational activities as throughout the Settlement's work the clientèle was almost entirely in the 20s and 30s, mostly female, and included a high proportion of people from ethnic minorities or of foreign origin. This is due to funding patterns which are directed entirely towards the young, and training, including English language work. There is therefore no money under these heads for work with the old, for outreach work or, currently, for community development.

The teaching groups are small, very informal and teaching is usually a mixture of individual and group work. All the students who were interviewed explained that they come to Bede House because it is local, cheaper than the FE College, and has a crèche they can afford. Moreover, 'numbers are smaller, you get individual attention' and (the tutor) 'lets you go at your own pace.' 'It's interesting. You want to go on and on' and the fact that they can drop in to ask questions or use a computer whenever they wish and feel the need for personal support is much appreciated. A typical individual instance is a middle-aged woman who owes virtually her whole functional education to Bede House. She first came for help with literacy, went on to the local FE College but could not cope with the formality, crowds and institutional atmosphere, and returned to Bede for more classes, culminating in word processing. She now does four hours a week of voluntary work in the office to build up her experience and confidence before applying for a job. In the case of someone who lacks the confidence to answer the telephone or the door this will require the kind of personal support which only the voluntary sector offers.

Formal education and training such as this (however informally delivered) is also an integral part of what is offered to the "slow-learning" Café trainees. Thus the Turkish girl who was interviewed has not just been learning something about simple cooking, relating to customers, taking orders and (with assistance) working the till. She is also receiving tuition in oral English, literacy and numeracy, some art, and experience in manipulating the computer keyboard whose value seems to derive mainly from

44

the confidence engendered. Another young woman from abroad, here to learn English and taking classes at Bede House, finds that her regular work as a voluntary helper in the Café Project is a source of enjoyment and learning about people as well as additional language practice.

The progression from student to volunteer (or the combination of these roles) can also be traced in those whose ability and vitality enable them to develop at impressive speed. One lone parent came, very nervously, to acquire marketable skills because she could not afford the cost of public sector classes and crêche. Her course involves three half days a week but the vagaries of public transport and child care make regularity difficult. The flexibility of the small teaching groups and open access at other times deal with the problem. 'We're allowed to work at our own pace and get on with it. You need these places.' It was clear that 'our own pace' here meant pushing the able rapidly ahead no less than endless patience with others. In this case the habit of "popping in" led on to regular and responsible voluntary work helping to organise the use of the computer room. 'I've learned so much up here, it's given me a lot of confidence. When I got into it I found it fascinating ... You know so much, and you want to know *more*. It would be terrible if I'd have to stop.'

A young woman graduate refugee who first came for language help and refuge from the culture shock of arrival in Bermondsey, sailed through other formal learning, 'fell in love with Bede' and volunteered for anything from decorating and secretarial work to the summer play scheme and taking the youth club mountaineering in North Wales. The settlement is the main source of the skills and knowledge which enable her to play a constructive part in her new environment and work confidently towards building a new role and career for herself. Another young woman immigrant who came for language and subject skills notes above all the managerial, organising, interpersonal and political skills she has acquired at the settlement as a result of taking on many voluntary responsibilities there, and outside representation on its behalf.

X, aged 20 and from a refugee family although she grew up here, first came to Bede as a Café volunteer but spread her interests into the youth club (for which substantial inservice training was provided) and into teaching of ABE and art to Café trainees and youth club members. She regarded her formal training as a matter of course and waxed vocal about more informal learning. How to deal with people, coping with racism in the area, including crises which 'can be serious and involve the safety of people', shouldering what she describes as 'enormous responsibility' and being 'trusted to use one's own judgment on the spur of the moment in situations which are often explosive.' She learned 'a different kind of patience' in work with the trainees which involves looking out for problems before they arise; finding the right pace, however slow, at which people can learn routines and teaching them to learn for themselves and become independent; 'finding the balance for each of them, not pushing too far, but challenging enough.' It is salutary to repeat that this respondent was aged 20.

Organisationally the next step, into formally established work, is illustrated by several respondents. Thus a computer engineer who also had experience as a volunteer of teaching English as a second language was attracted by the fact that even part-time work at Bede was offered in conjunction with training for it. He now enjoys the challenge of combining language and IT work. Two women, involved respectively in the Under Fives and the Youth Adventure projects, are examples of the deliberate policy of finding promising volunteers and providing them with experience and training to the point where, though perhaps somewhat lacking in formal qualifications, they are able to successfully discharge responsible paid duties. One, of West Indian origin, is as much concerned to develop informal parent education as the immediate task. The other came from office work into voluntary youth work; Bede House gave her both responsibility and extensive opportunities for professional inservice training for her task of informal education. However, as a result there has also been much personal learning, widening horizons of interest, motivation and activity and she now feels able to sustain all these and to take responsibility both for herself and for a rapidly growing variety of tasks.

Two respondents illustrate the tendency for professionally based full-time work and volunteering to blur into each other. One, who first came after marriage breakdown as a client, student and volunteer received the kind of work experience that enabled and taught her to learn and then take up formal training because 'here you can make mistakes in safety'. She feels that although her

46

formal training in community work was based elsewhere, it was here she developed what she regards as the central skills of community work: overcoming her own shyness, communicating, listening, the ability to help others and encourage them to build up their own confidence. She eventually returned (through open recruitment) to Bede House as a fulltime worker on a limited project, but this closed down. Now she continues as a volunteer although in the meantime she has found a full-time post elsewhere. Another, with a not dissimilar history, now has a very young family but continues to give voluntary help, training and supervision in various Bede House projects. This has meant a variety of contacts with adults with learning difficulties which 'has removed fears I hadn't even been aware of' and at the same time enabled her to learn and understand more about both these adults and her own toddler. She has become more aware of what she calls 'the paramountcy of process, not just task', and of the sense of achievement which can be conveyed by not just the Café training but the monthly walks in which she leads these and other people with learning difficulties and personality disorders.

Both of the full-time teachers responsible for the education programme are themselves products of the voluntary system, having started as volunteers, and moved on from part-time to full-time work while undertaking inservice training to a very high standard. Both appreciate the opportunity and the need offered by the Bede context to be learning new skills all the time in their subject fields and in awareness of and skills with people. In both respects they are 'learning continually that stereotypes don't work, that people's potential is enormous, it only needs unlocking'. The sense of a learning environment whose progressive challenge is shared by the teachers is potent.

Most students are women, 95% are unemployed, and a very high proportion are under-educated, former school drop-outs and the like. However, the desperate need students feel for work and any instrumental skills that may lead to it does not negate the unintended and underlying learning needs which facilitate the looked for occupational progression. For some at least the specific learning they do is essentially a vehicle for what may well be a more important underlying purpose which may or may not be hidden. However, it is anything but incidental and 'staff and

47

voluntary workers are always aware of these other agendas'. Some come with a need for involvement, learning to make relationships, political awareness in the sense of an ability to assert themselves and pursue their rights. Finally, ABE or IT may, in reality, be more and more often care and occupational therapy for psychiatric patients discharged from hospital into non-existent community care.

For all of these Bede House is a way back into the education system and virtually the first positive experience of it for many. Quite apart from the fact that people on social security cannot afford even the reduced fees charged to them by the FE college, Bede House is in their own area, thus saving much or all transport costs, and has that crucial adjunct to this form of education, a crêche which poor people can afford. The importance of open access, and the informality and intimate scale, to the ability to attend of harrassed, depressed and unconfident women who entrust themselves to the organisation has been recorded earlier from their own evidence. 'Adults' lives don't fit into two hours per week time tables. They cross all subject boundaries.' Therefore effective teaching needs individual work, small groups, open access. It also requires from the teacher 'more and deeper personal involvement', personal decision making and 'immediate responses to what people want'. This kind of learning and involvement are available in a voluntary organisation such as Bede House, and staff are prepared to put up with the drawbacks - insecurity, 'the continual waste of time on scratching round for funds' - for the sake of the personal responsibility, challenge, flexibility, and freedom of action they want for themselves and need for their students.

OCCUPATIONAL LEARNING
This standard section of our case studies has, on this occasion, been almost entirely absorbed into the preceding one. Occupational learning is the primary purpose of a large number of those who regularly use the facilities of Bede House, and an important part of the learning done by both volunteers and staff. The evidence is impressive, but so, too, is the way in which occupational and personal learning form a single process whose elements support each other. Both would be diminished by separation; the occupational element in particular might not materialise at all if it

48

were not for the personal one, 'the paramountcy of process' referred to by one of the respondents. This combination of elements is no less important where volunteers and paid staff are concerned, and it plays a major part in creating the unusual kind of Jacob's ladder between roles which was referred to in the introductory section on staff and volunteers. Beyond this only two points remain to be made. One is to note that both staff policy and student evidence show the systematic link which is developed for every learner at Bede House between learning itself, the development of practical experience, and help in finding appropriate employment. The other is to stress the great importance which is attached to both initial and inservice training for volunteers and staff in order to enhance individual professionalism and the continuous learning and development of the organisation itself.

These findings also apply to full-time staff, including senior members. The demands upon them, and consequent personal and occupational learning, may well be greater in proportion to a range of responsibilities which not only draws on all their previous experience but requires its continual extension into new areas.

POLITICAL EFFECTS
Staff are very much aware of political dimensions in their work. There is the continual struggle to key into the political system in order to obtain the resources which the Settlement needs to carry on its work. There is also their own professional engagement with local society and all its groupings and problems, and finally the educational need to help students to understand their own situation, and to pursue their personal rights in what must seem to many a hostile environment. Staff were too modest to make any such claim, but the evidence was clear that most if not all (including part-timers and volunteers) *chose* to accept the demanding conditions, the insecurity and the lack of prospects here in preference to working in the less demanding and better found ambience of public institutions. A young volunteer showed an intelligent appreciation of the way in which both of the Bede projects on which she works depend on Local Authority policies and decisions; she takes a continual interest in these, had collected up-to-date information, and participates in deputations to discuss youth work funding with councillors and officers; she informs the young members and takes

49

them to these meetings. A staff member confirmed this and mentioned that a notable proportion of youth club members had become informed, active and involved citizens more particularly in the wake of cuts in provision.

At a more immediate level it was clear that members, students and volunteers generally learn to co-operate and work in teams. Volunteers have to be taught to facilitate these processes, and to encourage people to speak out in front of each other and discuss issues. The volunteer typist who first came for ABE work told how the material she is typing has made her more aware of the social problems of the area, of facilities which are available and the 'organisations around the place'. 'I've become involved ... I'm more socially aware of what's going on locally ... things you don't really think about.'

Two others who had also started from ABE work but had progressed far into independence and responsible volunteering, were more deliberate and articulate. One had developed a clear-cut and conscious passion to serve her local community and showed herself inventive in devising means of doing so. She wanted to find ways of making her local community more friendly and open. Here was a civic consciousness that was fuelled by a desire to serve and help rather than merely get her dues. But her learning as a volunteer had also made her aware of links from these activities to personal career planning and an enriched *curriculum vitae*. The other said 'I have a sense of this community now, of owning it'. She had learned about the processes of central and local Government policy making and their effects on local people, for instance the elderly, or the single parents in her own group. She felt she had become 'more aware of the way the world is going, how it affects people, and wondering who's going to pick up the pieces'. She had 'learned that a community has to fight to hang on to things'. Her service had made her politically informed and aware, had her 'struggling to understand, to listen' and seek for solutions because 'just doing *something* is important for people'.

'Quite a few of our students become what you might call active citizens' and occasionally this leads to individuals taking action or acquiring formal responsibilities outside the Bede House penumbra. One former student became a local councillor. A deeply involved volunteer serves on one of the Settlement's committees, represents

Bede House on several other groups and acts as an adviser on its behalf. She finds her newly acquired responsibility as chair of her local tenants' association and the local family centre stressful and greatly appreciates the support she receives from Settlement staff. There is also a general sense of responsibility for the quality of society or its content. One respondent expressed it by claiming that she senses 'a feeling of sparkle and enthusiasm' in the Bede organisation as compared to her experience of the statutory sector, a 'sense of personal commitment to service'. This she saw as the reason why people's response in terms of learning and personal growth was all the greater: 'you're filled with a positive charge.'

All staff have had to learn what it means to be engaged in work which is a 'battleground between central and local Government', to be 'on the *inside* of pressure', and 'at the mercy of local politics'. Learning to cope with cuts, fund raising and the resulting mountains of paperwork and yet to hang on to the educational and social purpose of Bede's work, about the need for and the practice of inter-organisational co-operation, and learning how to teach the inexperienced to become active citizens, has become crucial to survival.

PERSONAL EFFECTS
Under this heading as others there is a wide range of response. Staff, very properly, are cautious in their claims regarding the users: 'you can encourage them to do things they wouldn't dare do on their own, or aren't ready for unless you support them. They progress very rapidly.' About their own learning and change they were outspoken. 'Here I'm at the raw edge all the time', being fully stretched, having to 'fall back on me as a person, not me as a role' but discovering that it is possible 'to survive professionally and support others' in the process. Learning in these ways to discover oneself, one's unexpected capacities, one's energy and creativity, and being able to accept and enjoy success, appreciation and support as well as retaining a sense of humility in the face of new tasks and responsibilities; taking satisfaction in both building and being part of a team and fostering its members; growing the patience to stand back and think and plan as well as the energy to respond - all these are ways in which staff members have to and indeed do grow very rapidly indeed under the stress of their tasks.

They learn to believe in themselves and discover that 'there are ways through ... despite all the insecurity'. This is why those who survive 'have grown hugely in their understanding of their own abilities. Given praise they are more confident in tackling the next job. Then they surprise themselves and others by the rapidity and extent of their personal progress.'

Users and volunteers on their own account - even the least articulate - made equally positive responses, such as 'it's given me an interest, personal satisfaction, keeps the mind going.' Of students, a teacher says that over the long periods some of them come and go and return their personal confidence grows, and above all their 'confidence in their ability to learn *something*'. They learn to make social contacts, to get on with other people. They acquire a feeling of belonging - to a place, to a group of people; they learn to make relationships and be committed. Bede House enables people 'to envisage the possibility, and then to have the ability' to learn, to 'push for something and push themselves, to have aims of their own'. More personally, 'it's very important (to a teacher) to see that women have confidence'. This gives her work 'intrinsic value and makes it satisfying. But it's also draining.' Yet she enjoys being fully committed and used, the autonomy of being able to have an idea and see it through to its fruition. All this has given her the confidence to experiment and plan by herself. She has become aware of owning a broad repertoire of skills rather than a narrow line of methodology. And this in turn is linked for her with the 'continual process of learning about people' which arises from the fact that she is 'privileged ... people are prepared to share bits of their lives with you ... you wouldn't learn this from books, or even your own circle of friends."

There is evidence that girl volunteer youth workers who are former members of the club have 'discovered that (they) *can be active'*. This has greatly enhanced their confidence to do what *they* want to do and freed them from the universal peer pressure to 'keep down ... be passive'. An ex-volunteer, now a staff member, has become much more confident and is able to take responsibility for herself and her tasks, to sustain her growing interests, and to share them with others. One of the young volunteers referred to here says quite simply that the 'responsibility Bede has given me has helped me to grow up'.

Two young mothers may be given the last word here. 'This is good for me. You're so out of contact once you've children. You're out of contact with everything. You're a mum and that's it.' This caused her nervousness and total lack of confidence when she first came. She was also very vague about what she actually wanted. The course she took at Bede House encouraged her, developed her confidence and gave her a sense of her own individuality and worth. It also gave her a sense of a definite goal, the determination to achieve it, and the good sense to go for instrumental interim goals like voluntary work as both pleasurable occupation and relevant work experience. 'It's a place where you could grow', said the other. 'It changed my life and helped me to find inner strength' after the breakdown of her marriage. 'It's given me a sense of my own worth, that I could do things ... I value myself now. I don't have to prove anything to anybody any more ... I learned to like myself (and) I'm much more able to accept other people as they are.'

EFFECTS ON OTHERS

Given the limits of the clintèle, interview responses suggested that these effects were mostly within a narrow range. The most obvious impact is upon the children of women who are involved. It is direct in the case of those who use the Under Fives project and the summer play scheme which 'was really good for my children' because it provided new and important experiences for them. Several mothers mentioned that their own learning enabled them to share their children's educational experiences and facilitated conversation on more equal terms. Informal chat in classes or the Bede House kitchen not uncommonly focuses on children and family relationships; in this way and also through the Under Fives some parent education takes place which respondents say is sometimes shared with friends and neighbours. The Youth Adventure Project, on the other hand, was reported to make a very considerable impact on friends who 'get dragged along' and then undergo the same personal and social development which was reported earlier.

All the women claimed that they were passing on their increased confidence, their discovery of themselves and their potential, the possibility of change, to their children and sometimes to other women. Transmission to husbands or partners was less common; it was said that 'it does not always work' and 'depends on the strength of the relationship': it makes social and emotional demands not all husbands can or are willing to meet. Instances of marital breakdown resulting from women's personal and social change were known to have occurred. The phenomenon is known from other, comparable, developments.

In a more general way the few middle-aged and older people interviewed pass on information rather than influencing their contacts more deeply. The group of old ladies who meet for tea and chat is fairly static but does let some others know that the facility exists. A middle-aged ex-student and current volunteer noted that 'when you work in an office you come out and forget. Here you educate other people about what (the people at the Settlement) do.' She herself claims to be doing this very thoroughly in the case of her daughter and her neighbours. Evidence of major influence upon others emerged mainly in the case of the necessarily few very exceptional individuals. These kept being mentioned with pleasure and admiration by other respondents as examples of social and learning gain, dedication, responsibility and personal influence on other people's development.

ORGANISATIONAL LEARNING AND WIDER EFFECTS

Because of the nature of a settlement's role these two topics are so closely related that they must be discussed together. Some of the evidence on them has been presented in an earlier context (cf. p. 35f. above) and some repetititon is inevitable. The most significant responses about effects on the catchment area will necessarily arise from the evidence of those who are not directly involved, which follows the present section.

It may well be the relationships which are demonstrated and fostered at Bede House that are responsible for the remarkable way in which a wide spectrum of roles has developed in the organisation. With people continually learning new skills and maturing into confidence, they move in and out of various activities from "client" (the Settlement wisely calls them "users"), to volunteer, part-time worker, occasionally staff member, trainee professional, move to a post elsewhere but return as a volunteer in a new capacity. It must be stressed that this fluidity is real; it enables the

54

organisation to ensure its own learning and development as well as that of the individuals concerned. It is also a contribution, albeit modest, to the local community's own leadership potential.

Respondents had learned from substantial experience that in one respect this pattern is perhaps too common. Because of the virtual absence of core funding most of Bede's work has to be done in the form of time-limited projects, and it is only in the current dire conditions that well-qualified people can sometimes be found to compete for such insecure posts. Moreover, the duration of project funding is almost invariably too short. Many ventures have therefore to be wound up before they are fully mature and effective; lack of permanent core staff means there cannot be a continuation by supervised volunteers. Nevertheless it is the researcher's impression that the Bede House Association has not, so far, sold its birthright for the mess of pottage offered by the "contract culture". Most of its work is still done on the basis of what the organisation itself has learned from competent enquiry is needed by its area. It has been planned as work appropriate to an independent voluntary organisation, and is being done as freely and conscientiously as limited and short-term resources permit. Professional staff, Council members, colleagues and Local Authority officers are all equally convinced of the need for organisations which engage in a general *and coherent* range of community work. This alone can enable needs to be properly identified, resources to be developed and deployed sensitively, accurately, and with the economy that arises from relating them to each other. The loss of such generalist organisation and expertise, or its conversion due to a concentration on separate specialist contracts, would reduce both the effectiveness and the economic efficiency of the work.

The concentration upon voluntary work and the training of volunteers is thus not just an imposed necessity but a deliberate policy, in that it enhances the permanent social and civic resources of the area. However, by focusing solely upon the needs and the training of those whom the imposed direction of its funding brings into its ambit, the Settlement may be limiting unnecessarily its own resources and the range and depth of its service. Some of the tasks that need to but cannot at present be discharged require experienced volunteers able to serve over a period of years rather than briefly until they find a job. Some might even be well qualified to start with, and since they would usually be older they would also give the organisation a more natural age balance, and facilitate organisational learning. So far, a respondent pointed out who has known Bede House almost as long as it has existed, it has shown itself to be 'flexible and responsive to need and able to change with the times', but it has also managed to 'retain its central objectives and its soul'. He was by no means the only respondent who drew attention to the pressures and temptations leading in the opposite direction.

The problems caused by funding patterns are shared with other settlements and comparable organisations in the area. Between them they have set up structures which enable them to collaborate in trying to mitigate the effects. They are learning from each other's experience, supporting each other professionally and sharing tasks. In these ways organisational learning proceeds co-operatively as well as in the individual organisations.

It is impossible to gauge from internal evidence the degree to which Bede House is able to influence the major social and civic problems to which it addresses itself. What does emerge from these sources is the way in which the very problems of funding and political support to which it is subjected contribute to the social and political education of trainees, students and volunteers as well as staff. It was clear that people had learned much about the decision making processes and finances of Local Government, and about ways in which they, as citizens, could attempt to influence them and defend their own rights and those of people too weak to do so themselves. The fact that the Bede House Association survives sturdily is evidence of its effectiveness in helping those who are associated with it to become active citizens.

EXTERNAL EVIDENCE
Nine external observers were formally consulted. They included officers of the Borough and the London Docklands Corporation whose duties include monitoring the effectiveness of Bede House and advising these bodies on the settlements' grant applications, a health visitor responsible for the area generally and a clinic serving it, and also staff of other organisations and projects which are active in the Borough. Some of the Local Authority views have already been noted in the preceding section.

The health visitor is particularly knowledgeable about the Under Fives and the Café training projects. In the former she finds that, apart from the advantages to the children, mothers learn about child care, parenting generally and play. Especially important for these particular women is that they learn to co-operate with each other and with other women. The work in this group also links them with ABE and, where needed, with English language classes. The Café provides them with food and consumer education. Bede House thus links closely with and greatly enhances her own work: it provides places, activities and services which her clients need, to which she can refer them or, more often, take them personally in the knowledge that they will be welcomed and cared for. By its provision Bede is a 'source of enormous long term savings to the Health Service, the Social Services and special education'.

In the respondent's experience this is possible only because the scale of the work is small and intensive, with 'lots of individual work in a small group context'. This approach is essential in the given area because it is 'extremely hard to get difficult or deprived people to go out or to any sort of organisation'. They are afraid of groups and institutions because they have 'been trained over generations to keep themselves to themselves'. However, she manages to take them to the Bede Centre, and once there they feel the benefits, and these affect families and whole neighbourhoods. Such work is slow, however, and there is the need to 'stick at things'. The respondent hopes that all may be well, but worries about the insecurity and brief span of Bede projects. Meanwhile she also appreciates the benefits from co-operation and joint work with Bede staff on identifying needs and planning how to meet them.

The various officers of grant-aiding arms of the Local Authority and the Docklands Corporation, though separately contacted, responded with remarkable unanimity. Like others they noted the importance of Bede's being a multi-project organisation, and managed in such a way that all its various activities reinforce each other. They found that this greatly enhances the resulting learning and personal development of users as well as paid staff and volunteers. It is accepted that the Settlement 'is responsive to the needs of a difficult area. It's successful because it has a caring staff who're very committed and courageous in their work, and that's despite being subject to personal physical attacks'.

Beyond this, officers find Bede's response to its area is effective because theirs is 'an ethos of quality rather than quantity'. It is accepted that to make an impact in the given conditions requires intensive work with necessarily small numbers: 'service contracts with us would have the opposite effect and make the work less effective.' Officers quoted evidence and evaluations to support their claim that *because* of its approach and methods the organisation is 'making a real contribution to the quality of life in a particularly deprived area'. They found that insecurity of financing was 'frustrating and wasteful of devoted and highly skilled effort'. They also praised the effectiveness with which users of the Settlement's services had learned more recently to understand local politics as they affected them, and to take an active part.

Individual professionals from other organisations in the area confirmed all these points and especially that about the political education of organisations and individuals. They added others: 'I have a feeling that it's one of those centres of excellence that understands the work and gives out a lot too to other schemes in the Borough. I quickly learned to expect support from them. I use them as a resource centre and a reference point.' All spoke of close relationships and mutual assistance which have developed more particularly from Bede's initiatives in setting up co-operative structures, providing advice and information, and seconding volunteers. 'It made me feel a lot more supported, less isolated ... one is desperately alone' was one development worker's personal response, but she also spoke of the benefits of co-operation and collaboration between her own and Bede's projects, the reciprocal learning, joint action, and the sense of a network of people working together in the area and being supported and fostered by Bede House. They make 'a notable impact locally on how to work, manage, involve locals (in community development) in a real way', and this is shared with the other organisations and accepted by the Authority as a general source of expertise. Bede is also respected for the contribution it makes at national and international levels through the settlements' national organisation.

After mentioning such external roles Bede's colleagues tended to recur to the evidence of work on the ground. 'They have to go for real and deep-seated changes in individuals so that they'll grow into oak trees ... we shouldn't underestimate the thing about empowering and the importance of (the quality of) process to end product. This, the breaking down of isolation, and the setting up of groups such as tenants' associations and 'the organisational changes they precipitate' lead to 'significant changes in personal attitudes'. And since 'communities are made up of individuals ... their quality of life's improved, and that's no mean achievement'.

Case Study 18

A WEST LONDON COMMUNITY CENTRE

BACKGROUND AND STRUCTURE

This Centre was chosen as a large organisation located in a London suburb, which included a variety of sports amongst its activities. The Centre is a very imposing mid-nineteenth century building, surrounded by a 1930s housing estate. In 1945 it was leased by the Local Authority to a Community Association. The Local Authority employed a warden to manage the Centre to the satisfaction of the Community Association, and also provided caretaking and cleaning staff and part-time clerical support. In April 1992 the Association became a company with fifteen directors, twelve of whom represent different interests and activities in the Centre. They and three Local Authority representatives were recruited from the existing management committee to serve for one year, after which they are eligible for re-election at the first Annual General Meeting. The warden, now designated manager and still employed by the Local Authority, acts as company secretary. The company has a 10 year fixed lease of the Centre at a reasonable rent.

The Board of Directors has in its business plan defined the Centre's purpose as 'to provide sporting, recreational and educational activities and other activities as may be deemed appropriate to a community centre', to operate the company prudently according to the law and to ensure financial viability. They define the whole Local Authority area as their catchment for the generation of income and the more immediate locality for community based activities, an area containing approximately 18,000 homes ranging from blocks of council flats to detached suburban residences.

Over the years, the Community Assocation has been an umbrella organisation for a large number of groups and activities. Uniformed youth organisations, a lunch club for the elderly, a major dramatic society, open youth clubs, a branch of the Citizens Advice Bureau, a health clinic, mothers and toddlers club as well as sports and single interest groups have featured in the Centre's programme. It has always housed an adult education programme which was provided until April 1993 by the Local Authority adult education service and thereafter by the local further education college in space rented from the Centre.

Forty one clubs and groups, twenty four of them sports groups, are at present based at or regularly use the Centre. A change to individual membership instead of group affiliation is taking place, and the administrative officer estimates from the incomplete records gathered so far that there will be around 900 members plus the adult education students (at present 300) and junior users (estimated at around 200). There has been no recent census of weekly usage but, aggregated from the booking sheets, visits total between 1500 and 2000 each week.

The researcher wishes to thank especially the manager and the administrative officer for their help and kindness, as well as the directors and other members, users, community workers and local people who gave generously of their time. She is grateful to the directors for permitting her to attend a Board Meeting.

THE INTERVIEWS
Information was gathered from fifty seven people. Thirty four of these were interviewed at some length, either singly or in two or three instances in small groups. Shorter, less formal conversations took place with other informants in the Centre and in its catchment area. Some of the respondents represented more than one interest or point of view, for example that of a director and a member of a user group, or that of a local resident who is also a part-time member of staff. Between them, the respondents represented a cross section of interests from within and from outside the Centre.

Interest	No. of respondents
Directors	11
Members of user groups (including adult education)	36
Outside observers	12
Members of full- and part-time staff	6

The total of 65 includes the duplications referred to.

THE DIRECTORS

The present Board is made up of twelve men and three women and eleven and the manager were interviewed.

The age distribution of the sixteen people involved in managing the Centre is:

20-30, 1; 31-40, 1; 41-50, 4; 51-60, 6; 61- 70, 2; 71+, 2.

They represent the following interests:

Sport - 8 (representing 3 of the badminton groups, 3 of the 5-a-side football groups, boxing and judo)

Single interest hobby groups - 3

Adult education - 1

Tenants' association - 1

Local Authority - 3

Three members have been serving on the committee for over twenty years and one for fourteen years. The remainder are relative newcomers, having served between two and six years except for one who joined as a director in April 1992.

In this section, I shall discuss the impact that being on the management committee and Board of Directors per se has had on members. In subsequent sections the impact of membership of particular groups and activities on the same respondents will be included where appropriate.

Social Impact

Directors agreed that belonging to the management committee and Board was of very little social significance to them. One of the council-sponsored directors, who was new both to the area and to local government four years ago, said how much he had appreciated the friendliness of other members of the Board and how involvement had helped him to get to know a lot of people in a groups that members find social satisfaction rather than from the Centre's committee meetings.

Educational and cultural impact

While most directors felt that they had learned a great deal from being involved in the management of the Centre, they found it difficult to describe this learning in detail. For most of them, the Association is the only voluntary organisation of its kind of which they have any experience, so they have no measure of comparison. They are all impressed by the complexity of the task and are very glad to leave the detailed running of the building to the knowledge and expertise of the manager. Until they came on to the management committee, most had little idea of what other activities apart from their own went on in the Centre. A tour of the Centre had shown some of them parts which they had never known about. For example, one director who had been coming for twenty years to a group which meets in the basement was amazed to see the second and third floor areas and what went on there. Several directors emphasised that although they came to the Board as representatives of particular groups, once there, group interests were laid aside and the good of the Centre as a whole is their only concern.

They spoke of learning how committees run and how, with a good chairman, issues can be fully discussed and negotiation can lead to decisions. One relative newcomer is 'impressed at the way people work together and pool their knowledge and expertise, giving their goodwill, time and often free labour' doing practical jobs for the good of the Centre. Another enjoys the meetings and always contributes opinions in discussions; he feels that he is 'a better opinionator than doer'. One had learned greater ease at speaking in public but one woman member had found it 'sometimes difficult to get a word in edgeways at meetings'. Several of the newer members would have welcomed more information and training when they first joined. One said that after three years he still perceives that there is an inner circle of directors and he feels on the edge.

Some said that becoming a company with a Board has released enthusiasm and creativity, made them feel more 'in charge' and encouraged them 'to take their responsibilities more seriously'. It has also sharpened their interest in making the Centre a commercial success. They want to generate more income so that there is a surplus to use for improvements, but there is a feeling that 'we must take no risks at present'. Stability, continuity and a pragmatic approach are valued; 'if it works, that's what we'll do'.

Several directors said sadly that they had learned a great deal about vandalism which one described as 'horrendous'. They were referring both to the casual damage to the outside of the building and to the more serious destruction inflicted by members of the youth club in recent years. There has been no youth club in the Centre since that time and the negative learning experience has made the Board very cautious about any proposals to restart work with young people. A small minority of the Board, representing the local community, is pressing for new youth provision but the initiative is slow to gain support. One member admitted that he 'has a conscience about there not being a youth club' because he recognises that young people lack the space and opportunities he had when he was growing up in the area, but 'the possibility of a youth club is a barrel of gunpowder'. Another feels that they do not understand all the issues surrounding the youth club. They believe that a youth club would be risky and therefore follow the lead of the senior members in their reluctance to agree to any proposals for a 14-19 club, but favour instead opening for younger children who may be easier to supervise. Because of past experiences and continued vandalism, a great deal of time and effort is put into improving security and any response to a new proposal has necessarily to include a security dimension.

Different opinions were expressed about how the Centre should relate to the community. A longstanding member regretted the lack of 'community spirit' and said that local people are not interested. 'Trying to get people involved is like banging your head against a brick wall' was another member's view. The chairman felt that the Centre is unable to respond to community needs. He admits that 'it appears as an alien force to the community outside', but justifies the present policy of running 'a tight ship' because the building has too many problems for open community use. Directors are struggling to find a balance between advertising the Centre's programme more widely to demonstrate to the local community the level of use, and controlling what goes on because publicity 'might attract the wrong sort of attention'. The resolution of this dilemma, often discussed at Board meetings, will involve the directors in new thinking and learning about the role and management of the Centre.

A director who has wider experience of working for and with voluntary organisations feels that though there is nothing wrong with the Centre as it is, change should take place more quickly. He finds the Centre 'a profoundly conservative institution' committed to an established way of doing things which suits the present user groups. From his involvement with the organisation he has learned that 'the practical limitations to change in a voluntary organisation are lack of vision, lack of professionalism and lack of commitment to change amongst the people involved'.

Occupational impact

For most of the directors there seemed to be little link between their occupation and their participation in the management of the Centre. One or two commented on the contrast between the hierarchical structure of their workplace and the democratic nature of the voluntary organisation. They contrasted the co-operation within the association with competition and conflict at work; 'there's no reward in a voluntary organisation in getting someone's back up. In business you can, but not in a voluntary organisation because personal feelings are entwined with the organisation'. One said that 'if anything, it's made me less aggressive, less adamant that I'm right, in dealings at work'. Another found that contributing to committee meetings at the Centre helps him to be a more effective shop spokesman at his workplace. Several have knowledge and contacts which are useful to the practical side of, for example, security and felt that they have business and commercial skills to offer to the Centre.

Some directors are involved in other voluntary organisations, for example the Hospital Savings Association, Community Transport, a residents association in another district and a Women's Group. However, none of these developed from involvement with the Association. The youngest member of the Board, now in his mid-twenties, spends 6-8 hours a week as a voluntary cub-scout leader. His enthusiasm and commitment are due to the positive influence of cubs first and then of the youth club, both active at the Centre when he was of an age to belong.

In contrast to most members of the Board, involvement with the Centre has made a profound impact on the occupation of the manager. He had been on the management committee since 1965, serving as vice-chairman and chairman of the association. When the post of warden at the Centre became vacant, he decided to capitalise on his experience as chairman of the community association to make a career change.

From his professional work he brought skills of dealing with people and preparing clear reports. From his long involvement at the Centre he knew the people and problems management had to tackle. As warden and manager, he has learned to take on the responsibilities of local government employment. He did not find the transition from voluntary chairman to paid manager difficult, and has always felt more part of the community than part of local government service. As paid manager he has had more scope and a more defined role. He has learned that the full time paid manager has the power despite being the servant of the voluntary organisation; 'an amateur has no chance against a full time professional.' He has learned that even if a chairman and a treasurer are keen, 'you can't expect too much of them.' He has learned to steer the committee and to use his influence to resolve disagreements between members. He admits that he sometimes finds it difficult to work with a committee and to accept its decisions.

He has found that managing caretaking and cleaning staff and dealing with their unions is often testing. He can cope best by 'sticking to the rule book 100% and playing the game down the line.' Being manager has taught him 'that if you let people treat you as a doormat, they will'. He finds that those with more education and status are more likely to take advantage and break the rules. He has learned the hard way that constant vigilance is needed to keep the building secure. His dream is to build a multi-purpose theatre for dance, drama and community arts events which would bring people and money to the Centre.

The part-time administrative officer, who has been working at the Centre for many years, is paid 10 hours per week by the Local Authority and another 10 by the Centre, and some weeks does almost as many again unpaid. She is the mainstay of the Centre, and her detailed knowledge of every quirk of the building, every need of the users and all the significant people involved with it make her a mine of information and an invaluable support to the manager. She has learned over the years every administrative procedure required to run the Centre and all the skills of dealing with people. Both the manager and the administrative officer have learned word processing and computing skills to assist their work.

Political impact

Most directors declared no interest in politics and felt that the raising of political awareness had no role to play in the Centre. The representative of the ruling party on the council said that politics should not come into local government either and the chairman said that he is 'not politically motivated at all.' A woman director has always been interested in politics, standing for the council on one occasion, but the Centre has played no part in developing her political awareness.

A director new to the Board agreed that politics are not directly brought up in meetings, but they are 'very much under the surface'. The representative of the local residents' association is perceived by other directors to be linked with the present minority party. They think he wishes to increase the influence of his group and its use of the Centre for political gain. He is supported discreetly by the minority representative but is always outvoted. Open conflict in the recent past resulted in a particular representative of the residents' association being asked to leave the management committee by the chairman.

The underlying political issue of the future of community associations in this Local Authority influences the running of the Centre and the response of the directors even if they wish it did not. One party favours more centralised management of Centres to bring about more openness and the implementation of 'equal opportunities' policies. The other favours handing over control to local people to operate on a 'market forces' basis. The Council owns the building and pays the manager and support staff, so even with a ten year lease, the directors, like it or not, operate within a political framework.

Since the creation of the company, directors have been more committed than before to their responsibility for the management of the Centre. Meetings of the Board have been notably better attended than those of the former management committee and discussions more focused on the need for commercial viability. The directors have agreed a business plan for the first year of the company and are monitoring the financial situation closely, from which, as the plan says, 'we will learn a lot in the coming year'. The chairman of the Board puts all issues to the vote to demonstrate clearly that decisions are taken democratically. The change to company status has involved a learning process which directors feel is just beginning.

Personal impact
The level of personal change described varied from 'very little' to 'significant', though not profound. One mentioned a gain in self confidence which enabled him to speak out in front of other people. Another very shy and reserved person still finds it difficult to participate in discussion at meetings but feels the effort is worthwhile. Involvement at the Centre together with the birth of his first son made one director realise 'there's more to life than work and just enjoying myself'. He is now keen to be, in his words, 'a participative citizen, putting something back by helping in what way I can'.

Appreciation of human nature, tolerance, personal satisfaction, ability to work flexibly and a respect for volunteering were mentioned as results of involvement. The chairman has found the work sometimes stressful, giving him sleepless nights, but the difficult times are balanced by a sense of achievement and pleasure at a job well done.

SPORTING ACTIVITIES
The building contains two very large halls and large attic areas which are used for sport. The ground floor hall is ideal for five-a-side football, played mainly by youth teams and leagues, but it is also a popular sport with adults. The upstairs hall has space for three badminton courts and there are plans for a fourth. Different all-adult clubs play on each weekday evening, at lunch times and at the weekend.

Part of the attic above the badminton hall is converted into a boxing gym which is used for training three evenings a week and on Sunday mornings. The Club's members range from boys of ten to young adults. Next to the boxing gym a large room is fitted with the special flooring required for judo and other martial arts. The members of the judo club are mostly under sixteen; few stay on to senior level.

During school term, there is some daytime use of the sports facilities by local schools.

Representatives from all four sports were interviewed and short conversations held with a number of participants.

Social impact
The social side of the sports groups is by and large incidental. Badminton players seem to be particularly serious about their sport; 'no one wants to join a badminton club that's just social'. Some clubs started as sections of firms' social clubs or as a group from a particular local government department. Friendships, indeed marriages, are cemented on the badminton courts but, 'It's not like the social life of a tennis club', said one respondent who plays both sports.

Some five-a-side groups seem to have a stronger social basis. An hour's session is an opportunity for ex-school friends or former workmates to get together regularly, and go to the pub afterwards. It is a legitimate framework in which to have 'a night out with the lads'.

Educational, cultural and personal impact
For those who play badminton and football, physical fitness and improving skills in their chosen sport are the dominant motivations. Badminton is particularly competitive and most clubs have teams which play regularly in leagues which are graded into divisions according to standard of play. Women players are in short supply so a woman of high standard is much sought after and may play for two or three different clubs. Each club has a match organiser who is the key person in the group.

Badminton clubs expect newcomers to know the game and play to a standard which will match that of other players in the club. No instruction or coaching is offered and improvement comes from match play and competition. One of the reasons given for difficulty in recruiting good match players was that badminton is not taught in schools, but the possibility of the clubs themselves providing tuition for beginners was not considered an option. It would mean a lower standard of play and club members would not get so many 'good games'.

One respondent is the organiser of one club and treasurer and organising secretary of another. She gets better at the skills of running clubs and arranging matches and feels personal satisfaction that she is putting something back into the game. Using her club experience, she is a member of the local Sports Council where she speaks on behalf of badminton. She is learning how difficult it is for minority sports to compete for funding and space. Another club secretary finds organising matches, dealing with members and keeping them happy a lot of hard work and the other members rely on her for the smooth running of the club. Keeping the membership up to a stable 28-30 is a technique that another club organiser finds demanding. He has learned how, in bringing new members into the group, to make them feel welcome and comfortable.

The organisers of boxing and judo and the juvenile football leagues participate as trainers and referees. They teach the basics of the sport to the youngsters and train them in techniques to improve their skills. The judo instructors are qualified to the level that entitles them to teach and the boxing trainer is registered with the Amateur Boxing Association (ABA) as a qualified instructor in the sport. They teach the young people self-discipline and skills of the sport, and help them to achieve their best. For many boxers in particular, general fitness training is as important as techniques of sparring.

The adults bear a heavy responsibility for the general wellbeing of the young people in their groups. The boxing organiser has been involved with the club for about 19 years. There is a committee but most of the work falls to him. This involves arranging fights and organising shows which takes a great deal of time both on the telephone and travelling around the country with young people to visit other clubs. Most of the young people in the club have personal problems and he is 'the listening ear, sorting things out, looking after the boys'. Although his knowledge of the world of amateur boxing, enhanced by membership of the ABA and the National Association of Boys' Clubs, is vast, he regards the development of skills in working at a personal level with his

70

members as the more significant learning experience.

The representative for the Judo club also identified the skills of dealing with the children as an important area of learning. He has also learned that running the club is hard work which gains little appreciation and quite a lot of criticism. He has used his experience to work as a volunteer in a youth club and boxing club in a neighbouring suburb.

For all who participate in sport at the Centre, their interest and personal commitment is to the enjoyment of the sport itself. The Centre does not offer adults systematic programmes of fitness training and coaching in the way that a specialist sports centre does. The players are looking for relaxation from stress at work, personal fitness and the enjoyment of 'a good game'. As one footballer said, 'we come, change, play, shower and go'. They rely on the one or two organisers in the club to take care of the logistics of bookings and schedules. The learning experience of the group leaders involves organisational skills and dealing with people and their personal satisfaction comes from helping to ensure that their sport flourishes and that good standards and results for the club are achieved. For some of them, election or co-option on to the management body of the Centre may lead to the learning they experience as directors.

ADULT EDUCATION CLASSES

The Association does not organise or manage the programme of adult education at the Centre but students of adult education classes form a distinctive and numerous user group. Until last year, a part-time head of centre with clerical support was in charge of the organisation of classes. With the changes in the structure of adult education, all heads of centre were made redundant last year and from April 1993 all classes have come under the local further education college. At present, a part-time clerical officer, now renamed the site receptionist, provides support for classes and their tutors. The future of adult classes is uncertain, as they were all closed at the beginning of the spring term of 1993 but then as suddenly reprieved.

The classes at present held at the Centre are upholstery (10 classes, day and evening), pottery (4, day and evening), car maintenance, furniture restoration and photography (all evening),

71

with a total of around 300 students. Day time classes have about 75% women students and evening classes are attended by equal numbers of men and women. The high fees and the recent abolition of concessions for the retired and unemployed have emphasised the middle class take up of classes. A representative of adult education, currently one of the upholstery tutors, has a place on the Board of Directors. The researcher talked with tutors and students in upholstery, pottery and car maintenance classes.

Social impact
The students value the social side of classes; they 'like the gossip and the friendly atmosphere'. Quite a few of them seemed to be people on their own for whom classes were an important source of social contact. However, there did not seem to be much continuation of social life outside the class environment. Some tutors try to develop the social life of classes by organising end of year lunches. One upholstery tutor numbers students among her personal friends and has, for example, been on holiday with one of them.

Educational and cultural impact
While it is not part of this study to examine the specific learning within each subject area, it was clear that the students felt that they had learned a great deal from their chosen course. In the craft classes, each worked on their own piece of furniture or pot with help both from the tutor and from each other. For car maintenance there is plenty of space for practical work and an authentic workshop atmosphere. As one student said, 'It serves its purpose - you don't need a smart place for upholstery' or for that matter for car maintenance. They become knowledgeable about different periods and techniques of furniture making, or about ways of firing and glazing their pots, or how to do routine maintenance on cars. They come for their specific activity and know little about what else happens in the Centre; 'people keep themselves to themselves'.

The tutors are more aware of the running of the Centre. The pottery tutor has to rely on the manager to operate the kiln and the site receptionist has to negotiate for use of space for classes. The representative on the Board, who was on the management committee for five years before the company was set up, has learned how much goes into running the building. She in particular has learned to appreciate the key roles played by cleaners, caretakers and canteen staff. She has learnt about committee work and that decisions in a community association should be taken democratically. Also she has come to believe strongly that people living locally should be involved with the running of the Centre and have a say in its policies.

Occupational impact

This case study provides two examples of that familiar phenomenon of adult education being an agent for women's career building. The upholstery tutor had started at the Centre as a student. Finding that she was good at the work, she did a year's course at the London College of Furniture and then worked voluntarily alongside her old tutor. When the tutor retired in 1981, she took over the classes which have now increased to ten per week of which she teaches six.

One of her upholstery students who happened to be principal of a local technical college, impressed by her teaching ability, suggested she built on her existing secretarial skills by taking a word processing course. This led to part-time teaching in computing and bookkeeping at two local colleges.

The area co-ordinator for craft classes started out as a pottery technician and tutor. Her job in the new structure of adult education is to develop a full and balanced programme of craft classes across the north of the area. For both these tutors, learning experiences within adult education have opened career doors and changed their working lives.

Political impact

Adult education students became suddenly very aware of political presssures when their classes were cancelled with no notice at all. This action, which was rescinded within a week and explained away as a misunderstanding, was further evidence to students that they need to lobby politicians to save adult education from extinction. Telephone calls, deputations and petitions flooded in to local councillors to prevent the closure of classes. This was a very similar upsurge of political awareness to that witnessed by the research team at the Percival Guildhouse a year earlier. The management of the Centre reacted as had the management committee at the Guildhouse by exploring ways of maintaining the classes under their own aegis.

Personal impact
Both tutors and students were aware of the therapeutic value of classes. As one student said, 'in class, there's no time to think of illness - you can unload your troubles'. The pottery tutor knew of three suicides of ex-students in the last six months since concessionary fees have been abolished. While the causes of suicide are deeper than the cost of evening classes, she is sure that for many people the classes provide that support and interest and outlet for emotion which gives them significant relief from difficult circumstances in their lives such as unemployment and loneliness. She fears for students' mental health in the future if more classes are lost.

THE LOCAL TENANTS AND RESIDENTS ASSOCIATION (LTRA)
LTRA is an independent organisation which rents a room in the Centre as an office and has a representative on the Board of Directors. It started in 1986 as an Action Group protesting at the Council's proposal to sell some playing fields behind the Centre for housing development. The group drew up its own plans for the use of the open space to include a wild life area, a sports area, a formal garden and equipped play areas. Whether in response to the campaign, or to other factors, the Council dropped their plans. The Action Group reformed itself into a TRA and took on issues of housing, the care of the estate and the provision of a link between residents and tenants and the Council. About 400 households on the estate are currently members.

The researcher interviewed three of the LTRA's committee, including the press officer and the assistant treasurer, and spoke with a number of members.

Social impact
The social side of LTRA's activities is important both for fundraising and for giving local people a social focus. Parties and outings for elderly people and children are well supported and appreciated by

74

local people. Three lettings a year for dances have been negotiated with the Centre though they believe that more such events would gain local support.

LTRA members spoke of the social benefit membership had brought to them personally. Knowing your neighbours better and making friendships within the local community contribute to making the estate a pleasanter place in which to live.

Educational, cultural and political impact

LTRA aims to draw local people into projects which will improve life on the estate. This involves raising political awareness and persuading people to take an active part in planning, managing and supporting local activities and events. The committee members are conscious that there is still a lot to achieve. They spoke of 'a long uphill struggle' which they like to feel they are winning. In a modest way, their efforts are bringing about learning and change in the community.

They have learned how to acquire and disseminate information so that people can understand local issues which affect their lives. For additional support they use the Tenants Resource Centre with which their vice-chairman is linked. Forming a tenants' and residents' association was in itself a learning experience about the political nature of local government. They have learned about the complexities of local govenment, how 'everying is interlinked with knock-on effects from department to department.' They have found that personal service is needed. Newsletters and a monthly 'street desk', a stall by the local shops, are useful in keeping people informed but members have to be visited in their own homes to gain support. They are confident that there is 'a great deal of community feeling under the surface that's not being tapped', and that LTRA has already brought different people in the community - residents and tenants - together to look at local issues. It just needs 'a little more push'.

They have learned through the Action Group how to bring about change and feel they have some solid achievements, such as the formal garden, tree planting and the wild life area, to show for their efforts. They see the Community Centre as the natural focus for community life on the estate. They have offices in the Centre and a representative on the Board of Directors. They have tried both by argument at meetings and by direct action to open up the Centre to more local use but have found that the committee 'is so locked into its present, traditional, strategy that there is no room for manoevre'. The LTRA put forward a bid for the lease of the Centre based on greater utilisation of space and more open use by the local community. This brought the response that the Council was satisfied with the way that the Centre is currently run. Some members feel disillusioned with the way in which tenants associations have become pawns of local politicians 'who play their games for political advantage'.

The issue of the social role of the Centre has been a source of conflict on the Board. LTRA questions why there are no social clubs at the Centre. It feels strongly that a welcoming and friendly open social club, probably with a bar, should be developed at the Centre for local people. This has been suggested and argued for by LTRA representatives on the management body but has always met with a negative response framed in a way that seems to the TRA committee to lack understanding of the needs of local people; 'When we try to suggest it, people who run the Centre feel that it just means lager louts.' LTRA is confident that local people want a social centre and would use it if it was attractive whereas the majority of the directors doubt whether the building is suitable and think that financial losses might be incurred.

Local people also look to the Centre to provide a social life for young people on the estate. Many of them who grew up on the estate went to a youth club in the Centre and would like to see a club for their teenage sons and daughters reopened. The attitude of many directors on this issue has already been mentioned. LTRA are trying now to negotiate a way of restarting youth work at the Centre.

Through gaining confidence and experience in working for LTRA, some of its committee have branched out from their local involvement: the vice-chairman is chairman of the Tenant Resource Centre, and the chairman is on the steering committee for the improvement of the local town centre.

Occupational impact

Some evidence emerged to show that participation in a tenants association has a positive impact on other aspects of work. For example, the assistant treasurer recently had to fill in a job application form and realized how much she could add arising from her work with LTRA. The press officer is by profession an architect. He was able to offer practical help to the Action Group and use his skills to interpret people's ideas for the use of the open space. LTRA involvement has made him more sensitive to local issues and feelings as he works on projects for his firm. He often feels that he wishes to advise local groups how to protest against schemes he has a part in planning. In terms of design, working with people who have no architectural training has sharpened his perceptions of scale and size. He has learned how to convey his ideas more effectively to untrained eyes.

Personal impact
The assistant treasurer has gained self-confidence from her involvement with LTRA. She used to be 'terrified' of making contacts and requests on behalf of the organisation, but now such initiatives are 'no bother'. She is 'more assertive, more bossy' and feels committed to her work with LTRA.

Another member said he has learned that things are achievable if you keep on trying; 'there are ways to conquer any problem'. He has become a more knowledgeable person, and more confident in his own effectiveness. Involvement with LTRA has 'helped me communicate with people better - at all levels' and given him insight into his community and himself as part of it.

OTHER GROUPS
The remaining groups within the Centre can be divided into single interest groups - such as the modelling group, the horticultural society and the junior theatre club; and the groups and interests concerned with disabled people.

The work with disabled people is the conscience of the Centre. These groups provide a response both to social need and to equal opportunities, and, from the point of view of the management, are controlled, risk free and profitable. A voluntary organisation to which Boroughs all over London send autistic adults for a sensitive and thoughtful learning programme uses the Centre five days a week from 9.30 to 5. The manager feels that 'they have become the backbone of the Centre and added a lot to it.'

There are some links between this organisation and a sign dance theatre company which rents space at the Centre for drama in which the deaf and the hearing work together. It is described by its co-ordinator as 'pioneering, two cultures coming together and coming up with something new'. The work of the group is becoming known nationally and it is also building a reputation abroad. Its workers believe that being based in a community centre means that they should work in and with the community both within and around the centre. They have initiated joint pieces of work with other groups in the Centre, run an evening junior dance group for deaf and hearing children on the estate and work in local schools.

They have also attempted to contribute ideas to change the impact of the Centre. They made proposals for creating a studio theatre in part of the hall which they wanted to share with all the groups in the Centre and tried to open up discussion about how the visual impact of the Centre could be improved. He feels that his suggestions are constantly 'blocked' but is learning 'not to accept "No" and to find alternative ways of getting things done when straightforward ways fail'.

A disabilities consultant worked with the theatre group and with the local Disablement Association before setting up independently at the Centre in 1991. She is a blind person who works together with a deaf colleague with non-disabled groups, educating the general public about disability. She runs disability awareness courses at the Centre to which commercial organisations send trainees. She has been asked by the Local Authority to work with their Access Group on a development plan for the area. She admires the work of self-help groups and thinks that they fill the need of disabled people for understanding and campaigning. But she fears that they tend to segregate disabled people from the rest of the community and for this reason she chose to set herself up in an independent mediating role rather than as a self-help group.

She has found the Centre supportive to her personally and to her work. In the Centre she feels she has achieved greater awareness of and acceptance for disabled people but would like to get more enthusiastic support for changes that would give them better access to a wider range of activities. Each of these organisations achieves impressive learning experiences for its client groups. By working co-operatively and by outreach into the community, they are indicating some directions for change for the Centre both in attitudes and practices.

By contrast, single interest groups have on the whole been static or in decline in recent years. Thus the horticultural society still has 200 members who use its trading store but has not enough support to run its traditional programme of meetings and annual shows, so that opportunities for learning by the group are restricted. Its organiser is using his experience in finance as treasurer of the Centre. The members of the small aircraft group have been improving ways of repairing and restoring light aircraft for more than 20 years and continue to learn new skills and techniques in their specialism. Their enthusiasm is comparable to that of the historic carriage restorers at the Midland Railway Centre.

A dramatic society which for many decades was a significant member of the Association recently disbanded. The dramatic tradition is carried on by a junior theatre club, a dance and drama group for 7-14 year olds run by a young woman and her mother who, as deputy head of a local middle school, has access to likely members. The club puts on annual performances, attracting an audience of 100 parents and friends for two successive evenings. Both the junior theatre club and LTRA make links with the groups concerned with disabled people to take part in what are some of the most dynamic recent learning experiences in the Centre.

IMPACT ON FAMILIES

A few respondents spoke of involvement in the Centre by other members of the family. Some who have lived on the estate for the greater part of their lives remembered activities that they had participated in many years ago. This confirmed that there is a local folk memory of more active involvement with the Centre which adds weight to pressure that the Centre should again be made more accessible to its immediate community.

For example, one of the LTRA committee belonged to guides and the youth club at the Centre in the '50s and brought her babies to the clinic as did other young mothers. Her husband has lived on the estate for 35 years but hardly came into the building until LTRA was established. Their son and daughter both came to the Centre for youth activities and five-a-side. Another respondent became

79

involved as a representative for judo because he came along to support his son 18 years ago. A footballer started at the Centre at the age of seven in the cubs, was a member of the youth club and is now a director; his brothers have also been involved in youth activities. Some badminton players bring their children to take part in judo while they are playing badminton. Husbands and wives together are often joint members of the horticultural society. The potential of family involvement seems to be tantalisingly apparent. However most respondents said that no other member of their family was involved in any activity at the Centre.

WIDER IMPACT
The local library is within the catchment area of the Centre's community-based activities as defined by the Directors, but the Librarian feels it makes little impact on the wider community. She knows about the Centre from its inclusion in the Local Authority adult education programme and she has also seen information from time to time about martial arts organisations who rent space there but she has never been asked to display a full programme of the Centre's activities. She feels that it is 'off the beaten track', but thinks that advertising in her Library would encourage more local support for it.

The manager of a complex of swimming pools on the main road about a quarter of a mile away, did not even know of the existence of the Centre. His complex offers teaching and coaching in swimming and is 'vastly used' with 650,000 attendances a year. The manager has had no contact with groups from the Centre and no approach from its management during the year he has been in post.

The minister of an active church on the estate is aware of the Centre which is only 200 yards from his front door. He came from the Midlands four years ago and has been amazed how people in London will travel only short distances to facilities even though public transport seems very good. From his work amongst local people, he hears that the Centre is valued by those who use it or who have members of the family involved in its activities. Especially for young people it offers almost the only recreational centre in the area. The needs of the elderly amongst whom much of his work lies are now met in other places. By people not engaged in its activities, the Centre is 'taken for granted'. The minister has never received any publicity or personal approach from the Centre though he would value contact; 'I sometimes feel I should make the move to involve myself, but there is not time for everything.'

The researcher spoke with a number of local people in neighbouring streets and shops. All were either unaware of what happened at the Centre or knew that it is a place where sport goes on and different clubs meet. Some knew someone who belonged to a club but generally the Centre was for 'other people', not for them. This local lack of awareness and contact with the Centre was illustrated by an attempt by the Local Authority's Leisure Services in 1990 to gather opinion about what the Centre should offer. Of 2750 locally distributed questionnaires, only 25, less than 1%, were completed and returned and the report on the results concluded that either local people were 'frustrated with the activities of the Centre to such an extent' that they ignored the questionnaire 'as an irrelevant and useless exercise' or that local people are satisfied with the Centre's programme. The Senior Community Officer, who has the Centre within his area of responsibility, said that he has worked within his advisory brief to influence the Centre to respond to the needs of people in the immediate area. He acknowledges there is a problem of balancing the expectations of the regular users who generate income and the needs of local people. He feels that not enough effort is made to meet those needs because local people are perceived as 'not respectable and not well disciplined', and he will advise and encourage the Board to take up LTRA's offer to start a new youth club for which the Authority will pay some workers.

No precise statistics exist about the numbers and residence of users of the Centre but the researcher would estimate that no more than 10% of the users come from the immediate area. During the day, the Centre is grossly underused and the heavy use of the car park in the evenings suggests that most users travel some distance.

The evidence suggests that the Centre's programme has little impact on the local area and has little to offer to meet the social and learning needs of local people. Opportunities to link with other local agencies, to advertise a programme and to encourage wider participation are not pursued and so the potential for the Centre to promote learning and change in its catchment remains unfulfilled.

81

CONCLUSION

In the late 1940s and 1950s, this Community Association was one of the flagships of the Community Association movement, not least because at that time 10% of its members and users were actively engaged in running the organisation. Today the Centre has to compete in the leisure market with other more modern facilities and it is experiencing difficulty in identifying and responding to the needs of the area. Indeed, the evidence suggests that the role of involving local volunteers and responding to the needs of the immediate community is being taken over by an alternative community association which lacks full access to the Centre.

This study has provided valuable evidence about issues of organisational development, raising questions of stability versus change, of eliciting and meeting the needs of local people or catering for a known paying clientèle, all of which have implications for the relationships between paid staff, board and membership, current and potential. While not published here, this material will enrich the discussion in our final report.

From the many individual testimonies, from staff, board members and those participating in different activities, the study bears further witness to the learning and personal growth that involvement in a voluntary organisation generates. The evidence confirms our findings that growth in confidence and self esteem and the experience of working with others towards common aims are significant though less recognised benefits of group membership.

Case Study 19

THE GARIBALDI AND NEWLANDS ESTATES RESIDENTS ASSOCIATION

INTRODUCTION

Mansfield, with a population of 60,000, developed through the industrial prosperity of western Nottinghamshire, and with its modern shops and supermarkets is an important shopping centre for the area. However, the decline of mining and hosiery has brought serious problems of unemployment, offset to some extent by the introduction of alternative industries. In one of the town's suburbs lie the Garibaldi and Newlands estates and the residents' association there agreed to be part of the Project. The estates border a beautiful countryside and are within easy reach of the heart of Sherwood Forest. Some of the houses on the estates were built in the last 40 years for mining families from the North East and Scotland. Sadly, the local mine where many worked was recently closed.

In the 1980s uncertainties about the future of Coal Board housing led to the formation of a number of groups of tenants, including one for the Garibaldi and Newlands area. This and others were disbanded as the housing position became settled. More recent concerns and issues led to the renewal or formation of such groups. The Social Services Community Development Worker gave 'terrific help' to them by bringing people together, printing leaflets, arranging meetings, informing councillors, offering a model constitution and continuing support after groups had been formed. He helped to build up people's confidence in running committees and directed them to the appropriate officers of the Mansfield District Council. Twelve groups have been formed in recent years and ten of these joined together in 1989 to form the Mansfield and District Federation of Tenants' and Residents' Associations (MDFTRA). The activities of the Federation, as of the tenants' and residents' groups, are concerned with improving the local environment and with helping tenants of council houses. County Social Services fund both the tenants' and residents' groups and the MDFTRA. Neither the groups nor the Federation have any paid staff. Mansfield District Council provides facilities such as printing, photocopying and rooms for meetings without charge. Both contribute to training opportunities.

One of the groups re-formed in 1989 was the Garibaldi and Newlands Estates Residents' Association (GNERA), and the researcher is very grateful to the ten members interviewed for their co-operation. Six members of MDFTRA were interviewed and also two officers of the District Council, an officer of a housing association and the Community Development Worker; to all these he gives his thanks.

On the Garibaldi and Newlands estates are about 800 houses, a quarter being council houses, over an eighth being owned by a housing association, some under private landlords and over a half privately owned. The proportion in the last category is said, in the Mansfield area, to be unusually high in a tenants' and residents' group. The Association meets monthly, everyone is eligible to participate and there is no membership fee.

While interviewing participants of GNERA it became clear that it gains support, a broadening experience, training and a stronger advocacy role through being in the Federation, and examining the relations of the tenants' and residents' groups to MDFTRA was thought to be helpful when considering the learning and experience of members of GNERA. These organisations kindly allowed the researcher to attend their meetings, and he attended three of GNERA's and four of MDFTRA's.

The participants of GNERA were interviewed separately and the age distribution of the six men and four women is:
31+ 1; 41+ 3; 51+ 4; 61+ 0; 71+ 1; 81+ 1.
Three were District councillors (2 men, 1 woman), two of them representing local wards and one a ward close by; the men had

been miners. Of the remaining seven, four are and one was in other voluntary organisations - welfare rights, social groups, girl guides, political and church groups. One of the seven worked as a secretary, one is a miner, one a redundant miner, two are unemployed and two are retired. All ten left school at the minimum age, but three of them have undertaken formal courses of study, two of them very recently - a councillor, the secretary and another member.

Three men and three women in MDFTRA were interviewed, four on their own and a husband and wife together. The distribution of ages is: 31+ 1; 41+ 4; 51+ 1, and again all had the minimum formal schooling. One of the men does voluntary work in welfare rights and is a member of a political party, and a woman has helped a voluntary group for the homeless and at present does voluntary youth work. The members of GNERA and MDFTRA who are in other voluntary groups say that it broadens their sympathies, increases their confidence and has provided them with skills.

SOCIAL EFFECTS
At their meetings GNERA participants greet each other warmly and there is a bond of good feeling. They come in a co-operative spirit to discuss matters of local concern. Since the formation of the Association, members say that they know more people in the neighbourhood and talk about the locality and the improvements made or sought; as a result 'people get to know each other better'. It is reported that from the start of the Association an informal atmosphere was established to put people at their ease, for 'it's like customer relations', and encourage them 'to say anything they want'. Originally new to this field of activity, the members work well together and have developed social skills as they meet Council officers, councillors and members of other tenants' groups and attend courses; they say 'you make a lot of friends'.

Very similar social effects are reported by those attending the Federation meetings. The Federation disperses the sense of isolation felt by some groups by providing a strong sense of support, for 'people feel they can work together'. They say that 'we stand and talk after the Federation meetings'. They form an informal support network, ringing each other up to talk about problems or seek advice and information.

85

EDUCATIONAL EFFECTS

As they go about their daily business the residents talk about the amenities and facilities in the neighbourhood; this leads them either to go to the Association meetings themselves or, more likely, to ask those who do attend to raise questions about, for instance, road and traffic conditions, dog fouling, lack of parking spaces, leaking water from roadworks. What the members learn is that, acting collectively, they can very often get something done, whereas individually they are unsuccessful. The Association contacts councillors or the appropriate officials from the District Council, the County Council or the housing association, and learns to explain its case, pointing out the dangers or adverse consequences for the neighbourhood or particular age groups. The councillors and officers inform the members of current plans, put issues in a wider context and explain what can or cannot be done. The members ask questions and 'challenge them'; they value these meetings for they 'learn what's going on'.

GNERA participants soon realise that there 'is a great deal to learn', whether it is about housing law, environmental issues or the range of residents' complaints. They also become more aware of 'the ability of people to educate each other'. About a dozen members attend the meetings but at times there may be several more, for 'we get different people all the time and it depends what they want to bring up'. 'You learn to keep people's interest... because when you talk it's got to be to the point'. The Association learns that certain people want their complaints seen to first and may not then come again. In listening to the issues members put before the Association, they become aware not only of the different views expressed but of 'people's different circumstances' and 'the things that bother them'. GNERA's Committee members realise the value of keeping the members up-to-date on the progress of improvements being applied for.

Some councillors, as residents of the area, attend the Association meetings whenever they can, and members learn a great deal from them about the District Council's regulations and also the councillors' points of view.

Members learn that 'you have to be careful in giving advice' as good legal or technical knowledge may be needed, but 'you learn to listen, to ask what they have done, who they have seen' and take

86

a sympathetic interest in their problems. In running the Committee, attending the Federation meetings and from time to time representing it, members acquire skills in managing and organising. They also learn to explain, to discuss, to speak in public, 'to be persistent', 'to have a constructive attitude'. When the work load is heavy they learn to cope with pressure, and when complaints are made with feeling or views put strongly 'you learn to stand your ground'. As they continue their work the members not only learn 'about what bothers people in the area' but how to set about putting local concerns right.

The members of GNERA who attend the Federation meetings say that they learn a great deal. Talks by District Council officers, pamphlets and the Federation discussions help them to learn of the complex issues in compulsory competitive tendering which the Government is introducing into housing management. Tenants in Council houses are keen to know just how they will be involved in drawing up specifications and the selection of contracts. The Federation and the separate groups are aware of the need to represent accurately the views and concerns of council tenants on issues specifically related to council housing.

Representatives of the tenants' associations say that they feel 'so inexperienced at first' and that they lack committee skills. Federation meetings form therefore learning and training opportunities. The associations recognise that they are at different stages and have different expectations; as a result the Federation is going to review its activities. People learn of the stronger voice the Federation provides on residents' issues and particularly on council tenants' issues in discussions with the District Council, and in seeking improved facilities from the Council for information. Learning about the experiences of other groups helps respondents to improve their negotiating skills, broadens their experience and helps them to think more clearly about the concerns of their groups. They also have access to training opportunities, for example, on equal opportunities and committee skills.

The District Council's Director of Housing had previous experience as chairman of a community association and member of a tenants' group. He and his staff see their role 'as trainers and educators', they talk to associations and the Federation on specific topics when requested, offer leaflets, allocate space in the housing department's newsletter and provide meeting rooms without charge and office facilities. In their turn the associations 'provide me with a window on the world and for my staff'.

OCCUPATIONAL EFFECTS
The comments from both GNERA and Federation participants mainly concern organisation and planning. The need to plan for meetings as well as to ensure that decisions made are carried out makes members aware of the value of planning in their other activities. They make time to fit things in and one looks ahead more over household finances. Being well organised for voluntary activities is transferred by some to ensuring that the needs of the family are met, especially those of children. The GNERA chairman, who had a responsible job in the mines, uses his management skills in creating an atmosphere where people feel comfortable in expressing their worries or views.

As they talk with neighbours members become more aware of people's circumstances and how situations can cause distress, particularly among the elderly; all this makes members 'listen more carefully and show a greater sympathy in dealing with people'. Participants in the tenants' groups realise that they cannot always take statements at face value and need to 'look for unstated assumptions'. The need for a questioning approach is being carried into their other activities. They 'realise that these things take time', and a few say that the persistence and patience required are useful qualities in general.

Appreciation of the value of discussing and working with others as a way of understanding issues and arriving at courses of action leads some to use these approaches in their other voluntary activities and with their families. One expressed it as 'the more consultation, the less frustation'.

POLITICAL EFFECTS
The purpose of a tenants' and residents' group is political in the sense of influencing the distribution of resources and bringing influence to bear on Councils' decisions, so that the effectiveness of such a group is its political effect. The GNERA Committee works hard to bring improvements to its area but is aware that determination is not enough; the Association needs some successes

and 'has to have the backing of the local population or it will fold'.

Committee members have worked hard at establishing good relationships with the local councillors; they know that their support is essential to get something done about the area's concerns. The members have become much better informed about housing and environmental matters and feel confident in putting their points to officers. They report that in the last few years officers' thinking has changed and 'the Council is starting to listen where it didn't before'. The views of councillors are likely to have been an influence, but the establishment of several tenants' and residents' groups and of the Federation have no doubt contributed. A member says that 'officers, councillors and the public are starting to mesh together', and councillors report that putting 'a neighbourhood view to the officials - that will get things done'. The residents in their turn learn that the councillors and the Council have to be fair to everyone.

GNERA participants do not always accept the argument of averagely distributed amenities over the District; at one meeting, the chairman, putting the case for the use of skips for extra waste, argued that people's ways are not always the same in different areas and said, 'everybody is striving for a better life, we are concerned for this area, not all Mansfield'. Training courses, supported by GNERA, MDFTRA or the Social Services, together with attendance at the Federation meetings have enabled three Committee members of GNERA to gain some knowledge of housing law and of the work and experience of other tenants' associations; these have been valuable in helping them to put forward the concerns of their Association. During 1991-2 the secretary attended a Tenant Participation National Certificate Course; she is also on the committees of the Tenants' Resources and Information Service, formed in 1990, the Tenants' Participation and Advisory Service, and the National Tenants' and Residents' Federation (NTRF), all national organisations which provide advice and support to tenants' and residents' groups. MDFTRA organised a meeting in Spring 1993 of NTRF and as it was open to the public the researcher attended. The knowledge thus gained by the Committee members of legislation and of the experience of councils, housing associations and tenants' and residents' groups is passed on to members of the

89

Federation and GNERA. Committee members of GNERA also report that the wider experience obtained enables them to present their concerns more effectively to officers and councillors and to anticipate objections.

The Federation's initial request for places on the District Council's Housing Committee was not accepted, but a Consultative Council has recently been set up consisting of representatives of residents' groups, councillors and officers. Federation members accept that the Council is, in a councillor's words, 'a consultative/liaison and not a negotiating body'. The members also see this work as providing valuable experience to help them to deal with local problems connected with housing associations and private landlords. The Federation successfully sought representation on the District Council's Housing Forum, a broader based group which includes building societies and businesses, for it is keen to protect what it sees as the interests of Council house tenants in every way it can.

Federation members extend their political awareness to groups such as miners who have lost their jobs, and pensioners. They pay particular attention to the needs of the elderly when seeking for improvements in their neighbourhoods. Many of the committee members of the tenants' groups report that they provide advice and comfort to old people and tend their gardens; a number convey them to the local association meetings. Members of the tenants' associations attend local rallies and sign petitions on behalf of miners and pensioners. A few belong to political parties and report that they speak in discussions there of their learning and experience in tenants' groups.

As Federation members attend to Federation and local residents' matters, and write and talk to officers and councillors about local concerns, they are more confident in questionning and probing. The members exchange their experiences of dealing with District Council and County Council officers. They report an improvement in their negotiating skills, putting their points clearly, listening, being ready to answer possible objections, compromising. One went on to say, 'it's how you talk to councillors and officials that matters'. The Federation learns that the annual tour of inspection, in which completed and ongoing projects and priority areas are visited, and to which two Federation representatives are invited, is very useful in obtaining tenants' groups acceptance of the Council's priorities.

PERSONAL EFFECTS

All respondents from GNERA and MDFTRA speak in the same way of the enhancement of personal qualities and feelings, especially confidence, satisfaction and working with others. They report that experience with the tenants' groups and with other voluntary organisations 'makes you confident that you can tackle things'. Working for voluntary organisations is valued and 'it makes you have more faith in yourself'. A member of the Federation says that after 11 years in voluntary work she 'can challenge things'. She believes in herself more, and her experience of writing and talking to officers and councillors 'has taken myths away about them, ... I see us all as equal'. Besides the value of experience in the voluntary sector, members, as volunteers, see the need for protection and support; the Federation provides a measure of this through being a forum to discuss problems and offer advice, and helping to arrange training.

The GNERA secretary confessed that she used to scoff at volunteers 'working for nothing', but now much of her time is spent on tenants' and residents' concerns and welfare rights, which she finds fulfilling. GNERA participants are heartened by the consistent support of local councillors to persevere in their efforts to serve the community.

Participants in the Federation and GNERA develop their listening skills and also become more tolerant as they learn of the variety of circumstances in which people live and of the difficulties with which some cope daily. They are more assertive and learn to keep calm 'so that your mind doesn't race ahead of your tongue'. People show a new sense of respect to others. They aim to tread a path between being passive, which does not help to meet needs, and aggressive, which 'can put people against you, ... you give them respect, that's the great thing'. Members find the work of the residents' associations satisfying and fulfilling. In the Federation and in their groups they work together and support each other; 'you get a fellow feeling for all are working for the same thing'. For all of them, 'when things get done for the neighbourhood you feel good'.

91

EFFECTS ON FAMILIES AND FRIENDS

Federation and GNERA members report that in general families support and show interest in their voluntary activities, and two instances were given of the development of skills being noticed. They also note the time spent in the house to prepare for meetings and contact others. The families also come to appreciate the improvements in the neighbourhood. Some members have taken up or increased their voluntary activities after children had grown up, after redundancy or unemployment after ill-health. A few older children have helped by taking out leaflets. However, complaints were reported that family members are 'out of the house too long', and in one case the family becomes angry when the member is thought to have done too much and comes home tired and irritable. One participant says she has shown the children how to take down telephone messages. The value of speaking to the family about voluntary activities is indicated when another member pointed out that at a time when some 'are looking after number one, we need to educate the family'.

Members of tenants' associations talk to friends about their activities and report that these become more aware of what local persistence and action achieve. Friends they meet locally thank them for recent improvements which have been made and discuss other matters which need attention. But it is reported that some are not interested 'because it's not happened to them'.

EFFECTS ON THE LOCAL COMMUNITY

Members of GNERA say that the work of the group has had an evident effect on the local community and, what may be more important, also on its outlook. Better parking and lighting amenities, the removal of dumped rubbish, and more traffic signs all improve the neighbourhood in which people live and work. Newly surfaced roads and altered kerbs improve the mobility of the disabled. The Association has been successful in obtaining a grant to buy garden tools to help keep gardens tidy. Besides tending their own gardens, members help disabled or elderly neighbours to keep theirs in good shape. The help is appreciated and the personal contacts made generate more social intercourse. Members report that they look on the environment 'with new eyes, to see it from the point of view of families with young children, the elderly'. They

92

say that people in the community generally appreciate the improvements, but some take them for granted.

What members also observe is the increase of pride in the area and a greater cheerfulness. Typical comments are: 'people feel proud when things get done' and 'people have a smile on their face and talk to you more cheerfully'. Members see the improvements they have helped to achieve and they feel that 'everybody knows what is happening at the local level'. They notice that as the area is cared for and neighbours keep their gardens tidy, people do more to look after their own surroundings - 'they tend the garden and paint'.

A member of GNERA who represents the tenants of a housing association reports that there is much more neighbourliness and pride in the neighbourhood; 'we've not even had a plant or tree broke, for we all stick together'. Another, however, pointed out the need for discretion when, for example, reporting dumping; if a household is suspected, 'you may get a brick through the window'.

As awareness of the achievements of GNERA has increased, a growing number of people, particularly the elderly, speak to its members about their troubles. Two of the members are able to help where welfare matters are involved, but even where no immediate help can be given members are gaining an up-to-date picture of people's circumstances.

The views of three District councillors, the District's Director of Housing, a housing officer, an officer of a housing association and a Social Services Community Development Worker are brought together on the effect of tenants' groups on their communities. They all see tenants' associations, when 'organised and knowledgeable', as 'a benefit to the community', as valuable and influential in indicating where resources for public services can best be used and in informing and educating the public. Some note the small numbers who actually attend the meetings at GNERA, as well as the commitment of the key members of the Committee to achieve improvements and ensure the continuation of the group.

CONCLUSION
Voluntary groups such as tenants' associations, focus the views and concerns of local communities to councillors and officers, and strengthen the participation of communities in the process of using

resources for the public good.

The individual groups seem to depend for their continuation and results on a few key people, who take the trouble to acquire a good deal of knowledge and apply it to seek improvements in their area. To the researcher this is one of the significant features of the study. This small number of active citizens respond energetically to the demands of the work to be done, gain satisfaction from their successes and broaden their sympathies. Within their groups and the Federation they receive the support to continue their work. In their separate groups they provide the drive and enthusiasm to carry on to achieve a measure of success. They form a strong inner core of commitment and growing expertise in their groups, and help other members and neighbours to appreciate the steps necessary within a complex organisation to implement an agreed improvement. To councillors and officers they can present a formidable force, making a case clearly and alert to counter points that may weaken their arguments. While ensuring they have public support for their actions, they realise that the generally small attendance at their meetings may not convey this impression to visiting officers. Within the Federation the groups may be at different stages, but together they have the potential and determination to form an influential spearhead, based on knowledge and some public support within their own neighbourhoods, to make an enduring impact on Councils' thinking.

Case Study 20

A WELSH WEA BRANCH

THE CONTEXT, THE BRANCH AND ITS PROGRAMME

This case study and its findings should be regarded as tentative because so few of the Branch members were available for interview and little external evidence was obtained. There were just three group interviews with a total of 13 individuals (9 men, 4 women, representing perhaps half the *active* Branch membership) and two interviews with three external observers. The project is grateful to the Branch Secretary for arranging member interviews and to all concerned for their helpful co-operation.

The Branch serves a South Wales village of some 6,000 people and draws upon a total catchment of perhaps 9 to 10,000. The men used to be employed in coal mining, tin plate or steel. These industries have gone, and the former industrial area has become a sour wilderness of waste ground additionally disfigured by garish box-shaped sheds dropped here and there in recent attempts to develop new sources of employment. There is very little of it and the small industrial estate on the edge of the village replaces only a small proportion of the lost jobs.

Meanwhile much of the traditional vibrant community activity of the area continues at least for the members of the Branch: all of them are involved with church, chapel, male voice choirs, rugby club and a variety of other organisations to the extent that it becomes hard to find a clear evening. In the circumstances of the study it was impossible to discover how representative of village activity this picture is, because the researcher only met Branch members who were of pensionable age. There are a few younger

95

ones but they were not available for interview. Following a lean period the membership has risen rapidly in the recent past. It is thought to be between 40 and 50 now and the recent members met by the researcher had joined on retirement from work. Between one third and half of the members are passive supporters, but as many as 37 have been known to turn up to the first meeting of a new class on a popular subject.

In the particular circumstances no attempt was made to administer individual anonymous questionnaires. However, only three of the respondents are known to have had high terminal education ages (TEAs) and related employment. One of these was an Englishman who, together with his Welsh wife, had settled in her original home on retirement. One other had risen through spare time study to graduate status and a managerial position. With the one exception of the English husband all respondents were local people. The membership was thus exceedingly stable and socially homogeneous.

The Branch draws upon a past which began just after the second world war when it was, and remained for a while, very active. Even for that time the activity was perhaps more typical of a particular kind of society which had reached its apogee in the 1930s and which now survives mainly among older members of the local population. The Branch reflected and served that society and continues to serve those who live in its particular social reality. Its role and its ethos differ from those more commonly assumed to be represented by WEA branches elsewhere in Britain.

Much of the early spirit is kept alive by the remaining long-term members and especially the Committee who look back to a golden past as something which they hold in trust for the local community. They remember the Branch of those days as a strong, egalitarian and united body, apparently of men only. It engaged in discussion and mutual education, and provided an admiring and loyal audience for the gladiatorial debates in which visiting experts, local polymath preachers and working class autodidacts locked horns. Since almost all the followers were working shifts, but no shift classes were held, irregular attendance was inevitable, and continuous, active and incremental learning would have been at best difficult. It may not have formed part of the ethos of the Branch and interview evidence suggests that it has not become customary

96

since then.

The Branch is led by a Committee which reflects this past, but it appears to be mainly the audience which remains from past personnel. The gladiatorial polymaths have gone, and experts are said to be hard to come by. Shift working has gone the way of the jobs and in any case almost all members are retired. However, the Branch maintains the tradition of organising a single evening class which every active member is expected to join. Owing to the variety of other village activities which claim both the loyalties of WEA members and space in the Mechanics' Institute, this must always be held on a Thursday evening. Notwithstanding the size of the membership, the option of holding more than one class has not been considered; Branch tradition is that a "proper" member attends regardless of the class subject, and the idea of giving a choice seems undesirable. Regardless of the fact that members are retired and have ample leisure, the possibility of day time classes which would not need to compete with other activities for time and space seemed positively surreal to Committee members. With only one class on a Thursday night, and a variety of tastes to satisfy, the Branch programme thus consists of a succession of six-meeting lecture courses, one before and one after Christmas each year. Topics are mostly broad and range widely ("Astronomy", "Comparative Religion", "Antiques"); specific ones ("Archaeology of the Gower Peninsula") are uncommon.

SOCIAL EFFECTS OF MEMBERSHIP

It was in keeping with tradition that, in all three interviews, the men showed initial reluctance to admit to any personal social benefits from membership, but they confirmed and illustrated them with some degree of enthusiasm once the women had identified them. Especially for recent members, classes enrich existing contacts and are a means of meeting new people. 'A convivial evening among people I like.' 'You meet people, it's like TESCO's ... companionship and interest in life.' Because everyone belongs to other organisations as well, it opens the way to new interests as well as wider contacts, is 'a door to a full life'.

EDUCATIONAL EFFECTS OF MEMBERSHIP

The evidence seems to point to the existence of three distinct groupings. It will be presented accordingly, but with the important caveat that neither the number of respondents nor the depth of the response justify absolute confidence in such a pattern.

The majority 'like to go out and hear experts. It gives you an insight into things I know nothing about'. They believe 'it broadens the mind' and that they become 'more aware'. If one is interested in the subject, the lectures can cause them 'to do a lot of thinking at the time'. However, 'we don't take part at all, there's no participation at all ... there *might* be a few questions'. This group draws a firm distinction between activities which are 'educational', 'demanding' and 'off-putting', 'like English and Accounts' and, on the other hand, their WEA classes which they attend 'to listen and enjoy'.

A smaller group of long-term members, while agreeing with the above description of the class meetings and their content, differ from the first in that they do, when the subject is of personal interest to them, follow it up actively outside the meetings by borrowing or even buying books about it. They want to 'go on learning something ... to improve my knowledge of things'. Above all, they continue to see the Branch as compensating for what they missed in their childhood and youth: 'I've had a terrific liberal education on which I missed out.' The WEA has 'enriched my life' and the varied class subjects continue to inspire new interests and activities, studies and educational travel. 'It's giving us something we've missed out on and there's a spin-off.'

Finally two recent members, retired technologists, see the class activity as no more than an initial trigger, to be exploited in long-term commitment to demanding personal study.

OCCUPATIONAL EFFECTS

With the exception of the two members just mentioned, membership of the Branch, even if it was combined with class attendance, does not represent a substantial commitment of time. It seems natural therefore that respondents (including the women, whose responsibilities had not ceased with their husbands' retirement) noted slight occupational effects of membership or none at all. Two of the men thought their letter writing at work had benefitted. The content of some courses, and the discussing and debating, had helped one who became a trade union official and spent some time in local government.

POLITICAL EFFECTS

There were marked differences in the reponses. Five were quite sure, regardless of prompts, that they were unaffected and that the idea of social or political awareness had no connection at all with their experience as WEA members. Three others had had their interest in international affairs deepened by one of the courses. One of these had been interested and actively involved in politics locally over many years, traversing the spectrum from left to right, but saw no connection with his experience of membership. The remaining five thought that social responsibility and membership of the WEA go hand in hand, and that this is a two-way traffic in which both are cause and effect. For them it was significant that it is the WEA which encourages them towards active citizenship and helps to make it informed. They regarded their own confidence to speak in public and to hold and express views and 'marshal your facts' as largely a direct product of their membership. Four of these five are currently officers of various organisations. One had been both a local trade union official and the founding Clerk of the Local Community Council, and another is a school governor.

PERSONAL EFFECTS

All seemed very conscious of their need to 'keep the brain active', and the success of membership in helping them to do so. 'If you go to these classes it triggers something off', and one of them illustrated this by describing how a geology class reference to the Andes had sent him via the Incas to his current reading about the social impact of the potato.

A number noted that they had become 'much more tolerant' and are able to appreciate the process of 'merging with people ... exchanging ideas, being at ease with my own ideas and other people's'. The experience of holding office in the Branch has taught one to trust his own experience. All of them, including one who described himself as 'a shy man', felt that the greater confidence which membership had developed in them had enabled them to make contacts more easily, and to speak in front of other people.

All were aware of the impossibility of clear distinctions between cause and effect in all this. They thought membership of the Branch

99

very much a cause, but also that 'there must be something there to begin with'.

INDIRECT EFFECTS ON OTHERS

According to one woman member a husband's commitment to the WEA can be awkward for his wife if she would need the car in order to attend something else on the same night, but another wife notes the advantage that 'it gets him out of the house'. Generally speaking wives 'take an interest'. One deliberately recruited her husband in order to help him overcome shyness and isolation and another did so as soon as her's retired from a shift job. Children and grandchildren in general are encouraged to share members' own excitements and interests, and one member who also belongs to the local rugby club has got its members so interested in the Branch's activities that they offered it accommodation at the club house and started to arrange lectures themselves. A few of them joined the WEA Branch. No other evidence of either impact or ways in which members might be perceived by others came to light. In view of the particular historical role, ethos and activities of this Branch it must be assumed that there will naturally be a gradual lessening of the degree to which its influence is felt by other people.

EFFECTS ON THE COMMUNITY

Questions and prompts under this heading produced the same diversity of responses from much the same individuals as under Political Effects. 'We enjoy it', some respondents say, but they do not see the Branch or its activities as affecting the community in any way. Some others are well represented by the following statement, regardless of whether their perception of the Branch's past is correct: 'In the past it was an educational thing. People used to sit in the reading room and look things up, and dictionaries. It was the only source of adult education, a bit like the Sunday School. It fed the Labour Party and fashioned a new way of life. But it's not like that now.'

On the other hand, what may certainly be described as the core group produced evidence of many and diverse activities and interests. All of these respondents were taking responsibility or had done so in all of them at various times - trade unions, chapel, church, choirs, angling club, bowls, rugby, women's organisations, and the Local Community Council itself. Whether all this was due to WEA experience, and whether the activities themselves were influenced by the WEA, is impossible to ascertain: 'I'd like to think so but I wouldn't like to claim.' What is certain is the impact of long term membership of the Branch and its committee upon the individuals concerned not just as individuals but as activists in this and a variety of other fields. The very caution of 'I wouldn't like to claim' is evidence of an ability to look for and assess the validity of evidence, of a hard-headed rationalism which is more likely to have developed through membership of the WEA, trade unions and local politics than in the minimal background of formal education which most members and especially this last group of them had received.

It thus seems very likely that past gains from membership of the Branch may have exerted some degree of beneficial influence upon the quality of life and the organisations and institutions of this particular community. However, none of the responses answer the question how real and how widespread that influence might be to-day. It is difficult to answer this question more than tentatively because appropriate external sources of evidence were few and limited.

The two sources which were tapped were at any rate consistent, and it must be admitted that their testimony seemed to mesh with the qualitative implications of the members' own evidence under all of our standard headings. In the local library the assistant did not know what the W.E.A. was or is. On being asked specifically if there had recently been an unusual level of demand for books about the Gower Peninsula (the subject of a class just finished), she replied in the affirmative, but knew of no reason. The Librarian herself knew that a W.E.A Branch exists in the village 'because I'm on the Local Community Council and we've just given them a grant' but she did not know anything else about it. The Chairman of the Community Council himself could only tell the researcher that the W.E.A. is 'a charitable group' which submits annual accounts as it must do and that it 'does good work for the community or they wouldn't get grant aid'. A number of prompts finally led him to connect this to a memory that the W.E.A. and AB's class (i.e. the Branch Chairman's) were one and the same thing, that there was a space problem in the Mechanics' Intitute, and that AB 'wouldn't be budged' from Thursday nights. Given the fact that in many and important ways this WEA Branch has a role which differs from that which is more commonly assumed, a comment such as the Community Council Chairman's should be regarded as positive. He clearly values a service which enables a group of elderly people to maintain a degree of intellectual and social activity which contributes to the maintainance of their health and self respect, and this is indeed consistent with their own direct evidence. The Branch has rather less in common than the researcher had assumed with organisations which engage partly or wholly in more specific educational activity, such as the Percival Guildhouse (Case Study 3), the Kelveden WEA Branch (Case Study 21) or even the Silverbridge group of the National Women's Register (Case Study 1). Considered in the same light as organisations such as the West Kirby 50 Plus Group (Case Study 16) or even certain self-help groups, a new role emerges, and this is the one which was discharged, and appreciated.

Case Study 21

THE KELVEDON (ESSEX) WEA BRANCH

THE CONTEXT, THE GROUP AND ITS MEMBERSHIP

Because the branch of the Workers' Educational Association which is the subject of Case Study 20 proved unusual in certain respects it was decided to include another, which would also cover geographical and social features not so far represented in our sample. The Kelvedon Branch has long served two contiguous villages, the other being Feering, which are joined rather than separated by the river Blackwater. Both are old and attractively representative of their area. Even as recently as 30 or 40 years ago they were fairly self-sufficient. Since then Feering in particular has expanded substantially. The joint population is now about 7,500 and employment is heavily commuter-based. Apart from those working at Chelmsford and Colchester, there are over 1,500 *annual* London season tickets issued here, and very many others people commute by car.

The demographic upheaval has been less dramatic at Kelvedon than at Feering, but its employment and commuting patterns appear to be much the same. Both villages are also home to substantial numbers of retired people, some of whom had worked from here while others came to live in this attractive area within easy reach of the facilities of two lively large towns and of London. The present population seems relatively stable, perhaps because a surprisingly high proportion of the many recent in-migrants are themselves Essex people. Twenty (91%) of the questionnaire returns were from people who had lived all, or almost all, their lives in Essex including its London fringe. Only 2 had come to the area in recent

103

years. The forest of estate agents' boards seemed rather thinner than one has come to expect recently in areas such as this. There were some remarks to indicate that the old and new populations have yet fully to merge, but all those respondents who commented said that they had done so fully in the WEA branch. Many WEA members also belong to the much larger Preservation Society, the Museum Society and some others, horticulture in particular. This suggests that for that very high proportion of the population which is active in voluntary organisations, distinctions of origin, residence and age are discarded in the face of shared interests.

Like the other Branch, this one is fairly traditional in that it usually runs one evening class at a time, whose topic is, however, decided in a large and argumentative meeting. There is also some degree of coherence in that, with occasional departures, the Branch tends to concentrate on courses in the visual arts, architecture and local history. The normal class is a "sessional", i.e. it extends over two full terms of weekly meetings 'so you can get your teeth into the subject'. It is usually supplemented by field work such as prepared visits or even holidays to study relevant sites or materials, by attendance at related one-day schools held at the University of Essex and by short residential courses. Study is taken seriously: the book boxes provided by the County Library are well used in addition to private borrowing, book purchase and the use of some personal collections. Note taking and the keeping of class logs are customary and members have also carried out local history research of their own, and published the results.

The Branch is in the midst of preparations for running a second, day time, course at a different venue in Feering, to which it hopes to attract mothers of young children in particular. Branches exist in one or two neighbouring villages and their activities tend to be similarly restricted to one class at a time; only Colchester is big enough to offer a choice. They keep each other informed of their programmes and a number of members sensibly follow their interests by joining in with neighbouring branches as appropriate. Such 'desertions' seem to attract amused understanding rather than ostracism, and there are some permanent exchanges. The number of active Branch members is in the region of 45, with usually 25 of them attending its own course while the rest tend to join in for one-day schools and field trips, and some others attend elsewhere.

The researcher is particularly grateful to the Branch Secretary who (with keen co-operation and the help of generous hospitality by members) succeeded in organising a tight programme of nine group interviews. There were altogether 32 respondents to these interviews, an unusually high proportion of the membership, though the timing may have caused some distortion of the age distribution towards the top of the range. There was, in addition, a brief interview with the two staff members of the local part-time branch of the County Library, from which emerged evidence on reading habits and the use made of book boxes.

QUESTIONNAIRE FINDINGS
A version of the standard questionnaire with the usual minor adaptations to take account of the group's characteristics was distributed to all interview respondents and a total of 22 (almost 69%) was returned in time to be taken into account in the following analysis. As far as could be judged, the returns differed from the total interview group in respect of age distribution, which follows:

31-40	41-50	51-60	61-70	71-80	81+
1	0	6	7	7	1

Here the 31-50 cohorts were very markedly under- represented by comparison with the interview sample. This means that members who have recently come to the district and joined the Branch may be equally under-represented. In all other respects findings from the questionnaires appear to be representative.

The findings from a comparison of terminal education ages (TEA) and present or last paid occupation were, however surprising. Including teachers there were 12 (54%) in professional occupations, 4 para-professionals and three in clerical posts. Three did not answer or gave their current (unpaid) occupation as housewives. The TEA distribution differed markedly, with 3 minimal (one at 14 and two at 15), 9 who had received a partial or complete secondary or further education to 16, 17 or 18 respectively, and only 9 with initial higher education. The discrepancy is explained by the high proportion of 5 (23%) of the minimal and secondary groups who had achieved higher qualifications and professional status through mature study.

Membership of the WEA was extremely stable. There were only two returns from people with less than 5 years' membership, though, as has been suggested, this group may be under-represented. Seven had been members for 5 - 10 years, another 7 for 11 - 20 and 4 for 21 or more. Two did not answer.

The question about what (other than the class subjects) members had learned from being *members* of the organisation (i.e. not just students) was misunderstood for the first time by a number of respondents, and this may have been responsible for absence of comment from 5. Where it was understood, the response was relatively thin. This may be a reflection of the exceedingly high level of organisational experience of most respondents, as shown below in their histories of participation. Even so there was a number of significant responses. Five commented on their learning about the WEA organisation itself, and learning from participation in organisational responsibilities. Four noted that membership had caused them to learn about the range of activities generally in the area, and had given them a stronger awareness of their surroundings, and the way in which their lives interact with these. Another four referred to various aspects of study or general intellectual activity: acquiring the ability to concentrate on the learning process, to 'really listen' to people and learn to co-operate with them, to develop research skills. Five mentioned coming to understand the value of friendship, of being members of a learning community, and of 'realising that learning not only should but can be pleasurable' and life-enhancing. It may have been a similar kind of experience that prompted 5 others to record their deep satisfaction from not just acquiring wide knowledge but an ability to 'manipulate' it, 'to appreciate life and look deeper into things' and to have confidence in one's ability to learn as an older person.

As many as 10 of the questionnaire respondents claimed not to be passing on the experience or knowledge they were acquiring in the Branch, and this, again, may bear some relationship to the skewed age distribution of this sample. However, of the remaining 12, 9 were passing some of their learning on to friends and acquaintances, 5 to their families, 3 to pupils present or former and 1 at work.

The amount of commitment involved in membership varied widely but was high for a branch running, at present, just one sessional class and encouraging its members to attend 1-day and similar courses regionally. Asked to estimate the number of hours

106

a year spent in actual attendance, preparation and follow-up of classes and on Branch business, 9 of the 20 who responded thought 50-60 hours. Four estimated 70-80 hours, three 80-90 and two 90-100. One very active member recorded 160, and the WEA's processes of reorganisation in addition to local duties, class attendance and related study had taken 650 hours of the Branch Secretary's time. Not surprisingly her social and family life had suffered and 4 of her other activities were in abeyance. The average commitment of these members had been 104 hours, which equals almost 6% of a normal full-time working year. The resulting personal expenditure on class fees in particular must have been high. It is likely to be an important factor determining the social composition of the membership. In this respect the Branch reflects the common misfortune of all adult education in recent years.

Twenty of the returns gave enough information to enable "histories of participation" to be constructed. In the case of the very high proportion of long-term WEA members the difference between "Past" and "Present Activities" ceased to be significant and the two lists tended to be more or less the same. However, the same appeared to be the case with more recent members, so that there was no significant difference between the two patterns. Neither was there any significant difference between those with different TEAs. In effect, respondents averaged 5.5 "Past" activities and interests with individuals ranging from 2 to 16, but clustering around 4 and 7. Present activities and interests rose to an astonishingly high average of 8.5, ranging from 3 to 20 and clustering around 5, 8 and 11. Almost all the individual lists represented a broad and liberal spectrum from intellectual and cultural to expressive, craft, physical and civic activity. These wide interests were also reflected in an equal range of memberships in other organisations. This averaged 6.1, ranged from 1 to 20, and clustered around 3 and 7. Apart from older members having to give up their more strenuous and competitive physical activities, nothing had been given up. The resulting pattern of expansion is thus typical of the trend which the Project has identified in all the "generalist" organisations it has studied.

Attendance at courses during the preceding 5 years, if confined to the Branch offering, would have yielded a maximum of 5 each. The recorded range was 4 to 'at least' 23 and 'very many'. The average was 8.5 but there were 6 returns of 10 or more. As would be expected in view of the age distribution, only a small proportion of the attendances were connected with inservice training for work. A high proportion were short courses arranged by the WEA and the University, and it was noticeable that many of these meshed with or supplemented the topics of Kelvedon Branch courses.

Asked which of the activities and interests recorded (other than WEA provided ones) had been stimulated by the WEA or fellow-members of the Branch, it became clear that most had been engaged in either prior to or independently of WEA membership. Three respondents (10.4%) claimed that none of their other interests and activities had been sparked off by the WEA, though 17 (85%) in contrast, reported that the WEA had introduced them to some of their present interests, hobbies and activities through classes or personal contact.

This suggests that the Branch is one in a network of reciprocally influential organisations with cross-membership, which between them stimulate an active and varied cultural life to which the Branch contributes and from which it benefits. In this the group is closely comparable to a number of other "generalist" organisations we have studied, such as Case Studies 1, 2, 3, 4, 5, the West Kirby 50+ Group (no. 16), the Welsh WEA Branch (No. 20), and the Sudbury Branch of the Suffolk Wildlife Trust (No.22). This pattern of what might almost be termed "syndromic involvement" will be found to emerge again and again in subsequent individual responses under our standard interview headings.

SOCIAL EFFECTS OF MEMBERSHIP
Three middle-aged ladies, well established and deeply involved in a variety of active pursuits, found it impossible to isolate the impact of the Branch from all their many other involvements. In a number of other interviews it was possible to discern some distinction between at any rate the relatively recent in-migrants and long-established members. One 'chose it as the focus of my social life' on moving to the village. A couple saw it as their introduction to the village on removal, 'a social outgoing activity' which led them on into membership of other organisations. 'It brings you in touch with people, especially if you haven't lived here before, (it is) amazingly friendly.' Quite generally the Branch is a source (and

sometimes *the* source) of personal friendships which persist, of mutual support and caring throughout the membership. People keep an eye upon each other, help out where there is illness or even permanent disability, give each other lifts to class and elsewhere.

What one of them sees as the 'very cosmopolitan' variety of members ensures that social contacts are richly varied: 'you meet people you wouldn't meet otherwise'; there is a strong sense of sharing interests which lead on to or spring from personal affinities. Existing bonds are also reinforced: 'it's something couples can do together'. Members of an elderly interview group produced comments such as 'It's very important: it fills my diary with things I enjoy.' 'We're all nice to each other; we *like* each other' and this group stressed not only the social satisfactions but the way in which their expanded social network was also providing them with a wider range of new interests and activities, reinforced by joint activity such as one day schools and trips, that kept them stretched.

None of this happened as it were of its own accord; it needed the deliberate effort of members to care for and help each other in a variety of practical ways. 'I felt extremely nervous when I joined, but got my confidence back' thanks to sensitive handling by tutors and the friendship and tolerance of fellow members. 'I'm very shy and it helped me with that ... I realise now that people are nothing to be frightened of.' And the perennial problem of young mothers: 'I used to absolutely long for that ... class ... it completely opened my mind'.

Branch members kept harping on their wish to extend the age and social distribution of their membership. They felt that its narrowness, and the severance (following a change of management) of their link with the local residential centre for spastics, were impoverishing the life of the Branch. The planning of an additional class aimed at young mothers from a housing estate was seen as an attempt to create a more satisfying social experience for themselves no less than to do their duty of making provision for all possible groups.

EDUCATIONAL EFFECTS

Members were extraordinarily vocal about this topic, and produced a great variety of responses. For quite a substantial proportion of them it was the Branch which helped them to learn 'to use time in

109

retirement constructively and intensively'. Thus two long established elderly women members took subject content for granted and seemed more concerned with certain generalities of learning. 'Life is wasted without something to do' and what better than learning to fill their time? Because 'lectures gather up for me the things one has always vaguely thought about, focus it, and make it usable.' But people also learn certain generic skills in the classes such as to discuss and to tolerate disagreement. Some of them acquire organising skills and take on responsible committee work. But for these respondents learning to understand the great variety of interests and of people involved is itself the greatest source of interest. Others, too, found that study in their classes developed an 'interest in life and things and people and putting something into life'.

Women, especially, can become 'horribly aware of gaps' in knowledge and understanding as their families grow up. Before joining the WEA, and despite very good schooling, 'I became aware of the most unbelievable gaps in my education'. Neither is this merely a matter of acquiring inert knowledge. Respondents spoke of the importance they attached to having acquired study skills or indeed the very capacity, for the first time, for real study. They were learning to concentrate on specific and specialised knowledge, 'going deeply into things', opening up awareness of previously undreamed-of areas of known subjects, becoming much more generally aware and observant and applying both skills and content as a result.

The experience of a variety of tutors with their own approaches was said to be stimulating critical thinking about both class content and various methods of teaching. In the process it developed an understanding of personal interaction and discussion, listening skills as well as the courage to challenge received opinion *including my own*. In consequence they feel strongly about having classes which are long and thorough enough to develop and to employ these skills, and the use of reading, writing, simple research tasks, and all the intervening short courses and field work. All these, regardless of the particular subject, are seen as parts of a coherent learning process and they issue naturally in a practice of keeping up with developments in the subject when the class is over. Respondents also spoke of the benefits of learning to be part of a working group and the way in which their field of interest broadens continually as their learning skills are brought to bear on their experience as members of other societies. Once awakened, the appetite for study feeds on itself, and progression to the Open University is by no means unknown.

These generic learnings (and the subject content itself) do not preclude more specific, ad hoc, tasks. Computer skills had to be acquired to support social research and its publication, as well as designing of Branch posters. Committee tasks and field work require organising and managerial skills, and these spread as office passes round the Branch.

It was a group of women who seemed to sum up all these experiences particularly well. 'You don't learn at school, you're too busy taking exams.' Now, in the WEA, you 'gain knowledge without having to prove it.' To be 'purely learning for learning's sake' is a new and deeply appreciated experience for members. It is voluntary, a pleasure, and there is time really to look into things and enjoy the process. This 'makes you look more closely at things' and 'more aware ... than before.' The respondents claim that they relate better and more intimately to new knowledge that is presented to them, and they use their own pre-existing experience in acquiring and understanding that knowledge. Doing it as a group makes all this learning more effective as well as more pleasurable, and one result of learning in the way they do in the Branch is that they are both more willing to help each other and to take responsibility for their own learning.

OCCUPATIONAL EFFECTS
Here responses fell into three separate groups. First of all there were some housewives for whom the Branch and classes had some slight secondary effects on the way they run their households. The second group (which also includes a few of the first) were all retired people, for whom the studies into which the Branch had initiated them had themselves become an absorbing occupation or the guiding principle of a related one. This last pattern is dramatically illustrated by the couple whose study of architecture and mediaeval buildings is guiding their life project, the reconstruction of the 14th century house in which they live.

The third group, of all those who were in paid jobs, claimed that

111

the class experience illuminated their work in one way or another. Historic background and material knowledge affected that of a journalist-author; openmindedness and the habit of using a variety of approaches to a single issue were making an engineer more creative; aesthetic training was influencing a potter's design practice. The teaching methods members were experiencing and which some analysed, were affecting their own teaching of their very different subjects, both to adults and young people. Personal and interactive skills acquired in the Branch were improving the ability to organise and manage a department of a business, a civil servant's work, and various others. All of these claimed that their experience with the WEA helped their work, whatever it happened to be, by making them more rounded personalities, giving them wider perspectives by which to judge their work and its requirements, and opening their eyes to the characteristics and conditions of people with whom they worked.

POLITICAL EFFECTS

In few, if any, of our case studies were the effects of membership as clearly and unanimously perceived as here. They begin with Branch democracy itself which is said to be 'carried to extraordinary lengths'. It is not only a 'group that belongs to its members'. The group deliberately encourages members to take part in village affairs, brings out their interests, varies and deepens their awareness of 'the village interest'. The view they take is a specifically inclusive one. They have so far resisted calls to make special provision for 'the disadvantaged' because they see it as a form of patronage of which they disapprove, because 'they're one of us'. Arrangements are in place to enable unemployed and other disadvantaged people to be absorbed into the mainstream. These used to include people from a local home for spastics as ordinary members of the Branch, who are now greatly missed. Members are encouraged to bring their social concerns to the Branch, and money-raising efforts are organised in aid of various good causes.

Almost all respondents pointed to the effect of classes in local and social history, in current affairs, and of discussions arising in other contexts, as stimuli which sharpened perception of the present and opened their eyes to current issues: 'it made me take it more seriously ... I now look at what's happening ... support action.' A

112

current affairs course some time ago seems to have had a particularly marked effect. Until then, a member said (and others agreed) 'I didn't question it, I voted as my parents did'. The class made them think and develop their own views because objective study 'cracks our prejudices'.

It seemed that in one way or another, and usually several, all respondents were actively involved citizens currently, or at least occasionally active in some form of service to the community. However, the Branch itself is perceived as part of a network of reciprocities involving other organisations, though there are instances where it can be shown to have been the original stimulant on some issue or other. Members have become involved in a variety of local issues such as planning matters, in the Parish Council, the work of local political parties, the churches and the Preservation Society. The questionnaire responses reported earlier (cf. p. 107f.) demonstrate this even more clearly and illustrate the quite extraordinary number of interacting organisational memberships which are involved. It may be even more difficult to identify the original stimulus because it is likely to have been multiple. However, the evidence also suggested that a disproportionate number of WEA members occupy leadership roles throughout the network. Interview evidence confirms this and suggests at least one reason for it. It is the class process itself which has developed the confidence to stand for office both in the WEA and elsewhere, and WEA members have a reputation of being ready and able to speak up at public and other meetings.

PERSONAL EFFECTS
As has been suggested, a few respondents found it difficult to isolate the impact of WEA membership from other concurrent influences, but most people had more definite views. At its simplest the effect was seen as interests and tastes being expanded and social relationships coming to include a specific personal and practical concern for the 'care of the decrepit'. Another respondent notes the way the interests and activities that make up life have become integrated and at the same time open-ended, leaving an intense desire to follow up new learning. 'My life wouldn't have been nearly as interesting if it werent for the WEA', says another. But this interest rests not just on formal learning but on personal

and attitudinal change. People have become more critical, more analytical, do not accept the world, and opinions, passively any longer; they demand and the group provides one avenue for, 'an *active* involvement in things around me'. The implication is that they have acquired greater confidence, but also a degree of tolerance and consideration for other people's feelings in what is a varied group with strong interests and convictions.

'Any learning changes you', and all these respondents are involved in other organisations as well, which must necessarily affect them. But it is the WEA of which a very elderly group said it has 'expanded our lives ... puts me in touch with new thinking ... keeps your mind moving, stops it drying up, ...' The new interests and following them up have made life richer but also more complex with new interests which meant having to become more organised generally. Without the pressures of examinations, members have 'recovered the learning instinct' and are now able to do more concentrated and more divergent thinking and learning across all their work and leisure interests.

Being able to attend classes with husbands or wives enriches both the relationship and the experience; the separate perceptions are integrated in discussion. Beyond this, several women members spoke of the way membership of the Branch rebuilt their confidence after years of domesticity, or while still immersed in it. The class is 'something *I have chosen* to do with my time'. This element of choice was of special importance to her because she had lost confidence in her own ability to cope with anything outside the home. The class was a first step, which enabled her to take subsequent ones into interests and activities, and finally into paid work: 'I wouldn't have met (others in the group), learned about music, changed the ways I've dealt with the rest of the world'. Intensive study in the Branch has brought a new experience of the potential richness of life, but it has also taught her patience over the demanding tasks she has chosen to undertake. With unconscious echoes she concludes 'I look at everything in a different way'.

EFFECTS ON FAMILY AND WIDER CONTACTS
The members' enthusiasm was obvious throughout the interviews and all of them spoke of sharing that enthusiasm with family, friends and neighbours, both in informal contexts and through the

network of local societies. Recruitment is thus an active and continual process, and it is based both on the general activity and on passion for particular subjects. There were accounts of spouses who, unable to attend a class, expect a detailed account of each meeting and share actively in follow-up. The age gap is frequently bridged both in families and elsewhere by interest in the class subject: 'it makes for a much happier family to have a granny who's interesting' and 'I tell my Rangers about it' because it enables them to see that there's life after school and 'learning that's enjoyable in its own right' and not bedevilled by exams. Transmission of the Branch's strong current interest in the visual arts has resulted in a son's taking it up and changing his occupation, while music, first taken up as a result of a course, has been passed on to a daughter. 'You can't help but reflect it ... you're the sum of your experiences' and therefore you share, pass on, discuss and influence others all the time. The most marked effects are of course the access of confidence and return to the habit of study which enabled several women to return to professional work after years of domesticity, and which led a few members to continue to Open University study and radically different occupations. More modest but probably no less important are the changes which are caused by the habit of applying the disciplines and skills of study in WEA classes to work tasks. The openmindedness developed through study has made some respondents more tolerant of other people's different views, insight or style, has taught them to respect and learn from these differences. Such changes of attitude are almost bound to be reciprocated by others, and thus have an important positive effect on the work place.

EFFECTS ON THE COMMUNITY
The members are modest about this. They realise that with 40 to 50 members in a population catchment of some 7,500 their's cannot be classed as a large and important organisation. The two villages are lively and active, with many and various societies some of which are bigger and better known than the WEA Branch. On the other hand nobody else in the village provides the kind of intellectually demanding and at the same time socially supportive group learning context which they organise year-in year-out, in a completely autonomous democratic context. Some of the single interest

societies are larger. The churches are equally good at integrating newcomers. But the Branch prides itself on offering something which is unique to itself, namely learning in depth in a co-operative group with the help of well qualified tutors. None of the other organisations stretch their members as they do. There is no series of one-off meetings here, nor short and superficial work. There is 'the opportunity to get one's teeth into a subject' and 'we *choose* what we're going to do'.

The Branch is seen by some of its members as part of a dense network of local organisations tied together by multiple memberships. This is carried by a number of key people who are very active in the WEA and other central activities and in public service, a kind of tacit collective. The existence of the WEA within the network, and its contribution both in training individuals in thought and study and the skills of public service, are important to the quality of both the network and the collective. Moreover, by its insistence on learning for learning's sake it contributes an important value to the total mixture. 'The essence of the situation', as one group put it, 'is that we're changed by it' - namely the experience of WEA class membership - and because of the positions held in other societies and public service by a significant number of members they are bound to contribute 'a leavening of the lump.'

Others pointed to various more detailed services. Being close to the class venue is regarded as a good selling point for a house; someone else has decided *not* to move in order to stay with the Branch. The WEA is said to help in ensuring that the village 'isn't stuffy or cliquey'. Their firmly held principle that anyone should be enabled to join the classes, rather than holding separate ones for the disadvantaged, and work on the additional new class underlies this. The Branch is also involved in supporting efforts by other organisations to meet a variety of other needs. Other organisations dealing with public issues through meetings and with speakers are larger, but 'the WEA is unique; there's nowhere else to go if you want to *learn*.'

A group of retired but exceedingly active members may be given the last word. They point out that there are many retired people in the village and in the Branch, and that this contributes centrally to their quality of life. Though relatively small, '(the Branch) is a well-known organisation in the village; they're glad we exist' not just because of their continuous standard offering but because they provide a base for anyone who wants to move on to mature study. They teach the skills that go with responsibility, and this is widely shared and turned over through their own committee. Having learned to carry responsibility and to do committee work, members often move on to other, including public, forms of service.

Case Study 22

THE SUDBURY BRANCH OF THE SUFFOLK WILDLIFE TRUST

BACKGROUND TO THE STUDY

The apparent stability of rural Suffolk conceals a surprisingly mobile population. Relative proximity to London and the availability of greenfield sites round Suffolk's large towns encouraged the development of large housing estates for London's overspill; attractive property prices brought London commuters and those looking for weekend and retirement homes. Declining job opportunities in agriculture and local industries such as the manufacture of coconut matting and wooden handles for hayrakes encouraged many young people to leave Suffolk to seek employment in London and elsewhere. Despite this population turnover and pockets of development such as the container port at Felixstowe, Suffolk remains deeply rural: no motorway yet crosses the county. It is therefore an appropriate setting for the study of wildlife and the conservation of natural habitats. The Suffolk Wildlife Trust (SWT) is justly proud of its 12,000 strong membership, a remarkable 2% of the total population of the county. Sixteen branches form the grassroots strength of the organisation. The Sudbury Branch, in the south-west of the county, is the subject of this case study. It was formed in April 1990 by the subdivision of a branch which had become too large. Its territory embraces the town of Sudbury and its satellites (population 20,000), the two ancient market towns of Long Melford (3,360) and Lavenham (1,710) and a scattering of villages and hamlets, a total population of around 30,000. The membership of the branch is 375 households, approximately 500 individuals, taking into account family memberships. Of these, about 10% are active, attending meetings regularly and taking part in surveys and working parties, and a further 10% attend occasionally and support open days and other special events. While the non-active members make a vital contribution to the strength and wider impact of the SWT, the case study concentrates on those who are actively involved in the Sudbury Branch.

The researcher attended the Annual General Meeting of the Branch, which took place in its regular meeting place in Long Melford Community Centre. About 35 people attended, of whom 23 (12 male and 11 female) agreed to be interviewed, including the Chairman, Secretary and Treasurer, and three other committee members. The respondents were scattered widely across the territory of the Branch, with a concentration of Long Melford residents probably because meetings take place regularly there rather than in Sudbury which lacks reasonably priced venues. A short anonymous questionnaire was given to each respondent, 22 of which were completed and returned. The researcher is grateful to the Branch for agreeing to be the subject of study and to members who gave time and hospitality so generously for the interviews.

In order to evaluate the wider impact of the organisation, opinions were sought from appropriate departments of the local council, from the local library and the local press. The Chairman of a neighbouring branch and a member of the SWT executive were also interviewed.

THE QUESTIONNAIRE

Twenty two of the respondents, 95%, very helpfully completed and returned questionnaires subsequent to the interviews. The analysis of the findings is supplemented by some unprompted comments by respondents made at the time of interview. Eleven (50%) of those who completed questionnaires have been members of the Sudbury Branch since it was formed in 1990; all of these belonged to the SWT before the Sudbury Branch was formed, ten of them for between three and nine years and one for over 20. The other eleven have belonged to the Branch for between 6 months and two years, and six of these had been members of the SWT for at least two years before they became active here. Unfortunately the questionnaire did not specifically ask if respondents had been active in other branches before they joined the Sudbury Branch, but four volunteered that they had. These responses suggest that the recruitment of new active members is steady despite two comments in interviews. The Chairman said that the recent recession had discouraged new recruits, especially as SWT has recently raised subscriptions by £3 to £14 for individuals and £16 for couples. One of the committee members commented on the difficulty of getting people to become actively involved despite encouragement at open days: 'they seem to lack the commitment and confidence'. Four of the questionnaires were completed by members who have lived in the area all their lives. Of the rest, seven have lived in the area up to ten years, 7 between 11 and 20 years and 4 over 21 years. This split of 18% 'natives' to 82% newcomers confirms the chairman's view that among active members newcomers predominate, and the opinions expressed by a born and bred Suffolk member and by a member who is a professional conservationist that newcomers are more active in working for the preservation of the countryside because, having moved into the area for its rural amenity, they have a special interest in seeing it preserved. The ages of those completing questionnaires are:

21-30, 1; 31-40, 4; 41-50, 3; 51-60, 7; 61-70, 4; 71+, 3

This pattern, 36% under 50 and 64% over 50, is illuminated by musings during interview of a young member who has just crept into the 31-40 age range. He was wondering why there are more retired and middle aged people actively involved and answered his own question by saying that in your thirties and forties, responsibilities of house, children, career take over and involvement in conservation is put on hold. This bothers him as he can see himself 'going that way and falling into the mould of non-involvement' until he reaches his fifties! Terminal education ages (TEA) from the questionnaires are:

15, 1; 16, 3; 17, 3; 18, 3; 21, 3; 22, 6; 24, 3

Seven have (or had) health and welfare related occupations - two doctors, an optometrist, various branches of nursing and social work. Five are (or were) secretaries or in office administration; two worked in industry, one is a teacher and five are self-employed: a bookseller, a smallholder, an artist, a restorer of antique furniture and a pet food distributor. Several members in interview commented on the middle class nature of the organisation and one asked himself the question, 'Is an organisation like his inevitably middle class?' His answer was that while the membership of some other organisations was predominantly 'county folk', the Wildlife Trust is 'not like this', but the flavour is still essentially middle class, though the Chairman saw the membership as 'broadly based socially'. The 22 who completed questionnaires belonged to an average of 3.8 other wildlife/environmental organisations. Only 2 belonged to no other comparable organisation, 16 belonged to between one and five and 4 belonged to between six and ten. Seventeen (77%) were attending adult education classes now or had done so within the past five years. These were a mixture of local authority, WEA and extra-mural classes, depending on local programmes. Natural history and local history were the favourite topics though as one respondent noted, 'Some topics studied arise because of availability at village evening class rather than direct choice and interest'. At least four are currently attending the same WEA wild flower identification course. Three mentioned the City and Guilds Conservation and Countryside Recreation Course and two the University of London Diploma in Countryside Management.

Responses to a question about membership of voluntary organisations with objectives other than environmental show that six, 27%, belong to none at all; the other sixteen belong to one, two or three each, an average of 1.3 per person. Among these other organisations, music and art groups are the most often mentioned. Overall, membership of voluntary organisations including the Wildlife Trust averages 6.1 per person, a substantial figure. Main leisure activities apart from those directly connected with wildlife are gardening (12), walking and 'the countryside' (11), reading (5), church activities (5), music (6), family history and photography (2 mentions each). Yoga, swimming, tennis, football, cycling, painting, philately, painting wild flowers, woodwork, cooking, winemaking, sailing, travel and cats all appear once each. Responses to the question 'which of your groups/interests arise directly from your involvement in the Wildlife Trust' closely paralleled those to Case Study 21, which was carried out in a not dissimilar community. One respondent found the question 'too tight' to answer. Nine replies of 'none' bear out that criticism, but the qualifications to this

121

negative response explain further: 'none directly but all are influenced by involvements', 'they all link together', 'several are related interests', 'they run parallel','probably the other way round, membership of other groups led to my joining SWT' and 'mostly the other way round'. The message was clearly that all these interests and involvements are interconnected and that the number of interests which are totally unconnected are relatively few. As one respondent said in interview, 'Once in, it snowballs.' An exceptional illustration of this was given by one respondent who listed six out of twelve groups and interests which arose directly from involvement with the Sudbury Branch.

THE INTERVIEWS
The interviews of members took place in people's homes, either one-to-one or with pairs and in one case with a threesome. Discussion was informally guided by the researcher, and the evidence is presented in the pattern established for all case studies.

SOCIAL IMPACT
Membership of the Wildlife Trust is motivated by a deep interest in and concern for the environment and no respondent mentioned social reasons for joining. However, for many the social benefits had become important. Many said that they valued 'contact with like-minded people' and that it was 'nice to be with people who have similar interests' and that 'meetings tend to be social events as much as meetings'. The social contact was especially enjoyed by respondents who described themselves as 'shy' and 'not naturally a social person' and by those who live alone or in isolated rural settings.

Seven of the respondents lived in Long Melford, where the regular evening meetings of the group take place. They each spoke of the value of having the meetings 'just up the road' and commented on what might be termed 'the Long Melford factor'. As one explained, 'there are lots of very bright retired people here' who form 'the core of active people who belong to everything'. Another saw the village divided into 'the joiners, whom you meet everywhere, and the non-joiners', the joiners being 'newcomers, in their 50s and above and middle class'. Membership of the Wildlife Trust branch, the church, the WEA, the community association and its off-shoots,

122

and the vigorous Historical and Archaeological Society creates a social network which is strong and supportive and pleasant for all concerned. These comments, again, are virtually identical to the "syndrome" found in Case Study 21.

A respondent who was 'born and bred' in Lavenham and has lived in the area all his life described the difference in attitudes and class between the more affluent newcomers - Them - and the local people - Us. He is an active member of the Branch who spreads widely his enthusiasm for local history and the countryside, and sees himself 'as a link person between us and them'. The Chairman too sees the Branch as a group where local people and newcomers like himself can share common interests, though he admitted that among the active members newcomers predominate.

An ex-foreman of a motorway construction gang has met a 'new sort of people' in the group. They are 'different from people in the building trade where there is a dog-eats-dog situation. He finds fellow members generous and sharing and has made significant friendships in the group. Sharing work projects such as flower surveys or reed cutting develops social bonding between people who might not make easy contact in more formal settings.

The study of wildlife is an activity which can often be pursued better in isolation. The chairman pointed out that active members can be 'loners' who do valuable work for the Trust entirely on their own, never attending a meeting or group event. But for those who attend Branch meetings, the social 'spin-off' is enjoyable and for some adds a significant dimension to their lives.

EDUCATIONAL IMPACT
Members come to Branch meetings to learn more about wildlife and about conservation of the environment. Most started off with some knowledge of natural history and often with a particular interest in one aspect, most often, in fact, in birds. All felt that their knowledge has been both widened and deepened through membership. Many mentioned how much they were learning about wild flowers, one saying that he has 'got a terrific amount out of the Branch as far as flowers are concerned - I'm a flower nutter now.' Several are now taking a WEA wildflower identification course arranged by one of the members who is also the local WEA Branch secretary. A course member said that this was 'getting down to the

fine detail', and 'I'm learning the Latin names and loving it.'

Other particular areas of learning mentioned were woodland management, dragonflies, butterflies, bats and badgers, and a detailed knowledge of local wildlife habitats and conservation techniques. 'I learn something from every meeting', 'good programme, good visits, good newsletter - all educational' and 'I've gained greater detailed knowledge of plants and particular species such as dragonflies' were typical comments. The regular Branch newsletters distributed to members with other wildlife publications provided by the SWT contain a mass of wildlife news and information about local surveys and workparties. A member who had been instrumental in getting a piece of woodland turned into a SWT reserve described what a complex learning process the long campaign had been. Through organising and joining in working parties to clear and coppice the woodland, he had learned a great deal about woodland management. One result of the greater involvementof members in the practical work of the upkeep of reserves has been, as this member pointed out, a closing of the gap between theoretical study of natural history and the practical skills of countryside management. Sharing is an important aspect of the learning process mentioned by several respondents. One spoke of 'the stimulation of meeting other people and getting other ideas'. Because different members bring different special interests to the group, there is a lot to be learned from each other. For example, bird song experts help other members to distinguish the nightingale and other bird song during shared walks in woodland reserves. Others spoke of their mutual learning about wild flower surveys. One member went to every one of the 31 survey sessions last year, learning from other members to identify the many species growing in the area. Most members belong, as the questionnaires showed, to other natural history and conservation groups and many have attended courses on environmental topics. One respondent had attended 58 courses on either history or natural history over the past 11 years, most sponsored by the WEA of which he is a Branch secretary. Coming to education as a mature student, he spoke of it as an 'unbelievable experience'. He plans to 'move on to' Cambridge extra-mural classes, on whose local committee he now serves, though he will continue to support the WEA. For him, the lectures at Branch meetings of the Wildlife Trust were 'topping up knowledge'. The Wildlife Trust is 'the medium which serves his hobby' and has interacted with the WEA to fill his time since becoming redundant 11 years ago. After working at what implicitly were rather boring jobs since the age of 14, redundancy turned out to be a totally liberating experience, 'the best thing that ever happened to me'. Another respondent made redundant from motorway construction has learnt that conservation is more enjoyable and satisfying than building work. He joined the Wildlife Trust and is taking a City and Guilds conservation course and finds that the lectures at Branch meetings and the practical work parties help with his college work. He has found great satisfaction in passing on his new knowledge and skills to groups of schoolchildren and to disabled people. He now has 'a hunger for education and I would like to go on studying for the rest of my life', and he sees his involvement in the Wildlife Trust as a part of this process.

The older members find satisfaction in having time to learn again and to build on childhood interest in natural history. They find involvement in the activities of the Branch a good way of keeping mentally stimulated. One of the younger members said how learning about conservation 'snowballs and takes over your life, because of your concern'. For newcomers to the area, membership of the group is a way of getting to know the area in depth. They value the group visits to reserves which they might not otherwise discover.

Members who have taken on the voluntary wardenship of reserves in the area have opportunities for more learning than the average member. The chairman has been the voluntary warden of Cornard Mere for eight years, since before the Sudbury Branch was formed. He organises nine work parties each year, which undertake under his direction reed cutting, willow cutting and clearing rides through the reserve. He takes groups on guided walks and visits each week to ring and make records of birds that visit the mere. He is supported by practical courses offered by the SWT and gets "perks" in the form of visits with other voluntary wardens to national nature reserves of special interest that are closed to the public. A committee member who has been voluntary warden of a local wood for about two years has broadened his knowledge from a special interest in birds to take in all the life of the woodland. The work has also brought him into closer contact with other members as voluntary wardens are expected to share knowledge and information within the Branch. For many committee members, organising a voluntary group was a new experience, which they found 'an interesting learning process'. One has learned how much work committee members have to do and finds that most is done by a small group within the committee. Members appreciate the amount of work the Chairman puts into the Branch and feel that he should share out the burden more. The Chairman, who is learning his role, and in particular 'how to organise people', still finds it difficult to delegate effectively. As a committee newly formed three years ago, one member perceived that 'it is going through a learning process of how to organise itself and the Branch better.' It is learning by experience not to overload the programme but to concentrate on fewer, "flagship", events and do them well. The Treasurer has learned how to keep accounts for a community group and responsibility for the sales stall at fundraising events has been a learning experience for another committee member.

OCCUPATIONAL IMPACT

For some members who are in employment, involvement in the activities of the group is a contrast and relief from their work. A busy general practitioner finds his long hours of work take too much of his time, leaving too little for wildlife pursuits, and his keen participation in football and tennis. An optometrist enjoys his wildlife activities because they bear no relationship to his work and are a contrast to the regimentation of his work pattern. A clerical worker values time spent in the open air after sitting at a desk all day. The Chairman has his own furniture restoration business which he fits in between his preferred voluntary work for the Trust. He finds that wildlife is taking over completely and is wondering if he should look for an opportunity for a career change.

For others, the relationship between work and wildlife interests is closer. Indeed, the GP said that wildlife sometimes comes up as a subject for discussion with patients. He feels that his aura of authority as a doctor gives wildlife and conservation respectability in the eyes of his patients. The bookshop owner values involvement in the Branch for the business it brings her. She has

126

the opportunity to advertise books relating to courses and lectures and, as a recent newcomer, it is good for her to be seen to be involved in local organisations. A young artist uses images of nature in her art: 'increased knowledge of wildlife gives me more accurate reference material for my paintings'. A young primary school teacher, who worked in the central office of the SWT for a year before taking up teaching and is now settled in the Sudbury area, is hoping to start a Watch Club, as the junior wing of the SWT is called, for the children at her school. A self-employed pet food distributor uses his travels in the area as an opportunity to spot wild flowers and to advertise the activities of the Branch to his customers. He talks about his hobby to all his 'ladies' so effectively that sixteen of them came to one of last year's open days. The two unemployed respondents have both been able to develop their interest in wildlife and give a substantial amount of time to the activities of the Branch. One of them is hoping, when he has gained his City and Guilds certificate, to be able to get a job in conservation. Two respondents are employed as conservation officers. One committee member's job as Ranger of the Sudbury town meadows interacts closely with the work of the wildlife trust. He was invited on to the committee of the Branch because of his job and as Ranger he organises walks and surveys on the meadows which forge links between the Branch, the management committee of the charitable trust which owns the meadowland and the Local Authority's Dedham Vale and Stour Valley Countryside Project. Another member has a local authority job in a countryside management project just outside the Branch's area. In his spare time he is using his conservation skills to convert his large new garden into a varied wildlife habitat. As a professional, he deplores the way that conservation has to be presented as fun to attract volunteers and would prefer to see jobs created for a trained work force.

The interviews revealed a considerable amount of interaction between members' occupations and their interest in wildlife and conservation. In some cases involvement with the group is a pivot of this interaction while for others Branch membership is just one thread in a complex web of activities.

127

POLITICAL IMPACT

The SWT is an environmental pressure group, so it is not surprising that membership has increased individual members' political awareness. Most said that their concern for environmental issues predated their joining of the Trust but that through membership they had learnt more about the politics of conservation. Environmental issues have led the Branch and individual members into negotiation with parish, district and county councils and this has raised awareness of local politics and the way 'in which power is distributed between the different layers' of local government. One retired member said that it was the first time he has belonged to an organisation which is so active politically and another said he had become aware of the importance of local pressure and more informed about wider issues, both national and international.

Several expressed their wish to act on their concerns in a practical way. 'I must feel useful, I've got to do something to help the community' said one member, whose father had set her an example of 'civic consciousness'. She worked for ten years as a volunteer in the Citizens' Advice Bureau and has now 'switched from people to the environment'. In a small way another respondent felt that he was' doing a bit to improve the world'. He does not expect a letter to a government minister to make any difference but 'I can say I tried'. A committee member said that it is 'nice to feel that I might have a bit of influence in local affairs' and through being on the committee he 'feels more in the know'. He gave as examples of action based on greater awareness his evidence given at local enquiry on the route of a new road and a letter he wrote to the local planning officer pointing out the whereabouts of a very rare tree that he had found. The result of the enquiry is pending and the planning department has taken note of the tree.

Most of the members belong to other wildlife and conservation organisations. Such cross-membership contributes to increased understanding and co-operation, but also exposes areas of conflict of interest between groups. For example, the secretary is also honorary membership secretary of the Suffolk Preservation Society and works two days a week in the SPS office in Lavenham. She has learnt that the emphasis on buildings by the SPS can conflict with the preservation of wildlife habitats, and on some issues the two organisations may be pulling in different directions. This can cause

128

her problems in sorting out where her loyalties lie. A committee member who described herself as 'highly political' feels that while the Branch is democratically run, the SWT is too authoritarian. She considers that it makes demands on the Branches for money and information but does not always listen to and support grass root aspirations. She feels strongly that the organisation should be more democratic from the top and personally strongly objects to the acceptance by SWT of sponsorship from a chemicals firm. In these ways, her commitment to the Branch is engaging her in difficult personal political debate. Another of the younger members agrees that there is not enough consultation by SWT of Branches but he feels that 'local members on the whole don't want to be bothered' with the internal politics of the organisation. Another respondent, significantly again one of the younger members, felt that involvement with the Branch 'does not make you a wiser political animal'. He feels that members are urged to raise money for SWT but 'cushioned from the political aspects.'

It would appear that all members of the Branch feel that their political awareness is being enhanced and have strong opinions about environmental issues and how they should be effectively promoted by both the Wildlife Trust and other environmental organisations.

PERSONAL IMPACT

Most respondents spoke of personal satisfaction from involvement with the group and joy and pleasure from the study of nature. Three respondents spoke of an increase in self confidence. One of these was a very shy person for whom working on a committee had resulted in 'an improvement in personality'. Another realised that 'you don't have to be an expert to make a contribution', which had made her more confident, and the wife of the third said that involvement had given her husband 'a lot of confidence' and had 'changed him for the better'. Two respondents commented on the therapeutic effects of involvement with the activities of the group; one valued the relief from stress and pressure of work and the other saw 'the interaction of self-help and help for the environment' as involvement which kept his 'mental muscles from drifting into inactivity'. Another spoke of a 'lot of fun and a good experience of commitment.' For the two who had taken up conservation after redundancy, involvement in the group was one of the influences which had effected profound personal change. However, the interviews produced less information about the personal effects of membership than has been usual in case studies made by this researcher. She hazards a guess that most people became members of conservation groups because of the kind of people they are, rather than membership contributing to their becoming such people.

IMPACT ON FAMILIES AND FRIENDS
The fact that the 500 strong membership of the Branch is distributed in 375 households suggests that about a quarter of the members belong as families rather than individuals. Indeed, there were five couples among the respondents, and a mother, daughter and son-in-law, and clearly all were stimulated by their common commitment to Branch activities. One partner specifically valued involvement as a shared interest. Other respondents spoke of the support families gave to the Branch by attendance at open days and tolerance of time spent on wildlife business. One member enjoys wildlife interests as 'her own space, an opportunity to do things independently of my husband', who is wholly supportive of her commitment and reciprocally enjoys his golf. Natural history appeals to children as much as to adults and brings the generations together in a common enthusiasm. One respondent had first been taken to Branch meetings by her son. Several had passed on their interest to children and grandchildren and brought them on walks and to open days. Those for whom detailed study of wildlife had become almost an obsession were eager to include family and friends in their hobby. One man has involved his girl friend in walks and badger watches as well as inspiring his nephew to look for qualifications in woodland management. Another member has been helping her brother over a difficult period in his life by persuading him to develop an interest in the activities of the Branch. Enthusiasm for wildlife is a hobby which people are keen to share with families and friends and one which seems particularly successfully transmitted across the generation gap.

THE WIDER IMPACT
The wider impact of the Sudbury Branch can be seen partly at local level, as its progamme of activities brings wildlife issues to the

130

attention of the general public, and partly at county level by virtue of the numerical and financial support that the Branch contributes. The wider impact is both educational and political. In addition to the opinions of members, evidence of wider impact was collected from representatives of a neighbouring branch and the SWT executive, from local agencies such as Sudbury library and the relevant departments of Babergh District Council, and the environment correspondent of the local newspaper, the East Anglian.

Educational effects
The Sudbury Branch takes its wider educational role very seriously. It aims to spread information about local natural history, and the Chairman and other members expressed their confidence that it was effective in raising awareness of conservation issues beyond its membership. Examples of 'spreading the word' are the open days: 300-400 people came to the last Groton Wood open day, many of them not members; and the street collections: £170 was recently collected in Sudbury and the collectors were able to talk about the Wildlife Trust to many interested shoppers. One of the Sudbury librarians, herself a member of the group, is called upon to answer queries on any topic relevant to wildlife or the environment. She reported considerable interest arising from the wild flower surveys in the town meadows. The chairman of a neighbouring branch said that the strength of the branches lies in their grassroot support and the relevance of local programmes to the interests and concerns of local people. The environment correspondent of the East Anglian said that the SWT as a County organisation has 'a significant educational function' both in its work with schools and with adults in the community. He described it as 'good at grassroots level, good on a community basis, and extremely good at stimulating community environmental projects'. At Branch leveleducational work with children is through Watch Clubs, which the Sudbury Branch is hoping to establish in its area in the near future, and at County level in two education centres which run courses and activities for 5000 schoolchildren from across the county each year.

Some more cautious views were expressed such as 'it's still a bit of a minority interest' and 'it's really catering for those who are interested - not the average man in the street. There is some way to go to capture the interest of ordinary people.' But even the most cynical respondent admitted that 'it chips away', and that helped by media coverage of wildlife and environmental issues, it contributes to a general increase in interest, knowledge and awareness.

Political effects
The political issues of conservation work have been highlighted by the campaign to stop the building of a link road round the south of Sudbury. There are a number of environmental arguments against this road and the one of particular concern to the Wildlife Trust is its cutting across an island in the river Stour which is a unique wildlife habitat. The Sudbury Branch joined in a consortium with 10 other organisations with a variety of concerns to argue against the road at a public enquiry.

The campaign has raised the public's awareness of environmental issues and has given the Branch experience of fighting such a campaign. There are some interesting aspects of the Branch's involvement which throw some light on its strengths and weaknesses as a pressure group. Initially it did not get the support of the SWT in its objections to the scheme. One of the committee members, who lives and works in Sudbury, took the initiative in forming the Action Group Consortium. He personally persuaded a Deputy Director of SWT of the merits of the campaign which in the end won over SWT support and funding for the consortium. The Branch has been active in joining in local protest, but the efforts of individual members seem to have been more committed and effective than any group action. No doubt the experience and knowledge gained will be useful for future campaigns, and the Branch has gained a higher profile locally as a participant in the consortium. In an earlier section the achievement of a member in the successful campaign to gain a preservation order on an area of ancient woodland was mentioned.

The success of this campaign in which the respondent took such a leading part, stimulated the SWT in its policy of acquiring wildlife reserves which now number around 60, most of them freely accessible to the public as well as to members of the Trust. The reserves in themselves are regarded as of great educational importance in providing places for the study of wildlife and for practical application of conservation techniques and habitat management. They have played a crucial part in the build-up of the membership of SWT, and illustrated how effectively grass roots support can be mobilised. This led to the decision to form a network of local branches which stimulate local excitement and enthusiasm for involvement in local projects.

Having established a spread of reserves, the SWT is now concentrating on persuading and educating landowners and farmers to manage their land sensitively for wildlife, while the EC regulations leading to the increase of land set aside from cultivation reward environmentally beneficial management schemes. Further, with the agreement of the Local Authorities in charge of road maintenance, over 100 roadside verges are now protected and managed, forming miniature nature reserves. Within the structure of local government, environmental issues are dealt with at District Council level from their offices in Hadleigh. In both Parks and Planning departments the work of the Wildlife Trust was well known. Volunteers from the Trust provide working parties for conservation work not suitable for contractors in local authority parks and country sites. Their work is reliable and much appreciated by the departments. The Trust has succeeded after years of pressure in gaining an influence on planning applications. The planning officer sends for consultation to the Wildlife Trust any application which he feels has implications for wild life and takes into consideration opinions expressed. Some Branch members were critical that not enough account is taken by SWT of knowledge and opinions at grass roots level. The member of the executive of SWT made the point that the Wildlife Trust 'is effective in bringing influence and bringing about action because it exercises pressure rather than makes protest'. He said that the growing influence of the Trust on Planners is due to the large membership in the County backing up the skill of the paid Director and his staff. The policy for the future is to secure the same status for listed wildlife sites as for listed buildings. Media publicity is regarded as crucial to maintaining a high profile for the work of the organisation. The environment correspondent on the East Anglian reports fully about the Trust's activities because it is, in his opinion, 'a very effective conservation organisation'.

CONCLUSION

The interviews showed that involvement in the Sudbury Branch of the SWT has a very great impact on its active members. The Wildlife Trust is characteristically one of a number of environmental and natural history organisations to which they belong, but because it has a vigorous and locally based Branch, it is one which is of considerable importance to them. It adds significantly to the quality of life both of individuals and of the community, and helps to safeguard that quality for the future. Concern with the immediate environment is a strong impetus to active citizenship. Members take seriously their role as protectors of the countryside and conservers of wildlife habitats not just for their own interest and pleasure but for what they see as the good of the community and for future generations. As part of a county-wide organisation (which is itself part of the national Royal Society for Nature Conservation) through their numbers, their publicity, their campaigning and their policy of open reserves, their work raises public awareness and has an influence on local planners. They are not only making members of the public more knowledgeable but winning their sympathy and support. Individual members add to their own knowledge and pleasure while at the same time contributing to the development of good management of the countryside.

Case Study 23

THE GORGIE DALRY WRITERS WORKSHOP

INTRODUCTION

This group was chosen both for intrinsic reasons and to widen the project's geographical spread. It is an associated group of the Adult Learning Project (ALP) which is based in a shop in Dalry Road, Edinburgh. ALP was started in 1979 to assist the regeneration of the depressed Gorgie Dalry area by the application of selected parts of the educational philosophy of Paulo Freire. Methods and progress of the project up to 1987 have been described in *Living Adult Education: Freire in Scotland*[1.] ALP has now (1992) become part of the Local Authority's community education service, is still working in the area, and continuing to build 'programmes of learning and action' to assist local people in their efforts to meet perceived local needs.

The Workshop itself was started by the ALP workers in 1981 to provide a forum for writing about themes other parts of ALP were working on through music and photography, and by studying local issues such as the take-up of welfare rights, health and local history. Support was obtained from the Lothian Regional Council Community Education Department with some involvement from the Adult Basic Education service of the Scottish Community Education Council (SCEC), as it comes within the broad definition of basic education[2]. The members of the Writers Workshop soon 'broke loose from the themes of the project' to pursue their own concerns. Their common interest lay in creative writing and in their aspiration

135

to improve their writing skills, starting from their varied levels of competence. The workers handed over the workshop to its members, and it became an autonomous group, still associated with ALP and committed to the ALP culture.

THE GORGIE DALRY AREA

Gorgie Dalry is an area of densely packed streets and tenements, sandwiched between Haymarket, at the west end of the city centre, and the suburbs. Following the closure in the 1960s of many local works many families moved out to new council housing in the outer suburbs. Today there is still a core of the old skilled and unskilled working population, but new people have been moving in, taking advantage of cheap housing near the city centre. Many travel to work in other parts of the city and to new industrial estates beyond. Apart from a small concentration of families of Asian origin, the social character and appearance of the neighbourhood have changed little. The drab and rundown late nineteenth century terraces, grey and clifflike, remain and the typical 'house' is a flat approached by a bleak and steep stone staircase. The volume of traffic thundering down Dalry Road is new and seems to mirror in its movement the feeling of a whole community being on the move.

The development of ALP was just one of a number of initiatives in the late 70s and early 80s which recognised the needs of the area; others were the Gorgie Dalry Community Shop which is the base for the Gorgie Dalry Community Council, the Better Gorgie Dalry Campaign and the local newsletter, the Gorgie City Farm, and two adult education centres with an emphasis on drama and the arts. In fact one respondent went so far as to describe the area as 'saturated' with community projects which have, in the words of another, made it 'highly politicised' and 'vibrant'.

THE GORGIE DALRY WRITERS WORKSHOP

Since September 1981, a great many people have passed through the Workshop, though its membership at any time has remained fairly constant between 10 and 20. Today there is a hard core of around 20 people with a penumbra of 20 more who may appear sometimes or reappear after an absence of months or even years or be members by correspondence, having moved to distant places. The group now has two parts which overlap and interact. The Writers Workshop meets on first and third Tuesday evenings and is mixed and open to all, but in practice predominantly male. The second part, Words, which meets on Sunday afternoons, developed three years ago in recognition of the need for women to have their own space in which to find their voice. Some Words members go to the Tuesday sessions and occasionally a male member comes to Words, 'not just out of tokenism but when it feels right'. The two parts meet and mingle at events, readings and performances, and in the pub sessions afterwards.

The groups are organised as a collective, without constitution, committees or officers. Different members, by pre-arranged agreement, act as co-ordinators for sessions. It is the responsibility of the co-ordinator to decide on the format of the session, which may include a stimulus and discussion, readings of poems and prose by those present followed by criticism, or a stimulus followed by writing during the session itself. The Words group do more writing while meeting together than the Tuesday group. Each session includes a business spot when information and news are exchanged and plans for special events and performances may be made. Recording the content of each session is given high priority and different members 'write the book' each week during the meeting. Sessions shift to the pub at an appropriate time where discussion continues.

When the Writers Workshop started, the only other writers' groups in the city were three or four Workers' Educational Association (WEA) classes, but now over 20 groups are known to flourish. Gorgie Dalry Writers Workshop took a lead in bringing workshops together in the Edinburgh Writers Association (EWA) which meets every 'First Friday' in the month for a Poems and Pints night. There is usually a 'billed' performer for part of the evening but anyone can claim a floorspot and read out their work - poems or prose - to a limit of five minutes.

The researcher attended a Tuesday evening Workshop session, a Words session and a First Friday. She interviewed eight members individually and four members as a group. Questionnaires were distributed to members. The researcher also spoke with the workers at ALP and a senior development officer at SCEC, and with people at two other major projects in Gorgie Dalry. Many shorter

137

conversations with members' partners, colleagues, fellow writers, ALP tutors and passing observers of the scene contribute to this study. Because of the long distance from base, as much material as possible had to be collected in one short preparatory visit and one longer visit of six days. The researcher wishes to thank all those who gave time and information so generously.

THE QUESTIONNAIRES

Ten of the twelve members interviewed filled in questionnaires. With the addition of impressions and information gained in interview, these provide useful information about the membership.

The most striking aspect of the group is how very different the members are in almost every way except for their interest in and commitment to writing. In age, they range from early twenties to over sixty:

20-31: 2; 31-40: 4; 41-50: 1; 51-60: 2; 61-70: 1

They have been members of the workshop for as long as 11 years or as little as 3 months; four have belonged for 7 years or more and six for 5 years or less. Six of the ten live locally and four in other partsof Edinburgh.

In terminal education age (TEA), they range from 15 to 24+, with six in the 15-17 age group and four in the 21-24+ group. Bearing in mind the stronger emphasis in Scotland on further and higher education, the proportion of early leavers is high. There is no correlation between age and TEA and little between TEA and occupation:

Occupation	TEA
unemployed actress	16
labourer (decided not to build career on his qualification)	23
civil servant	16
mature student (end of schooling)	15
part-time tutor	17
lecturer	24+
scientific/medical technologist now redundant/early retired	15
laboratory technician	23
project engineer in distillery	21
retired	15

138

The dominant social affiliation of the group is working class despite upward mobility in occupation and income for some, and the adherence of one or two members from a middle class background. Nine respondents listed 29 other organisations to which they belonged, 13 of which were different writers' groups. Other organisations included the Scottish National Party, National Union of Students, WEA, the Scottish and the International Herpetological Societies, local community associations, the Woodcraft Folk and Amnesty International.

Two had between them attended at least 25 classes or conferences and seven others at least 21 within the last five years. Fifteen of these, spread amongst eight respondents, were connected with either the Writers Workshop or the ALP. Other subjects studied were languages (8), the arts (10 - music, drama, dance and painting), and vocational courses. All the arts were represented in the listings of other activities, together with physical recreations and a variety of sports.

Seven of the respondents affirmed that many of their activities and interests grew from involvement with the Workshop. This applied particularly to those concerning writing and writers' groups, the arts and community events. One respondent wrote, 'All of (my activities) developed more because of Writers Workshop involvement since my level of self confidence significantly improved via WW and this allowed me to "risk" more'.

THE INTERVIEWS - IMPACT ON MEMBERS
Social Impact
The social side does not bring members into the Workshop but once part of the group it becomes of great significance. All spoke of the conviviality in the pub after meetings and events. This opportunity to relax with each other after sessions which are often charged with high emotion is greatly welcomed. The friendships formed over a post-session pint often 'become a significant part of social life'.

One respondent wrote 'I suppose the majority of my social contacts are either in the Workshop, or at some time were so. This would suggest the depth of influence it has had upon my life'. Others commented that 'the most important friends in my life' were fellow members, and illustrated the closeness of the ties by saying 'we remember each other's birthdays'. Several felt that the Writers

Workshop was a good basis of friendship because 'you have at least one interest in common'. Because many of the members live geographically close to each other, they meet frequently in shops, streets and local pubs and developing from the friendship network 'You get a feeling of community here. I feel part of it.'

The women in the Words group spoke of 'rich relationships' developing within the group and they enjoy being in the company of other women. One member, reflecting on the sudden death of a local acquaintance of all of them, said 'you don't always realise the close bonds you make with people'.

Educational and Cultural Impact

Not surprisingly, the greatest impact of membership of the Writers Workshop described by the respondents comes into this category. It falls into four sub-sections: the effects on writing and critical perception; extension of learning into other areas; practical skills associated with magazine production; and process skills associated with organising groups and events.

(i) Writing and Critical Perception

Respondents all felt that belonging to the Workshop had improved the quality of their writing. Most said that if they had written before, they had kept it to themselves and been unsure if it was 'any good'. Some said that they had written little since leaving school; they felt the urge to write but had not been sure how to go about it. Sharing their writing in the group and getting supportive criticism helped them to recognise their weaknesses and strengths. 'Reading something out loud in itself shows what parts are good and bad', and the comments of the group help to improve expression. Others spoke of enlarging vocabulary, learning to punctuate and learning technical terms of writing and of literature. Several spoke of the 'two way process of learning to receive criticism and to give it'. They felt that they had become better critics with experience of listening to each other's work, but stressed that it is always 'criticism of the written word, not of the person.'

One respondent recognised writing as a therapeutic process and workshop members always receive shared personal experiences supportively. But therapy and technique are kept in balance; 'sometimes there is stress on one, sometimes on the other - both are

140

enjoyable'. For some members, group meetings are no longer the only learning environment and one-to-one critical assessment between pairs is proving an additional and rewarding experience. Continuity of learning experience and support is valued; one commented that the group was always there when he needed it, and another found 'the group worthwhile as it keeps me writing especially at times of pressures at work and other events which are not conducive to writing'.

Several respondents said that they had started out writing only in prose but the Writers Workshop had opened up for them a whole new world of poetry. One young woman found the Workshop very supportive when she changed from writing in 'proper' English taught at school to writing in Scots, her first language. She said that 'you never feel that you're being yourself when you are speaking or writing in English' and she finds Scots 'better for expressing feelings'.

(ii) Extension of Learning into other Areas
Topics chosen by different members in turn to stimulate discussion in sessions give insight into new areas. For example, Chinese poetry and culture, and Urdu ghazals (traditional love songs) and their sitar and drum music, were chosen recently by Words' members as starting points for creative writing. Most members have taken the opportunity to join in other ALP activities, such as photography, music, local and Scottish history and combined projects, 'to a whole cultural awakening'. Another did a presentation to a seminar on Scots language and literature, the preparation for which extended her own knowledge. Another had been led to an awareness of theatre and now goes regularly to plays at St Brides Centre and other Edinburgh theatres; 'I would never have thought of going to a play'.

Two members had rejected returning to formal education because it 'looked boring' and the whole formal education system seemed 'patronising and I don't think I would fit its system'. One who had returned to learning was moved by her wider experience in ALP to switch from an Educational Technology to a Community Education degree course. Several members attend other writing groups and classes and at least two now teach other workshops as paid tutors. They have learned, without formal qualification, how 'to impart

141

knowledge and experience to others'.

(iii) Getting into Print
Members of the Workshop have different aspirations in terms of writing. Some have ambitions to be published and become recognised writers. Others want their writing 'to be the best it can be' for their own satisfaction. Readings to the group and then to larger audiences gave members the confidence to set up their own modest publishing enterprise. Using ALP duplicating equipment, the few copies of the first productions were passed from hand to hand. Five members set up a small publishing venture and with more sophisticated equipment and growing skill in layout and production, small editions of pleasant looking anthologies were published with the support of grants from Edinburgh District Council. From these ventures, members have learned editorial skills, typing and word processing, layout, desktop publishing and how to produce with simple equipment a good looking book and market it. One member uses these skills to help with the production of ALP newsletters and posters while another has become assistant editor of a controversial new magazine.

Perhaps the most original regular publication which comes from the Writers Workshop is the Yonkly (a yonk being an indeterminate period of time). It 'aims to be a Writers Workshop in print, issued eight times a year' and its policy is to include every piece sent in. Pieces are printed anonymously, but attributed in a listing a few issues later. A major section of the magazine is 'Everybody's a Critic', where all criticism of items that appear in Yonkly is printed. These, too, are anonymous, and in this case authorship is never disclosed. There is a further 'Right to Reply' section so discussion of a piece of writing can continue through several issues. Four Writers Workshop members currently make up the editorial panel of Yonkly, plus one non-member. All Workshop members contribute to the magazine from time to time, together with some writers from other workshops and some, like the fifth editor, who prefer to be part only of a workshop in print. Forty copies of Yonkly are produced each issue and its readership is much wider. For all concerned it involves learning in writing, criticism, communication and magazine production.

(iv) Process
A great deal of the learning considered of importance by members of the Writers Workshop involved process. This emphasis reflects the ethos of the Adult Learning Project which gives as much value to the process as to the content of learning, following its application of what it sees as the principles of Paulo Freire.

Members valued the style of co-operative learning of the Writers Workshop. One who attended a writing course for two ten week terms before hearing about the Workshop had found the 'hierarchical' class structure very offputting and the holiday breaks very frustrating. He liked the Workshop for its lack of structure, its continuity, and its freedom from a 'tutor's saying what's right or wrong'. There is equality in the Workshop, 'a multiplicity of views, no one more true than others' and 'all views are accepted as valid'. For another member, the Workshop was immediately attractive because 'it was not a classroom in a school with janitors with bells' and so 'phenomenally different from night school'. Reflecting on his experiences of education, he said that he had 'wanted school to be like ALP' but it was not, and coming to the Workshop was 'like coming home'. Other comments on the style of learning included 'learning on the basis of doing it', 'learning by example, not by the book', and 'having permission to disagree'.

They spoke of the 'culture' of the Workshop which they share with other ALP groups. Several of the members had been on courses for group co-ordinators run by ALP where they had learned skills such as managing groups, listening skills, and leading group discussions. 'What makes a good group', 'what it is to be a good member', 'giving people opportunities to speak', 'being able to communicate with people, especially people with writing problems', 'listening to the quiet voice', and 'people who don't say anything may have something to say' were some of the ways that members identified what they had learned. One member described the experience of co-ordinating the group as 'hefty' at the beginning, but he is now confident in his skills and hopes to extend his expertise at a new co-ordinator's course to be put on by ALP shortly. In a questionnaire, a respondent wrote, 'In developing my co-ordinating skills, I have realised that the smallest voice usually has something important to say and that consensus can be obtained if everyone has access to all available information.'

143

The group regularly reviews its own process and tries to improve its way of operating. For example, they decided to make greater efforts to help newcomers feel welcome by talking less about past events and avoiding in-jokes. They recognise that it is important to respond to people's needs and to let new members make their own mistakes. One member reflected on the one occasion when a new member caused disruption and offence which threatened to destroy the group. After all reasonable persuasion over a number of weeks had failed, an ALP worker was asked to give support at a meeting when the difficult individual was asked to leave.

Members have taken their process skills into other situations and learned more. For example, one has been co-opted on to the committee of the Edinburgh Writers Association which has a more formal structure in order to be eligible for arts funding from Edinburgh District Council. Another is leading a WEA writers' class and finding it difficult to run in the way she would wish because of the expectations that she will act an a conventional tutor.

Organising events is a further extension of process learning. Setting up and publicising poetry readings, ceilidhs and local 'fringe' festival events is shared by everybody and involves learning how to cope under pressure to 'get the show on the road'. From all the discussions with members it was clear to the researcher that the learning about group organisation and the process of working together to achieve their aims were accorded as much significance and value as the improvements in writing technique and the blossoming of creativity.

Occupational Impact
Some members have full time jobs; some are retired; some have part time work and take jobs as and when they need to; some are unemployed; one is a full time mature student. Involvement in the Writers Workshop has an occupational impact for most of them, but to different degrees and in different ways.

The mature student felt that it was the experience of the Writers Workshop and ALP which influenced her to change to the Community Education course. She feels that her learning with the group helps her to relate the theory of the course to practice. Recently when set the task of role playing a tenants meeting, she felt at an advantage over the other students because of her experience at the Workshop. She is committed both to writing and to the course and feels that her future career will be a job in community education.

One member, with no paper qualification, got the job of arts worker in the recreation department of Edinburgh District Council on the strength of his involvement with the Writers Workshop. He said that this was an 'amazing' experience as one year he was trying to get money for the publishing activities of the group and the next he was advising the council on which groups should be funded from the arts budget. Involvement with the Workshop had 'a profound effect on my occupation'. Especially, he found the negotiating skills, 'instead of swearing and shouting', learnt at the Workshop were helpful for dealing with committees. In the end he found that the job interfered with his writing so he left the post, though he still does some part-time tutoring. He would like to enhance his desktop publishing skills to be able to get a job which would pay the bills but leave his mind free for writing.

Two members in full time jobs both feel that the skills learned at the Workshop benefit their work. They are more competent at expressing themselves and more effective at managing situations. One said that the skills learned in co-ordinating Workshop sessions 'gave me insight' which he could use at meetings at work. Though he had training at his work for the technical side of his job, courses did not include management skills; 'no one gives you these opportunities', which, in his opinion, accounts for much bad management in industry. A part-time college lecturer said that while co-ordinating skills did not affect his teaching style, performance skills did; he was aware that his ability to keep his students interested had been enhanced by his experience of holding the attention of a Workshop audience.

Another member's experiences at the Workshop have led to part-time tutoring and assistant editorship of a poetry magazine. She is keen to collect a portfolio of relevant jobs and experience to lead to a writer-in-residence post with a local authority or institution. Part of her feels that she would not fit into any conventional work situation but the other part says 'why not go for it?'

Some of the members, perhaps more ambitious, hope one day to make a living from their writing. They see other work as necessary

145

but distracting; at best it keeps them in touch with everyday life and gives them material to enrich their work.

Political Impact

ALP members find that by-products of the learning process include consciousness-raising and empowerment, and involvement in community action leading eventually to heightened political awareness. The same process occurs within the Writers Workshop and is recognised by the members. The concerns with Scots culture and Scottish nationalism give an added dimension to this politicisation.

The respondents were unanimous in identifying increased political awareness as one of the outcomes of their involvement with the Workshop. 'Talking with people at the Writers Workshop and in the pub afterwards, talking about what's going on, has been a politicising experience.' Being on the dole, being on low income as a student or part time worker, the poll tax and the issues of Scottish democracy and the Scots language are all political issues which they write about and discuss in workshop sessions. Recent stimulus sessions in Words arose from members' commitment to anti-racism, a theme which is a current concern because of the National Front propaganda rife in the community. One respondent identified the culture of the Workshop as 'subversive' in the sense that members use their writing as a vehicle for political protest, and another said she now 'likes to get involved in political action' such as the recent Democracy for Scotland march. One respondent said that she had never before regarded herself as a political person but finds she is becoming very politically aware; 'you are a political person and you have a voice'.

The group sees itself firmly grounded in working class culture. The assertion that 'Any working class Scot who writes something which is read is making a political statement' was deeply felt. A founder member recollected that in the early days the group was very 'defensive' and would not have accepted a non-working class person, though now 'we are more tolerant'. They have learned 'ways of getting groups together to change things for the better' and that 'you can bring about changes and affect others and the situation'. One said that he had 'learned the political lesson that to get things done you must do it yourself' while another felt it 'confidence-inspiring to know that you're not at the mercy of alleged powers to get things done effectively'. Some of the changes to which the Workshop has contributed are discussed below.

Personal Impact
Learning 'to be tolerant, to listen to other people', 'to be outgoing', 'to feel empowered', 'to feel that I'm meeting my aspirations', 'to be ready to take risks', 'to have faith in myself', 'to have confidence in groups, especially with men', 'to be a lot more confident in my own abilities' were all expressed as positive personal outcomes. One woman said that the Workshop has helped her 'to come round to my own sense of self and my own opinions'. For her, personal development supported through group activities had come before political action; 'you need a sense of yourself personally before you can go out and demonstrate'.

Membership of Words has enabled women to enjoy a safe environment in which to start writing. One woman said that Words is 'full of energy' which gives confidence as well as friendship to its members. One member who has only been writing for a year said that 'at the beginning it is extremely important to have support'. The group not only 'keeps you motivated to write' but also 'gives you an all-round outlook on life and living' by exploring issues of importance to women such as violence in society and sexual harassment. One elderly woman who has been coming to Words for only a few months said that she 'feels uplifted' by the experience.

Being part of the group is seen as a therapeutic encounter which enables members to explore feelings and life experiences which they have found difficult to talk about in any other context. Several reflected that they felt able to take emotional risks in the safe environment of the group which helped in their search for personal identity.

Growth in self-confidence is a universal outcome of involvement in any sort of voluntary organisation so far studied, but performing made a special impact on the writers. All said how nervous they had felt when they first stood up to read at an event. In overcoming that nervousness, they have learned 'performing skills and self-presentation - interesting in themselves as well as having an effect on character'. 'It's all about building up confidence' to reject an unsatisfactory meal in a restaurant as well as to perform in front of an audience. A comment on a questionnaire reads 'Involvement in the Workshop and in ALP has developed my confidence and range of experience. I can and do organise a lot of things I would never have believed!'

IMPACT ON FAMILY AND PERSONAL CONTACTS
Both positive and negative impacts on family and friends were mentioned, both by members and those in close contact with them. One respondent noted the break-up of three marriages, his own and those of two core workshop members, a consequence, he felt, of the 'growth in confidence, self-assertion and dissatisfaction' gained from the group. One partner felt that the Writers had a 'primadonna mentality' and tended to be exclusive.

On the positive side, family members have been drawn into new experiences. One member's brothers had attended a festival fringe event and now will try new things and admit to enjoying poetry. His mother took up photography and surprised him by the skill and creativity she displayed. Another member's family come to poetry and music performances which they would never have gone to without his encouragement; 'they said they enjoyed it and they did'. A work colleague was persuaded to a first poetry reading to hear him read and now goes to readings regularly. She commented on the effect she felt that membership of the Workshop has on him; 'he is one of the fairest people I know; he will listen to both sides' of arguments about work.

The partner of one respondent has been involved in many ALP groups - the skills exchange, the women's group, the democracy group. Another member's partner now herself writes and, though not a member of the Workshop, is deeply involved with EWA, with Yonkly and has many close friends in the Workshop. These are two examples of partners whose interests and sympathies are closely linked and mutually supportive.

WIDER IMPACT
The impact that the Gorgie Dalry Writers Workshop has had on the writers workshop movement in Edinburgh and beyond has been significant. In evaluating its influence on the local community, it is often difficult to distinguish between the part played by the Gorgie

148

Dalry Writers Workshop directly and indirectly through ALP, and by ALP itself.

From its earliest days, the Writers Workshop became a significant contributor to the development of an intricate and far flung network of writing groups. Many people have spun out from Gorgie Dalry to form their own workshops, in Aberdeen, in Falkirk and Glasgow as well as in Edinburgh. There are strong links with workshops in Newcastle and Durham and through Yonkly the network is reaching places in the Midlands and south.

As we have seen, Gorgie Dalry Writers Workshop was one of the instigators of the EWA and its members form a large part of its committee. Through First Fridays the Workshop spreads its work to a wider audience not only of other writers but to many people who may be attracted to performance through a personal contact and gain from it new experience and a new interest. The finals of the annual poetry competition, attended by the researcher, attracted an audience of over seventy people, packed into the upstairs room of a large pub. The researcher talked to people who were regulars and to some who had never been to a poetry reading before and were enjoying it. The occasion was not without drama as supporters of one poet, an aggressive young man, on one side of the room exchanged invective (not always understood by the researcher!) with those of a feminist poetess on the other. The atmosphere was a far cry from an orderly middle class poetry reading and more reminiscent of descriptions of performances of popular poetry and song in Victorian pubs and music halls.

The First Friday rule that anyone can claim a floorspot of up to five minutes ensures a rich variety of readings. In the first years of the competition, recognised poets were invited to judge, but now the audience is the judge, each person voting in secret ballot for first to fourth places. This audience participation has increased the popularity of the occasion, at which serious listening to poetry is combined with a good night out. In this competition, the young feminist was voted winner to much acclamation from her supporters.

The ALP worker, who has observed the activities of the Workshop since it started, sees the Writers as people trying to gain confidence in their own culture. Gorgie Dalry Writers Workshop has participated in Scottish Writers Workshops, 'Come all ye', and in the development of the 'fringe' festival in Edinburgh, as well as taking a leading role in establishing First Fridays as a platform for aspiring performers. The Workshop reflects the linguistic diversity and debate in Scotland and gives members the opportunity to explore the use of Scots language, both literary Scots and urban dialect Scots. An indication of the focus on the language as a vehicle for Scottish identity is the growing demand on one of the Workshop poets for readings of her Scots poetry.

Impact on the Local Community
The Writers Workshop has begun to change local attitudes towards writing and poetry in particular, making people more aware of poetry and a Scots culture that has greater depths than Burns night. One member explained that ten years ago a poet in a local pub would have had a hard time whereas now they are more or less accepted. Some people are even starting to look for and buy their books at local festivals.

The Writers Workshop makes an effective contribution to the work of ALP.   Members contribute through readings and performances to ALP celebrations and campaigns, and through assisting with the production of newsletters and publicity material. A workshop member reports on its programme and progress at the ALP Associaton meeting. Although autonomous in its organisation and style of working, there are many links with other ALP groups and all acknowledge the importance of the common culture they share.

Observers value the contribution of the Writers Workshop when groups form under the ALP umbrella for special projects, such as setting up safe play areas for children, combatting racism in the community by initiating cross-cultural events and opening a Health Shop to be a source of health information.   The worker at the Gorgie Dalry Shop, who is a local resident, felt that ALP as a whole has played a significant part in politicising the local community. She knows of the Workshop through a writer who is a member of the Gorgie Dalry Festival Committee and involved in many local projects. This person is typical of the network of local activists who appear with different hats in different situations, like the musician who performed at the First Friday and works with some of the writers, putting their words to his music, and who is also on the

150

management committee of Gorgie City Farm. It is difficult to pinpoint responsibility for the increase in people's confidence and success in bringing improvements to the environment and amenities of the area, but observers agree that the Writers Workshop is one of the groups that have played a part in bringing about change.

CONCLUSION

In one dimension, the Gorgie Dalry Writers Workshop falls into the category of a specialist group, akin to the Sherwood Archaeologists and the Newstead Singers (Case Studies 13 and 14). The 'all-devouring' interest in this group is writing and, as the personal histories illustrate, many other activities and interests, and often occupations, reflect this central commitment. In contrast to choral singing, while writers need an audience, mutual support and opportunities for celebration, writing itself is usually a solitary occupation and an individual experience. Writers can, and as the evidence shows do, leave the workshop when they have gained the confidence they were looking for, and seek a fresh stimulus or work on their own. Thus the group is a collective of individuals, a looser association than a choir who are dependent on each other for the sounds they make. Another difference between the Newstead Singers and the Writers Workshop lies in their place within the definition of culture. The choir strives to reach the absolute standard of excellence in its field, and can claim a place in musical 'high culture'. The work of the Writers, like that of nineteenth century popular poets, may never be given high cultural status. It has none of the set standards that the Singers recognise, and would be unlikely to have a place in the literary canon, but it is nevertheless part of the development of a self-defined Scots working class sub-culture and has a place among modern popular cultures.

There is another dimension to membership, which is perceived as special to Gorgie Dalry, which arises from its origins in and continued association with ALP. The learning impact of the emphasis on process and the political commitment to community organisation gives the members an outward-looking and questioning attitude which in turn enriches their writing.

The enhanced political awareness of Workshop members is not translated into conventional voluntary service or civic participation. What they experience and learn takes them towards the kinds of local community action which many Scots, feeling alienated from and marginalised within British political processes, feel is their way forward to Scottish democracy. 'Writing your own word' is an important part of the Freirean way of raising political consciousness and the Writers Workshop contributes this dimension to ALP.

The processes which have become part of the Workshop culture have given members an attitude towards 'professionals' which they readily admit is 'ambivalent'. On the one hand they have a suspicion of 'professional writers' and those who have become 'big names'; on the other hand some of them would like to enjoy the same sort of success. Equally they are critical of professional community workers. One respondent felt there was a great divide between volunteers and professionals working in the community, and that while local people 'know what's good for the community', professionals are 'just promoting themselves'. A comment on a questionnaire seemed to be reflecting this negative experience with community workers; 'sometimes it's noted that voluntary groups are more active when set up by local people for local people, then once the 'professionals' appear, they wish to dictate their views which are at a tangent with the group so it collapses'. Another member criticised 'the full-time administrators from various organisations who make up the local Arts Council committee'. On the other hand, the Workshop originated as part of ALP, members value the training and support they have received and still receive from the professional ALP workers, wish to remain an associate group of the project and feel that it has brought benefit to them individually, to the Workshop and to the community. Several recognise that they are themselves in the process of compromising with and adapting to professionalism by working part time for the community education service as tutors and group leaders and one is looking forward to a career in community education. When one Workshop member was in the post of arts worker, the opportunites offered for tapping into arts funding were not ignored. This is a telling example of how the Writers Workshop offers an interesting window on to the interplay between the voluntary and the professional contributions to community work.

References

[1] G. Kirkwood and C. Kirkwood, 1989, *Living adult education: Freire in Scotland*, Open University Press in assocation with the Scottish Institute of Adult and Continuing Education.

[2] Adult Basic Education in Scotland 'includes the skills that are essential to leading an adult life in the community. Skills like literacy, numeracy, communication skills and life management skills.'
The Senior Development Officer at SCES said that the present policy is to merge ABE with adult education in Scotland 'to form one seamless robe of adult education.'

Case Study 24

THE LONG REIGN ALLOTMENT GARDENS SOCIETY

INTRODUCTION

An allotment group was selected as an example of a single interest out-of-doors activity. It differs from other voluntary organisations studied in that each member is responsibile for a particular plot, but there is collective responsibility for relations with the public, especially those living nearby, for the upkeep of the hedges and verges, and the appearance of the allotment area. The researcher would like to thank the Chairman and the Committee members for agreeing to assist the project, and is grateful to all who were interviewed for their friendly co-operation.

The Long Reign Allotment Gardens are at Stanton Hill, in the parish of Skegby, which is part of Sutton-in-Ashfield. The area, on the western side of Nottinghamshire, near the start of the Pennines, has suffered over the years a reduction in its traditional industries of mining and hosiery, and alternatives are only patchily replacing them. The closure in 1988 of one colliery and the expected closure of another, both within two miles of Stanton Hill, have devastated the morale of local people. Family stability, long cherished in the villages, has been eroded as younger family members seek work elsewhere and as substantial numbers of newcomers move in. Until a few years ago 'generations of families lived near each other and you could always call on someone to help you'. People who have lived a long time in the area say that 'families are now scattered' and that 'neighbourliness has to some extent gone'. However, the area is still seen, though less so now, as having the 'attributes of mining - industrious, loyal, close-knit'.

The changes in employment in the area have affected the allotments. The adjacent Miners' Welfare Institute has recently closed. There is strong and growing interest among redundant workers, especially miners, in taking up an allotment and there is a waiting list of 10.

Old people who have lived in Stanton Hill and Skegby all their lives say that the Long Reign Allotments go back over 100 years. The land originally belonged to the squire of Skegby and still remains in the family; it may continue to be used as allotments so long as there are no more than three plots in a rough state and one untended. The allotments stand on a level piece of land nearly 600 feet above sea level and 'the area is a windy one with little to break it'. There are 108 plots each of approximately 330 square yards; all but one of their widths face in a north-south direction, traditionally thought to be ideal for growing crops. The gardens are enclosed by a well-kept hawthorn hedge. Near the main entrance stand two large well-padlocked sheds which hold the group's seeds, fertilisers and tools for keeping its area tidy. The allotment holders are required to abide by the Council's by-laws such as not causing a nuisance with bonfires or pets.

The Committee is very keen that all the gardens are cultivated and sends out warning letters without hesitation where any have been neglected. While it remains mindful of personal or family circumstances, its paramount concern is the continuation of the allotments; the Committee cannot afford to renew bad tenancies. Allotments are vacated almost entirely through members becoming too old to carry on. Tenancies are renewed in Spring, but where an allotment has been neglected, incoming gardeners, particularly young ones, respond promptly and have shown their keenness by helping members who cannot do heavy work. They are allowed to take over in winter to prepare the ground for Spring sowing. As one of the Committee members put it, 'we want to encourage the young ones for they will be future Committee members'.

Each allotment holder pays an annual rent and a Committee of nine looks after the rent collection, the running of the gardens and the buying, care and sale of seeds and fertilisers. The Committee is elected annually, but where there is a need to complete numbers likely members are sounded out in advance. It is an informally run

The Gardens are affiliated to the National Allotments and Gardens Society (NAGS) from which the group obtains most of its seeds and fertilisers, and these are sold during the hours allowed. The Society is a source of support and advice if there are any difficulties or fears of losing the allotments to other purposes.

THE ENQUIRY

Forty gardeners were interviewed, 35 men and 5 women. The actual number of allotments held was 38 as two couples are included; two of the allotment holders were women. The great majority, 33, including all the women, left school at 14 or 15, five at 16 and two at 18. Almost all come from the area and many have lived within a few miles of the allotments all their lives.

The two couples were interviewed together and three other pairs were seen; all the other interviews were with individuals. Six were held at members' homes, where there were also brief talks with the gardeners' wives, and the others in the sheds or greenhouses on the allotments. The gardeners work in their allotments on different days and at various times, many of the retired or redundant attending several days a week. Morning, afternoon and evening visits were made on various days of the week in an attempt to meet a representative sample of gardeners.

The age distribution of the gardeners was as follows:

	21-30	1-40	41-50	51-60	61-70	71-80
men	1	5	5	12	9	3
women	0	0	1	3	1	0
total	1	5	6	15	10	3
miners						
work	0	1	1	1	0	0
ret'd	0	0	1	7	7	0
non-miners (men)						
work	1	3	3	4	1	1
ret'd	0	1	0	1	2	2
women						
work	0	0	0	2	0	0
ret'd	0	0	1	1	1	0

Sixty two and a half per cent of the gardeners were in the age range 51-70 (21 men and four women), but only three men (7.5%) were between the ages of 65 and 70. Three gardeners (7.5%), all range 51-70 (21 men and four women), but only three men (7.5%) were between the ages of 65 and 70. Three gardeners (7.5%), all men, were aged 71 or more. All the miners who were not at work had been made redundant. Most of the tenants who were interviewed believe that most of their number are redundant miners; in view of this it is possible that the researcher's sample under-represents the miners in spite of efforts to meet a representative sample. Since miners in the main now become redundant in their early 50s, the 'young' gardeners may be thought of as 50 or under. 12 of the respondents were in this category (30% - 11 men and one woman). The miners in the colliery that is likely to close have an average age of 32 years and a number have expressed an interest in an allotment.

The details for men given in the table show that there are almost equal numbers of miners and non-miners (18 and 17 respectively), and, interestingly enough the average age in each group is approximately 57 years. Their age distributions, however, are quite different; 14 from the mining industry are aged between 51 and 70 and only four under 51, while eight of the 17 who are not miners are under 51 although three are over 70 - two were landlords and one was on the railways. Their employment positions contrast strongly with only three out of 18 working at the mines as against 13 out of 17 non-miners at work. The average age of the women is about 55 and of the two employed one works at a shop and the other at a factory. A number of men hold or had held responsible posts at work in mining, the police, photography, the railways, building, hosiery and the post office.

For many, gardening has always been a strong interest and most also look after a garden at home. The great majority were introduced to gardening when children, some during the Second World War. Nearly all look back on their early experiences with pleasure and reported that 'they learned the basic things'. Some had taken up an allotment when their children had grown up or on retirement or redundancy; besides being a physical activity or an interest, for some the contribution it can make to the family economy is important. The members have varied interests and they lead active and fulfilling lives. Besides time with their families and friends, sport and home maintainance are popular, and for some pubs and pub games figure large. Joint activities with

157

partners include visits to gardens, and grandchildren and dogs are brought to the allotments. A few serve on committees of organisations concerned with miners' welfare and gardens.

SOCIAL EFFECTS

Without exception the gardeners speak with pleasure and anticipation of the social side of gardening; 'socially gardening is a great thing'. Every day brings opportunities for them to talk together and the occasions individuals go to their allotment determine who they talk to. As they pass other plots or walk round to compare, they also pass the time of day with those they meet. One described the tenants as 'a gardening community, a second home to me', to another the group 'is a nice club - genteel and there is excellent camaraderie', and to a third 'you have comradeship like in the army'. The members see each other as friendly and dependable, and 'there is no backbiting; we talk with each other about gardening and other things'. Several bring flasks of hot drink and gather in small groups in a shed or greenhouse to talk. In the summer particularly a couple or a family will bring refreshments and spend some time at the allotment. Many see each other at one of the local pubs in the evenings or at the weekends and some play dominoes there. Quite often wives and other members of the family visit the allotments and 'so you get to know them as well'.

While many work individually with occasional help from their wives, there are a number of instances where family members work together. The gardeners tend their separate plots but move and work in close proximity; they can see what each is doing as well as, in time, the results of the activity. All this generates a natural opportunity for entering into conversation about gardening or other topics.

A friendly rivalry develops among the tenants from time to time as to who will produce the earliest or largest crops; there is discussion about the factors which lead to early maturity and an inspection of the allotments in question. One says 'if somebody gets something earlier, there is competition and they are proud to display what they've grown'. Occasionally those with 'a particularly fine early crop casually walk round the allotments with a sample'! These give rise to opportunities for animated discussion, praise and laughter. Almost all report that 'we help each other a lot', and 'when you're busy, people give you a hand'. 'They're there like flies' to work as a team to put up sheds and greenhouses on the gardens and replace large plastic tunnels. This joint activity fosters a sense of acceptance and value. When allotment holders plan a holiday, others volunteer to look after shed or greenhouse keys, water plants as necessary and keep an eye on the gardens. A few gardeners have disabilities or have had heart attacks; they greatly appreciate the regular help of others with the heavy work. They do not have to worry about the progression of the work, and they find it a strong incentive to continue to maintain their interest. When one of these members was in hospital during part of the summer, others kept his allotment going. Some gardeners, especially the older ones, have known each other for many years and a number may have worked at the same colliery; they give each other a hand with jobs in their gardens at home. Talking and working together through a common interest fosters their sense of contentment and wellbeing.

Very few gardeners enter their produce in shows; those who do are well known locally and regionally and one acts as a judge. One who enters shows says that the 'best part of competitions is the social side'. Many visit shows, gardens and nurseries with their families; they find them enjoyable occasions for sharing experiences and talk about them afterwards to other tenants.

For gardeners who are at work, time is often at a premium and they get to know best 'those who are in the immediate vicinity'. They enjoy a few minutes chat between jobs and feel they belong to a group. Quite often they have specific tasks they want to achieve and, particularly for those with young families, time on the allotment is limited. While their social contact when on the allotments is much less than that of retired gardeners, they enjoy meeting them and have the same access to advice and information. They notice that 'the older gardeners talk a lot to each other'.

For the retired and redundant, being an allotment holder is in effect a second career giving them purpose and a social life. Many of them spend three or more hours a day at the allotments for several days a week, meeting old and new friends. 'When we meet we talk about the pit, about gardening, about local events and about world-wide topics'. They also discuss their experience of life. Most have known each other for some years and, particularly the miners, have worked only with men, which leads, they say, to 'good humoured banter' and 'we rag one another and have a laugh'.

The Chairman and other Committee members make it their business to walk frequently round the allotments and talk to the gardeners; they warmly welcome newcomers to the area from a few miles away and the few who have come from other parts of the country. They note carefully anything the tenants have to say and are ready with information or advice where they can provide it; by keeping in close touch they hope to settle promptly any concerns expressed.

One of the women allotment holders has been associated with the allotments for 38 years, taking over her husband's allotment on his death. She said that up to the last 10 years it was very unusual to see women working, but now a number give a hand. Initial doubt on the part of some men quickly dissipated and they are welcomed.

The women gardeners spoke in the same way as the men about the social effects; one who is at work said 'there is goodwill with the gardeners, who are sociable, they help each other', and another at work was enthusiastic, saying, 'there's a fantastic atmosphere here, it's part and parcel of the allotments, the friendliness of the place is great'. Another who is retired says that 'the gardeners sit relaxed in chairs and drink coffee, always time for a chat and smoke'.

LEARNING EFFECTS

Learning about many aspects of gardening takes place on the allotments. While the gardeners attend at different times and for different lengths of time, a substantial number come regularly. These could be regarded as a community. This cohesive group, with its setting of acceptance and friendship, has a common purpose; its members, although independent, work in close proximity which facilitates learning and observation of practice. Their readiness to discuss current methods, alternatives and their consequences is a feature of their learning.

The Committee is an important source of new ideas and practices to members. It introduces new seeds and fertilisers, especially organic ones. Committee members often try them out and talk to other tenants about them. At the same time the Committee is alert to tenants' interests and queries, and responds to their requests. Members of the Committee are very willing to advise gardeners or

160

refer them to others. The secretary, a former pub landlord, who has only been doing the work for three years takes 'in my stride' the tasks of ordering, stocking and selling seeds and fertilisers.

When tenants try out a new variety of seed or a new vegetable or alter the time of sowing, they note carefully the results in terms, for example, of family reaction, the trouble in growing and the health and weight of the crop and, before deciding what to do, discuss them with others, for they learn 'to value others' opinions, some know a lot about nature's ways'. Several examples of allotment holders learning from others were mentioned. Generally the younger ones who want to know something ask their 'father or other gardeners'. Those who are new to vegetable gardening appreciate the fact that they can readily obtain advice if they need it and they are given spare seeds and plants; 'D was a great help when I started' and 'I have learned from the lads round here, they are fantastic'. Another who liked gladioli said that he 'asked a gardener who knew a lot about gladioli how to grow them', and a young gardener planned to get in touch with an old gardener who knew how to grow leeks. Examples of new gardeners not taking advice or being unwilling to ask for it were rare. A great amount of knowledge and advice is passed between gardeners as they talk in shed or greenhouse; one elderly gardener strongly asserted that people learn about gardening 'mostly by talking to each other'. One added a cautionary note when asked for advice: 'they don't tell you exactly what they have done, so you don't always know just what to do'. The tenants also watch each other and 'learn to do the right thing at the right time'. When they go to shows a number ask questions 'to learn how they do things'. Having so many allotments together means that examples of good practice are quickly passed on.

There is a strong belief that 'you only get out what you put in'. Learning from mistakes and how to deal with crop diseases is taken seriously for 'you always fail in something every year'. They look at possible causes, try remedial action and note the results. To one 'a gardener has to be like a doctor, see to the diseases of the plants'.

As allotment holders meet, they readily enquire about or pass on information concerning useful materials, especially those which people or firms want to get rid of, such as barrels, doors and

161

windows. This informal network of information often enables the gardeners to obtain materials cheaply, an important consideration for some. They help each other to collect them, and learn to co-operate in erecting sheds, compost boxes and greenhouses, setting up guttering and putting in reliable foundations.

The rotation and continuity of crops are seen as most important. One gardener put it, 'I have to plan the garden well to get variety and not too much of one sort', and another says, 'you need to think ahead, be mindful that winter vegetables are in one place for some months'. A few couples plan the garden together. The times for setting seeds or plants have to be considered and the length of time they are in the soil. Many members, especially those not at work, 'learn that you have to work as much in winter as in summer'. They have learned the value of discussing their plans, thinking about the place of new vegetables and examining seed catalogues critically. Many write down their plans and a few compare them annually.

There is a strong interest in flowers and a growing one in herbs, especially among wives, many of whom gather both along with vegetables. The allotment holders learn not only tips from each other about growing certain flowers but also that they play a part in attracting bees or in deterring certain insects. A few declared that 'people are going back to herbs' as they learn of the flavours they bring to meals.

The gardeners learn about a variety of organic and synthetic fertilisers, the uses of mulching and compost, and discuss both artificial and natural insecticides. Growing mistrust of excessive use of synthetics also leads to mutual education about shop vegetables. The older ones, especially, insist that 'you've got to work with nature'.

Gardeners have noticed 'a change in the seasons over the last 10-15 years', the winters generally being experienced as milder; 'you go from summer to winter, the winters are milder and don't kill the filth'. The observed absence of prolonged cold weather is causing a number of allotment holders to rethink their approach to the traditional times of setting seeds and plants.

Tenants, especially the older ones, have learned of the stable ways in gardening, seeing it as labour-intensive, and consisting of planning, 'feeding the soil' and tending the plants. One who has

162

gardened for over 50 years said, 'the way of gardening has more or less stayed the same during my lifetime but there are improved seeds, more greenhouses and pest control, and a few use rotavators'. However, they have come to appreciate stainless steel tools and learned about the advantages of small greenhouses, cloches and ready made compost for starting seeds in beds. They have learned to appreciate the qualities of the wider range of commonly set vegetable and flower seeds available in extending colours, flavours and setting times.

Over the years several gardeners have started enthusiastically to grow vegetables that are new to them, for example salsify, garlic, sweetcorn and asparagus; 'I experiment with one or two new vegetables each year', says one, and another, 'I want to grow melons'. One has grown and cured tobacco and smoked it. They say that their families welcome the wider range of produce. The gardeners compare notes and think how they can use the experience for the following year. However, 'some gardeners are conservative, some keep to the same seed, others change seed, they tell each other about new crops they grow, it leads some to try it but others say no'. As tenants learn which seeds do well on the allotments and what they cost, they also learn how to save and store them.

Gardeners and their families have learned the economic and dietary uses of producing their own frozen vegetables. They report that 'we have frozen more and more' and 'that it avoids waste when a crop comes all at once'. Families have worked out a routine for collection and preparation, and say with pride that freezers enable them to eat fresh vegetables for most of the year.

Almost all the respondents read about gardening in books, magazines, catalogues and newspaper articles. A number do so in the library, where the librarian reports a very strong interest in gardening. None has heard of evening classes in gardening. They enjoy radio and TV programmes on gardening; 'TV programmes show you how to do things', but they are critical and weigh them against experience. One wife tapes programmes which they then look at together.

A few have a strong interest in nature generally. As they garden they learn more widely not only about the progress of their crops but about the birds, insects and weeds around the allotments. They note their habits and when they go for a walk or drive in the countryside take an interest in the wildlife. A man who has gardened for over 40 years finds that 'gardening makes me think about how nature works, why are poisonous plants so colourful and attractive? It makes me reflect on the working of the universe'. He believes that things have to be done in due order in the garden - 'this extends to other things and makes you think'. His interest in nature 'has led to an interest in poetry'.

Collectively the members have a tremendous expertise in gardening. An active quest for knowledge is fostered by the Committee, and members report that they are continually learning from their own experience and from others. One of the oldest expressed the typical feeling when he said 'you've never finished learning, you're learning all the time'.

OCCUPATIONAL EFFECTS

Although a number thought that their approach to gardening activities did not extend to their other interests, a good proportion commented on the value of planning and thinking ahead in all their activities especially those who have been gardening a long time. Often the timing of holidays and of jobs about the home 'so as not to interfere with planting and harvest time' were mentioned. One said that planning in gardening had helped him in thinking about DIY work. A gardener at the allotments for about 50 years, now a widower, plans ahead in domestic work and fits 'gardening and taking the dog for a walk around it'. While their own nature and sense of providing for their family substantially influence how they garden, most of the older people, after experience of growing plants under conditions they cannot fully control, reported that gardening gave them a thoughtful and patient approach to their activities.

The importance of rotation and continuity has encouraged many to adopt a systematic approach to gardening and has for some led to or reinforced being systematic in other activities; one sees the 'need for an orderly mind in gardening, so when at home I am orderly and methodical'; this redundant miner is a member of the Committee and has transferred 'man-management from work to the Committee'. Another retired miner says that things have to be done in due order in a garden and 'this extends to other things and makes you think'. A man with a very responsible job has learned the value of being 'consistently methodical in work and play' and

164

finds 'it pays in gardening, work and other activities'.

The comments of some of the women gardeners emphasise the value of joint activity with their husbands. Two couples plan their allotment together and also other activities. Another couple report that 'we continue our education, for example, by looking at gardens in hot countries and noting how they save water'. The wife of a couple, both of whom are at work, finds that 'through gardening, having to go when we can, even in the rain, we accept things more both in the garden and in the home'. One female gardener says that being systematic in the allotment does not make her systematic with housework, while another finds it does. Many retired people who have gardened for most of their lives learn to be patient and to stand back; their unhurried approach to gardening is carried over to other tasks they do. They realise there are limits to influencing the growth processes of plants; they see the gardeners' tasks of preparing, tending and reaping extending to the lives of people. 'Gardening makes you philosophical,...in gardening you always have to plan ahead, so in your life you plan ahead, decide what you're doing and arrange it'. 'You can't expect instant changes in people, it takes time to change a system or a person'. One applied his own needs to plants; 'you need looking after, it's the same with plants, they like a bit of a change'. One respondent says that 'gardening has taught me to have a practical approach to things and to think about it before you do anything'.

POLITICAL EFFECTS
The issues put forward by allotment holders under this heading tend to be limited to immediate concerns. They include the organic approach to gardening, provision of water, relations with the public and security.

Members have learned over the years about the effects of the extensive use of fertilisers and insecticides; 'I read how deleterious pollution is to plants' and there is concern over 'people getting illnesses, there's dioxin a few miles away'. While the focus is on the effects on food, there is also a concern for the environment and animals, especially from those who love the countryside. The Committee has obtained information about organic fertilisers from NAGS and the secretary reports that sales, both to the allotment holders and to the public, have increased substantially in recent years.

The tenants discuss among themselves and with friends the effects of the use of chemicals on food and shop vegetables. The Committee takes practical steps to help members to learn and to decide for themselves; it does not impose. It orders introductory quantities of new environmentally friendly fertilisers and insecticides and offers advice. Advice is sought of those who have adopted an organic approach and gardeners observe what others are doing, but the action taken is individual. More are using manure in spite of some seeing it as expensive, and the use of compost boxes has increased.

That there is no water supply to the allotments is a source of frustration to a number, but 'there is a lot to think about before you introduce water': cost, metering, placing of taps and rent increases. The Committee is conscious of the high proportion of retired or redundant tenants and its members realise that the question is most prominent during the infrequent dry spells. Most relieve the problem by collecting rainwater from greenhouses and sheds.

The Committee is conscious of its relations with the public and impresses on all its members the need to abide by its rules. Particular care is taken over garden fires and keeping the paths and hedges clean and tidy; gardeners see the 'need to be careful and not cause a nuisance to neighbours'.

Stealing and damage to gardeners' property occasionally occur; however, several say that it is much less than what they know happens on many other allotment gardens. While at the allotments members keep an eye open for damage to hedges; they also take home any valuable tools. Committee members constantly walk round the allotments at various times during the light evenings and they encourage all the allotment holders to be security conscious.

PERSONAL EFFECTS
Having an allotment means a great deal to the gardeners, and this feeling was elaborated in terms of pleasure, keeping the mind and body active, achievement and relief from stress.

'Gardening means a lot to me' is reported by many and this sentiment was supported as they spoke with enthusiasm about the sense of purpose that it brought them. They have something to think about, not only from time to time but during any season of

166

the year. 'It has given us fresh vegetables for 40 years', 'if it is not tidy and planned you are not a gardener', 'you feel proud' and 'when I talk about it to friends, it keeps me going' are typical comments. Those retiring or being made redundant see the need for continued activity and for them gardening is ideal; one put it, 'when not at work you have a sense of not being part of the community, not contributing, no responsibility'.

Gardening brings the tenants pleasure, apart from one exception whose first words to the researcher, said with feeling, were 'I hate gardening!'. As a boy, 'football crazy', he had been compelled to do certain tasks in the garden while seeing friends play football. Now retired, and after helping a friend who had 'taught me a lot about gardening', he had taken to an allotment as 'you've got to keep active'. Other gardeners speak of the pleasure in terms of 'you can't find a finer pastime', 'such a change, it's quiet, you go at your own pace' and 'after you set seed it's a pleasure to see the plants growing'. The quiet summer mornings, the singing of the birds, the feel of the warm soil and the neat, growing rows of plants are spoken of as a joy. One says that 'you lose yourself in gardening' and tenants commonly say that they would give up the garden only if it became a burden.

Almost all the allotment holders report that gardening keeps them physically and mentally active. Those not at work particularly see it as 'exercise for me, something to think about, I don't know what I'd do all day in the house'. They feel the benefit of the regular exercise and keeping their 'mind awake and reasoning', and look on gardening as helping them to remain independent and to keep going.

There is a strong sense of personal achievement among the gardeners. Comments such as 'you get the satisfaction that I've grown that', 'I've got to be active, you can achieve something when gardening', 'you see the results of your labour, everything is fresher and cheaper' represent the views of the gardeners. One gardener says that through gardening 'I feel good, you can see what you've done and you have cabbage, cauliflower and potatoes on your Sunday plate'. They feel proud that they can grow a good range of fresh vegetables and fruit. Growth of confidence in gardening and through gardening is quite often mentioned, and most are ready to 'have a go' with vegetables new to them. 'If you are good at

167

growing something, you are looked up to, people ask you how to grow it'. Younger gardeners feel confident that they can produce good crops as they engage in gardening and see and talk to others. One who had just retired said that 'my job helped me a lot in life - gave me a certain assurance', as he took up gardening more extensively. The tenants report that success with the allotment extends their confidence, 'I become confident, know I can do things' and 'people are confident in making their own judgments'.

The allotment holders report how important it is to them to provide their families with fresh and tasty food. They say 'it keeps my family in fresh food all the year'. 'you grow for the table, know it's fresh, you go and cut when you want it'. In addition, for many, gardening is an important economic activity. Tenants' comments on the expenses involved in buying seeds, manure and fertiliser make it clear that a return from the allotments of fresh vegetables and fruit is essential, for example, 'I more than cover my expenses, not counting labour', 'helps with the budget' and 'not ripped off by the shopkeeper'.

The last but by no means least personal effect mentioned, mainly in relation to paid work, is that gardening helps to relieve stress; 'it is a stress-buster'. Gardening is said to be peaceful, the telephone does not ring, and 'you work and relax'. Choosing what to do, the physical activity and working at one's own pace are mentioned as helping people 'to unwind'. One who has always worked in an office environment says he 'feels mentally scarred because of the times we live in. With gardening it's the diversion, it's physically active, you ache at first then are physically tired which is wonderful'. Another, recently retired, says that when at work 'through gardening I got rid of frustration which built up during the day, felt better to go work the next day, also solved the problems brought from work'.

EFFECTS ON FAMILIES AND FRIENDS

The gardeners encourage members of the family to work with them on the allotments from time to time; examples noted were mother and son, brother and brother-in-law and of course husband and wife. Several wives and mothers help on the allotments, mainly weeding and gathering vegetables and flowers, but a few also spend much time digging and sowing. Where a husband is at work wives play a crucial role, for example one dug up potatoes and wheeled a barrowful home. Sometimes couples 'plan what we set together'.

For some couples gardening is a common interest at times extending to a love of the countryside. There is often a division of the work with the wife tending more to the flowers and the husband to the fruit and vegetables. It is the wives mainly who pickle and freeze the garden produce and one or two looked on that as 'her department'. Where the husband is unwell or is unable to do the heavy work, the wives, with help from others, ensure that the allotment is tended.

However, where neither husband nor wife is at work, each values an opportunity to pursue their tasks separately. One wife says that 'his going to the garden gives me a break' and another wife, active in the allotment, that 'many gardeners go several days a week to the allotments and stay some hours; this means that their routine is similar to when they went to work, also it enables the wife to carry out her usual domestic tasks without hindrance'. It seems that for retired couples an allotment provides a safety valve to help them adjust to their change of circumstances.

To be able to obtain fresh vegetables from the garden or the freezer at almost any time of the year is a great pleasure to them. The delights are evident in 'the dinners on Sunday, fresh and organic' and 'I come up on Sunday morning, get some fresh air and an appetite, then we'll enjoy dinner with a bottle of wine'.

Gardeners quite often bring their children to the allotments and explain 'what you do in a garden, it makes them aware of seeds and I explain about setting and tending plants'. The children are often given a patch of garden with various seeds to set and water. They gather produce, but one parent added that they 'gather onions and pick gooseberries, but sometimes get bored'. One father is keen that his 'children get a good education as regards food'. In spite of that thought a father said, 'I can escape to the garden when the children are noisy'. In summer families come for a picnic to the allotments and the fathers teach the children 'about gardening'.

Parents report that they give vegetables regularly to their married sons and daughters who help to gather them when they are able to do so. Gardeners give garden produce to their parents and in-laws. The parents also give advice to their sons and daughters on gardening matters or encourage them to take up gardening. Spare vegetables are also given to friends and neighbours.

EFFECTS ON THE LOCAL COMMUNITY

A number of local people were interviewed and asked about any effects the Long Reign allotments might have on the local community. Within the locality are two complexes, each warden controlled, where over 60 single elderly people live. The two wardens and a general practitioner who has worked locally for many years opposite the allotments were briefly interviewed and 13 of the elderly people from the complexes, mainly in small groups. In addition interviews took place with six people who have lived in the area for several years and a recently arrived pub landlord. All the information in this section comes from these interviews.

One warden knew little about the allotments but the other said that a number of elderly men walked down to the allotments in the warmer weather and talked to the gardeners; a number had been keen gardeners, 'it is an interest, there is talk about local events, people pass on the news'. She had asked the allotment holders for contributions to the harvest festival service and was pleased with the generous response. The produce was sold afterwards and the proceeds given to a local hospice; 'so we pass it on and benefit others'. All the residents the researcher spoke to in the complexes knew about the allotments and a few had 'fond memories' of them as their husbands had gardened there. Families and friends had bought seeds and fertilisers there and some still have friends among the gardeners. They see the allotments as helping the gardeners to be independent and keep 'the grey matter busy'; 'you feel good when you are independent'. A number of the residents are 'given fresh vegetables' by the allotment holders. A gardener and his wife visit a group of residents each week taking them vegetables when they can; the gardener says 'we all enjoy a chat and bring them news'.

The allotments Committee has arranged that two local chimney sweeps deposit their soot at the allotments for the gardeners to use as they wish. The general practioner knows a number of the allotment holders as patients. He encourages his elderly patients to take up constructive hobbies, anything that interests them, 'for if you don't you become depressed and die'. Those who have been ill or had heart attacks he advises to garden steadily and not to

170

overdo it. One retired gardener who thought of giving up the garden was told by his doctor, 'don't give it up whatever you do, it's the finest therapy you can have'.

For the last two years a charity event has been held in the locality over a weekend to raise money for local causes. It is planned to make it an annual event. It is organised by a committee which has personal links with allotment holders. The activities are based on a pub frequented by them and the landlord says that they make generous contributions of their garden produce, collecting them at the allotments and transporting them to the pub, for use at an auction and a sale of goods. The landlord reports that the gardeners are enthusiastic about the charity and help to sell raffle tickets.

The six local people interviewed, four women and two men, all know about the Long Reign allotments, although one knew only a little about them. Five of them know some gardeners. They think that the allotments are well known in the area and see them as beneficial, both for the families of the allotment holders and for the community as a whole. One says that 'some families have had allotment holders for three or more generations, they pass their knowledge on'.

Members of the public who are not allotment holders can join the Long Reign Allotment Gardens as associate members, which enables them to buy fertilisers, insecticides, seeds and canes more cheaply from the association. It is said that the local people 'value this service', which is very convenient, 'especially for those at work'. The members give advice on seeds, fertilisers and insecticides, and 'a group of men are always there talking and they will lift things into your car'.

The respondents report a great deal of social activity in and about the allotments. The gardeners are seen as friendly, quietly tending their gardens. 'At spring and summer weekends a knot of people can be seen talking near the main gate' and a couple who live very close to the allotments say 'it's the social centre of Skegby, the gardeners talk of local news and of their gardens, they help each other'. The wife reports that young children go to the gardens with their grandfathers and set seeds, 'they talk and write about it at school'. She sees the gardeners and her family as having the same interest in protecting the land for they make the allotments 'as secure as they can' and on most evenings will walk through the gardens on their way to or from social occasions.

The allotments are looked on as a blessing for the area as gardeners grow food for the table and freezer, and also give produce to the family, friends and neighbours. 'The gardens offer a regular occupation for retired men and are a place to go to when the wife is washing and they won't get under her feet'.

CONCLUSION

The Long Reign Allotment Gardens promote personal and social wellbeing among their members. For all of them there are the benefits of regular exercise and of keeping their minds active. Those at work attend in a more relaxed and purposeful way after releasing their tensions through gardening. The retired or redundant know that they have a hobby that can keep them busy several days a week. The value of the allotments as 'a substitute for the workplace, it keeps them occupied' is widely realised in the locality, and the anticipated closure of a local pit is expected to lead to an increase in those applying for allotments.

Gardening on the allotments provides a great deal of social satisfaction for the gardeners. They have a common bond in maintaining the good name of the Society, and the public display of activity on each plot offers such golden opportunities for them to get together on their joint interest and extend their friendships. The retired and redundant in particular have regular companions and also a variety of others to get to know, and have an opportunity of doing something together with their spouses. The wide range of topics discussed, including current affairs, local and family news, extends gardeners' understanding and awareness and creates strong social bonds among them.

Gardening offers the elderly especially a purpose; this and the opportunities for learning local news and exchanging ideas on all sorts of topics helps the gardeners to maintain their health and interest in current affairs. Most, especially the older ones, have an air of contentment and an awareness of achievement for their families and themselves. Their advice and gifts of surplus produce to friends and neighbours are appreciated. It is noteworthy that in the community elderly gardeners are respected for their knowledge.

The great majority of the members have had only the minimum

of formal education, and by the nature of their culture and jobs come from a working class environment. The amount of knowledge and expertise demonstrated are very impressive and they show a great enthusiasm to continue learning. They learn not only while working individually on their plots and through reading and the media, but also through discussion and seeing how others tend their gardens. It is characteristic of the learning that any theory or generalisation made is drawn from experience and discussion.

Allotment gardening is a public and visible activity, but each gardener is responsible for his or her particular plot; 'it is your own kingdom, something you have produced from a seed, you have fed and looked after it'. They also observe each other at work. This encourages the transmission of good and makes evident poor practice, providing incentives for everyone to aim for high standards. Their discussions of their approaches and plans help them to final decisions, but they emphasise that they 'never impose my way on others'.

All the members have, through gardening, something to talk about to their families and friends. The activity of tending the garden and the resulting companionship improve their quality of life; all see that the vegetables and fruit produced increase their families' standard of living, for the much reduced need to buy vegetables means money is available for other purposes.

With their cheerful and patient but determined approach to gardening and indeed, particularly for elderly gardeners, to life, they provide fresh wholesome food for their families, friends and neighbours, and enjoy individual and social activities which sustain an active mind and body.

Case Study 25

THE SUTTON CENTRAL FLYING CLUB

INTRODUCTION

Pigeon fancying i.e., the care, breeding, training and competitive showing and racing of pigeons, is an exceedingly complex activity and so is the organisation which sustains it. Few who are not fanciers can have much understanding of what it involves, or be aware of its fascination. The purpose of the present case study is precisely the same as all of the others, but on this occasion it will be helpful to provide a brief introductory explanation of the hobby and of its local and wider organisation. This will be followed by the usual description of the local background of the club visited and then the standard sections of the case study.

PIGEON FANCYING: ITS CONTENT AND ORGANISATION

Pigeon fancying remains a popular hobby in many parts of the country. The fanciers are always conscious that they deal with quality birds 'like top class athletes'. Daily care and attention are vital and prompt action follows the discovery of signs of disease. Fanciers take great pride in their lofts and aim at all times to make the birds comfortable and content. Internally the structure is designed for breeding and for the adoption of various racing strategies. Maintenance includes hygiene, ventilation and control of moisture. In front of each loft is an area where the pigeons strut and peck after exercise. Almost always it includes a lawn and border; high fences surround each loft and its immediate area to keep the birds safe from marauders.

The great majority of fanciers run their lofts by themselves, but a few work with a partner. This they appreciate not only because the task of caring is shared but because of the discussions on breeding, racing and the progress and programme of individual birds. In a few cases husbands and wives are partners, a joint enterprise reported to bring much pleasure.

An annual cycle of processes and activities governs both fancier and pigeon. The fancier decides routines, develops skills, observes and acts on the analysis made of the pigeons' behaviour, always with great expectations and on race days great excitement; the pigeons mate, bring up the young and race. Breeding starts early in the new year, some looking on it as propitious to pair the pigeons on 14 February; a few days after hatching each pigeon is ringed, the number on the ring identifying it and the owner. The six months long racing season, starting in April, is strenuous and exciting for both pigeon and fancier, the latter part of it also being the introduction to racing of the young birds, i.e. those born in the Spring, which can be entered in races when 12 weeks old. Soon after the end of the racing season the birds moult, and enter into a period of peace and quiet. Autumn is the traditional time for club pigeon shows, for buying pigeons to renew stock and introduce new blood, and for attending the enormous national and international shows, where fanciers are immersed among the milling enthusiasts, meet friends and keep up-to-date with pigeon practices, lore and equipment. It is also a period of reflection for the fancier to see where modification of routines and practice can give a competitive edge and also a time to think about Spring pairings. During winter comes the payout, the annual coming together of fanciers, their families and friends to celebrate the awarding of trophies, certificates, and prize money.

The excitement of racing days stands out most vividly in all fanciers' minds and a typical racing day is described in their own words: 'race day is the high day', 'the air is electric', 'you're all keyed up', 'they come over the houses and you see them dip', 'the heart starts to race', 'you see their wings close and they sail towards the loft', 'the excitement is terrific', 'when you win you feel great'. To all fanciers, win or not, pigeons are fascinating and 'money can't buy the excitement of racing'.

The grid references of each loft and liberation point enable flying distances to be determined, the pigeons' times are found from the members' clocks and so the birds' speeds can be calculated, the one with the fastest speed being the winner.   Entering pigeons for a race and preparing them for transportation to the liberation point are 'meticulously done'.   Fanciers' clocks are checked, the fee is paid, each pigeon's number is recorded, a race ring is put on one of the bird's feet, the ring's counterfoil (for checking after the race against the number on the inside of the bird's ring) is carefully saved, and the pigeon is placed in a crate.

On returning at the end of a race it is important to get the bird into the loft as soon as possible, take off the race ring, place it in a small cup or thimble and put that into the clock to register the time taken. Later the members meet, the clock setter takes the thimbles out of the clocks, checks the numbers on the race rings against the counterfoils, the times are recorded and speeds computed, results made known.

The cloth cap image of pigeon fancying has to some extent been modified as people from a wider range of backgrounds have taken it up. The character of the sport has changed during the lifetime of most fanciers, the great majority of those interviewed being in their 50s. In the eyes of this older generation the hobby has become 'big business' to the detriment of camaraderie; some fanciers are making a business of pigeons and breeding them for profit while continuing their enthusiasm for racing.   The independent and determined characteristics of the traditional fancier are still there in abundance, but competition is fiercer.   A number hold that there is 'less sportsmanship' and perhaps not as much affability. Some feel that less prize money is now available; ten years ago the 'pool' on a typical local race is said to have yielded over £70 while now it is more likely to be £30 to £40. The price of birds has soared and the cost and range of equipment, food and drugs have increased enormously.   National and international contacts have been developed.

Until quite recently pigeons were transported by rail for training and races. The closure of branch lines has led to the regular use of vans and cars for training pigeons and to huge transporters for conveying them to racing points.

To race each fancier must belong to a club, and each club defines the area within which the lofts of all its members must lie. Any person wishing to join a club has to be proposed and seconded by members; a majority vote by members present is necessary for election. Clubs are grouped into federations which in their turn, where desired, are amalgamated into combines. The officers, elected annually, of each of the organisations at these different levels, consist of a president, vice-presidents, chairman, secretary, treasurer and committee. Almost all of the business of the organisations is done by volunteers; the secretary and clock setter each receive a small payment. It is the pigeon fanciers themselves who by their annual subscriptions and race fees keep the racing and showing of pigeons going. Through a system of delegates between the different levels of organisation a strong network for discussions, decisions and dissemination operates. The organisations, which are all affiliated to the national body, the Royal Pigeon Racing Association (RPRA), are principally concerned with racing and showing; in all their activities they must follow the 'Standard' rules, comprehensive, detailed and strict, of the RPRA. All organisations belong to a Local Region which deals with membership and the interests of the Region. These Regions send delegates based on the numbers of members to the RPRA's Council which controls the national affairs of all fanciers. The RPRA regulates the racing and showing of homing pigeons and has established a uniform system for timing and for measuring race distances. The RPRA Council's attention to detail is demonstrated by its long established committees on clocks, rings and weather forecasts; on rules; on liberation sites.

Within pigeon fancying there is a built-in tension which causes an inescapable ambivalence in each individual member; on the one hand the 'fascination' for pigeons inevitably draws them to spend as much time as possible observing and training the birds to win at all costs. On the other hand they know that in order to compete they have to be members of a club and co-operate, working to strict rules.

THE AREA, THE CLUB AND ITS MEMBERS
The Club which kindly agreed to take part in the project is in the north midlands town of Sutton-in-Ashfield with a population of 40,000. The one-time key industry of the area, mining, is much less prominent than it was. The town, part of a large urban and

industrial development based between the Pennines and the more agricultural eastern part of Nottinghamshire, is striving hard to gain a new prosperity and identity. Within the area there has long been a strong interest in pigeons, and Sutton Central Club, with 55 members, is numerically the largest in the Notts and Derby Border Federation to which it belongs. Fanciers describe it as 'a strong club', with many members gaining prizes in national, regional and local races. It is in good heart but aware that in recent years it has not been able to attract as many new members as it would like.

The Club's meeting place is a local pub which has been used for many years for shows and the weekly display of race results. One of the landlords gave the Club a trophy. Although not many members live close to the pub, there are recognised times of the week when pigeon fanciers are likely to visit to meet friends. Members give good support to the federation, combine and national races which start in the North. They send about 500 pigeons to the weekly federation races which generally have 3000-4000 birds in them; combine and national races also attract several thousand birds.

Eighteen members of the Club were interviewed, four with their wives and the others individually, a few for a short time only. Telephone conversations were held with the federation chairman and his wife. In addition conversations were held with a number of gardeners on the allotments where seven of the fanciers interviewed have their lofts, a librarian and a few local people. The researcher was received by everyone with enthusiasm and kindness, and he is very grateful to them.

Of the 18 members interviewed there were two each in the age ranges 21-30 and 31-40, eight between 51 and 60, five aged betwen 61 and 70 and one over 70; so 72% of those seen were in the 51-70 age range. From visits to three Club shows and a national one the majority of members appear to be middle aged and so the sample interviewed is likely to be fairly typical.

All the respondents left school at the minimum age, but the federation chairman, a keen flyer, is a medical practioner. Eleven of the members (61%) had started their interest in pigeons while still at school, often with encouragement and guidance from members of family or friends. Seven (39%) expressed a lifelong interest in animals and birds. Most of these were family pets, with budgerigars and greyhounds often being mentioned, but what characterises the respondents are the variety and number of pets they looked after simultaneously. The delight and affection in looking after and observing all the pets stands out clearly.

Nine (50%) of those interviewed are retired or redundant, six (33%) of them from the mines. For all of these, maintaining their enthusiasm for pigeons is a 'lifeline', it means responsibility and activity for 'they all depend on you for food, water and shelter'. It is noteworthy that those retired members who are married are encouraged by their wives to continue their hobby. The range of jobs mentioned by Club members still at work were: caretaker, shopkeeper, fireman, self-employed corn merchant, engineering, hosiery and miner.

SOCIAL EFFECTS

There is a strong and enduring social aspect to pigeon fancying. On the one hand keen competition tends to place bounds on it, and on the other fanciers enjoy talking at length to others 'as they know what you're talking about'. Most Club members have known each other for years and besides sharing, often over a drink after meetings, their experiences about pigeons and to some extent their learning, they talk about their families and local and national events; 'I've known them for years and there's a fellow feeling'. Those with lofts on allotments often come together in small groups.

Pigeon fanciers on the whole enjoy getting together and one respondent's wife says that when they meet, 'it's worse than a gang of women'. Some discuss race results over the telephone. In addition, members get to know a number of casual aquaintances at local and regional shows, auctions and sales of pigeons and equipment. However, it is pointed out that in their talk, members 'don't tell you anything that will help you as a competitor'. Those who are delegates or show judges come into contact with a large number of fanciers and enjoy exchanging experiences and news of mutual friends. Members say that through the hobby people of different backgrounds and ages become friends. The warm, friendly ambience is real and valued, but nevertheless members' determination to win may overide common courtesies.

To enable them to keep lofts in good condition and renew equipment, pigeon fanciers tell each other about any cheap materials

179

that are available such as dismantled garages, and help to collect and fix them. Such information and support are appreciated as they enable members to continue their interest at what they see as a reasonable financial outlay. They also take each others' pigeons for training and will work in pairs when the pigeons require injections. When a fancier is ill or on holiday other members will readily take over the job of looking after the birds. Members report that this kind of help can always be relied on and it is appreciated.

All members go out of their way to help and encourage new members, especially young ones. They give pigeons and advice, and explain and demonstrate to newcomers how to deal with all aspects of caring, breeding and racing. Members support them strongly in the early stages and show a kindly interest in them. However, when they gain good positions in races, it is felt that they are no longer novices and so, while the encouragement continues, the regular support is gradually withdrawn.

Groups of members join together quite frequently to visit local or regional shows and auctions; a member also organises annually a weekend at the national show which is held in Blackpool. Committee members arrange winter shows as they 'realise the value of meeting and socialising during the winter months'. Members look forward to all these occasions not only because they are good social opportunities but because they help them to keep up-to-date with all aspects of the sport. Wives and other members of the family often come to the shows and may separate from Club members for part of the time 'to look round the shops'. These events provide happy social gatherings for members and their families.

However, a number of fanciers point out certain changes. Wives used to get together to organise social events, raffles and jumble sales, 'but not now'. Good support for each pay-out was a feature but 'there is less support' for them and the last pay-out was not held because of lack of support. One longstanding member recalls that 'in the old days if you won 50 bob you would all go for a drink, but not today'. It is reported that 'jealousies come in so they want to change things to suit themselves'. One member went so far as to say that 'I'd like to think that I could trust people in what they're telling me about pigeons, but I can't'.

It is clear that, while pigeon clubs offer fanciers many

opportunities for meeting socially, when there is enthusiastic talk about a subject they find fascinating, there seems to be declining support for certain local social gatherings. Together the members form a network of information, social exchange and practical help so long as there is no seeking, however subtle, for anything that could confer an advantage on a competitor. Cost and effort feed the keen determination to win; this and displays of jealousy could be regarded as factors which in time inhibit the development of social opportunities and the information network within the Club. While there is social interaction, there would seem to be very little social learning or development.

EDUCATIONAL EFFECTS
Pigeon fanciers universally report that with pigeons 'you never stop learning' no matter how long they have had them, and that 'you need to be dedicated to win'. One admits that 'I have only been doing it for five years, so I have a lot to learn'. They spend such a great amount of thought, time and effort partly because they learn that 'pigeons are fascinating little creatures' and partly because of the will to win races. Most of this is individual, but members value meeting each other to talk in depth and at length about their hobby, and to clarify their knowledge. They listen to what people say, they read, they 'consider' and then, as members emphasised time and again, they learn to make their own judgements and critically appraise them; 'if things don't work out, you have to go through it in your mind and find what has caused the difference'. They learn that 'you've got to be well organised' and that to do well both good pigeons and good management are necessary. Fanciers learn that 'pigeons have to suit your lifestyle', and become aware that others' routines and methods may not be suitable because their circumstances are different.

Pigeon fancying is a very technical activity, yet the Club members interviewed, with no extended education and mainly having experience in practical trades, willingly take on difficult learning. While knowledge is passed on 'from one generation to another', fanciers are generally avid readers. They read and exchange magazines, they read and re-read books and study a variety of pamphlets. One of the local librarians reports that since a library can only buy books through the net book agreement, he regrets that it is not possible for libraries to buy specialist pigeon books which he knows fanciers would appreciate. None reported having attended evening classes and only one thought there might have been classes years ago. While greater sophistication in food, drugs, training and racing methods contribute to the need to keep up-to-date, there appears no doubt that learning is stimulated by competition as many members see their reputation at stake. Fanciers, including those who are from a background in which traditional adult education finds it most difficult to recruit, demonstrate a consistent willingness to learn and reflect within their strong but narrow interest.

Theoretical and practical learning are integrated in observing and handling pigeons; fanciers learn about the physical characteristics of the birds, for example, bone and muscle structure and plumage. They observe the pigeons 'for hours', noting such details as eating habits, relations with the others and their 'individual quirks'. Through long observation and racing records fanciers are able to build up a detailed picture of the characteristics and prowess of individual birds. By these means they hope to pick out pigeons 'with a big heart, with spirit' which should develop well for racing and breeding. They 'learn that pigeons tell you when they're right', for example, bright eyes, white wattles, shiny tight feathers; it is typical that fanciers give different weight to these various factors.

Breeding pigeons and improving the quality of their stock is of vital importance to all fanciers; 'a stockman looks for parentage with winning genes, it's the same with pigeons'. Some follow line breeding with the occasional outcross; they learn from older members that using this method 'to breed a champion it takes years'. Others put their faith in 'putting winner to winner'. Past performance, pedigrees and the characters of the birds are studied, and members 'learn to watch out for too much inbreeding' and its inherent weaknesses. They have a practical approach to breeding and realise that it will always produce a high proportion of unremarkable birds. The importance of 'working to a timetable and keeping records' is recognised. When assigned pairs do not hit it off a limited choice is often given. Hens look after the young although 'some cocks mother and look after them but others kill them - pigeons are the same as human beings in their temperament'. Members learn of the excitement of rearing pigeons, 'you breed them, you feel they are yours, they need looking after'.

All members quickly realise the need to start training the young birds systematically as soon as they leave the nest for from these come the future champions and breeders. Typical comments are: 'you learn good habits have to be taught', 'you've got to train them right or they'll get fat and idle'. As soon as the young birds can walk, training begins to enable them to 'get their bearings' and to accustom them to a calm, daily routine within a welcoming environment of food, water and shelter. Stimuli such as dogs, children, adults and washing flapping in the breeze are introduced to get the birds used to the characteristics of the immediate loft area. Members learn that 'you've got to control them and you do it by their bellies'. They find that it takes patience to train pigeons in good habits and to get rid of bad ones such as perching on loft roofs.

Training is taken as seriously as that of 'athletes' or of 'racehorses'. To develop the right combination of speed and stamina pigeons, young and old, are trained through practice flights at varying distances and through races. The training also helps them to become familiar with the last few miles of a race so that, the fanciers hope, the birds resist the 'pull of the pigeons' and fly straight home. They know by the direction from which the birds come at the end of a race whether they have flown too long with the bulk of the pigeons or come directly; they learn to pick out those 'that use their brains'. They find, sometimes to their cost, that with regard to training, 'nothing is left to chance'.

Different systems of racing have been developed based on degrees of withholding or offering access to the birds' mates; all are aimed at motivating the pigeons to return home as quickly as possible. The fanciers learn about them, try some and judge which to adopt according to the number and sex of birds they race and whether they enter sprints or long distance races. They monitor performances and select the distances at which individual pigeons do best, and learn to 'handle the (novice) bird gently' as 'it knows when you are excited'.

For most races the birds are released so as to aim for a Saturday afternoon return. All fanciers learn the systematic procedures necessary for conducting races, and soon become aware of the need for co-operation for such a complex operation to succeed; they know that what are to them valuable pigeons in terms of stock and potential prizes should be handled carefully and made comfortable while being transported to the liberation sites. Stories of past attempts to cheat are occasionally brought up, and fanciers adopt a realistic attitude by acknowledging the need to take every precaution against fraud in human or animal competition where money or prizes are at stake.

A great deal is learned about nutrition and its effect on health and performance. Members follow well established principles of feeding, but learn to vary their application according to the needs thrown up by practice. They also learn to be reticent about the food they give their pigeons; 'they don't tell you anything that will help you as a competitor'.

Maintaining pigeons in good health is vital and fanciers learn to recognise and deal with standard ailments. Some are sceptical about the powers and apprehensive about the effects of new drugs. They believe that 'not many vets know about birds' and they aim to rely on themselves and other members to cope with pigeons' illnesses.

Respondents report that they acquire a certain amount of geographical knowledge - about the effects of the wind, physical terrain and weather on pigeon flights. At the start of a race fanciers are told about the weather conditions for the flight and use the information to estimate the expected time of return. They learn that the birds can fly at 60-80mph with the wind and that 'a nose ender means a hard race' at half that speed. The fanciers learn for several lofts near them the advantage or handicap of distance, which helps them to compare the pigeons' speeds. Some learn to use calculators. Secretaries of clubs and the federation learn to use computers to obtain and print out the race results.

Pigeons stray at times mainly through gruelling races or adverse weather conditions, and fanciers learn about the procedures and expenses for dealing with them. Where they have the opportunity of keeping a stray, they learn of the persistence necessary in persuading it that it has a new home. 'There are brainy pigeons and others, like people; brainy pigeons soon get to know the new loft, but some don't seem to learn.' Fanciers learn to accept the loss of a number of birds each year through predators, being shot, injury and not returning from a race. One member 'bred 60 pigeons last year and lost 33'. They learn to kill pigeons because of old age, illness, injury or not doing well or 'you would be over-run'. 'You've got to be ruthless' is often said. Many pigeons race for six or seven years and one fancier keeps a pigeon which is 15 years old as it has done well for him; 'you get fond of them but eventually they've got to give way to young ones'.

A few members have learned to act as judges, mainly locally, but one or two at national levels. They are aware of its value to 'the pigeon fraternity by maintaining interest', and learn the RPRA detailed criteria.

Whether they have few or many birds, members learn to become well organised in looking after them. If they are at work they decide on a routine which fits in best with it and with their family, although where there is shift work they may have to vary the routine; those on shifts observe that when they have a run on one shift the birds always do better. They plan carefully the tasks required at different times of the year, 'you're always thinking ahead'. Whenever they make a change in their practice they always look at how the birds are affected by it.

All members learn skills in handling the finances connected with their hobby. What fanciers have to balance are costs due to the number of birds they maintain, the price of new birds, the number to race, the frequency of racing and the amount of pool money. They recognise the uncertainties of breeding, but 'if you pay £100 for a pigeon you give them another chance'. They are conscious that 'poor birds take as much to feed as good ones'. Those who race a large number of pigeons say that because of costs, 'you've got to win'. Some older fanciers with a small number of birds believe that modern practice 'is putting pigeons beyond the reach of the ordinary working man'. Fanciers are conscious of the very high costs of starting up for young people.

Pigeon fanciers enjoy tremendously their 'absorbing hobby'; their love of the birds and desire to win seem to stimulate them to learn. The list of competencies involved in that learning is very impressive indeed, ranging from anatomy and genetics to nutrition, simple mathematics, and diseases. It develops analytical and organising skills. It is notable, however, that the educational benefits are acquired individually, though subsequently clarified and extended in discussion.

185

OCCUPATIONAL EFFECTS

The daily commitment of fanciers to caring for livestock gives rise to an awareness of the value of planning and 'thinking things through first'. The majority of those interviewed have been involved with pigeons since childhood and have learned over many years the benefits in what they do of suitable routines, thinking ahead and examining the effects of changes made. Members also see the value of good management not only for pigeons but for all their affairs. They say that 'being systematic with pigeons shows the benefit of being systematic with other things', for instance, 'for work and gardening', decorating and holidays. Others report that they follow their practical approach to pigeons 'in other activities'.

The importance of food, minerals and vitamins for pigeons to keep them in peak condition for breeding and racing makes many fanciers aware of their own diet and they 'are more careful in what they eat'. The need for patience in carrying out changes with pigeons makes some realise that patience is needed in personal and family affairs, for example, in dealing with children and grandchildren. Also, through long experience with pigeons, several say that 'being kind to people brings the best out of them'.

The success members have in racing pigeons enhances their confidence not only as fanciers, but at work and in day-to-day activities. Through making decisions about pigeons and dealing with the consequences they develop faith in themselves to have control over their lives.

POLITICAL EFFECTS

The individualism and independence of learning and activity which have been noted in other contexts become most pronounced in this sphere. None of the other organisations we have studied is as completely concentrated upon its immediate area of interest or has so few if any points of contact with its local community. The commitment of the great majority of members is focused on pigeons, though a number do take an interest in gardening. Nothing was said to indicate that activity with pigeons leads to an extension of political awareness in other aspects of their lives. This section therefore concerns members' learning of "political" issues within pigeon fancying.

Respondents recognise that it is only with other fanciers they can speak in depth and at length about pigeon fancying; this, apart from the social contact, seems to be a necessary part of the learning process. Time for such discussions, the desire to spend much time with their pigeons, and the need to co-operate to compete raise tensions within members, and contribute to political learning at club and federation levels. The Club and all other levels of organisation are organisations of rivals. The RPRA's elaborate procedures and precautions for racing are fully accepted because fanciers know they represent the Association's experience of keeping rivalry within acceptable bounds and ensuring fair play. Officers quickly learn that they need to be firm and fair, for 'if you're not doing it right, they'll ride on your back'. Members learn as they talk together of the willingness of some people to take unfair advantage wherever money or prizes are at stake.

Members become aware that a love of pigeons, money and competition are inextricably linked. They know that in the Club, 'there are some good flyers and so the prizes are distributed and that keeps it a strong Club'. This feeling that prizes are within the reach of every member helps to maintain enthusiasm. But the tightness of money depresses both the amount of prize money and the number of new entrants. Finance is 'sometimes very difficult, leads to arguments', and in races the prizes cannot be 'more than the money coming in'. Clubs and federations are sometimes in conflict over money and members have to recognise the claim of transporter and race administration costs and prize funds on all clubs.

Decisions are made at Club meetings about Club matters. It is reported that 'members fall out if things aren't going right'; occasionally some who do not attend meetings then 'criticise what's decided', but these are given short shrift. Members learn to express their views forcefully, but in the end accept democratically made decisions. Delegates to the federation transmit Club views and bring back details of federation decisions and discussions.

In terms of personal finance respondents realise that they balance risks. They learn to weigh up the pros and cons as regards costs, effort and immediate or long term effects, for example, of buying a more expensive bird for stock or of modifying the racing method adopted. Family commitments, health and stage of life all help to shape their decisions. While as enthusiastic as ever to breed and

187

race pigeons, the general willingness of most members to join in the co-operative work required to prepare the birds for transporting appears to be less evident. Allowances are made for those on shift work or who are unwell, but members are aware that 'a pigeon fancier can be a good pigeon man but not a good club man'. And they still like their birds to be placed last into the crates! Some are inclined to think that pigeon fancying has 'got past a hobby, it's what you can get out of it'. There seems to be a greater awareness of the payments received by the secretary and clock setter for their services, which of course come from the members, who note 'the cost of their pigeons is covered'. While there is greater expectation of those who are paid, 'you get the same hard core to help'. A few like to be Club officers but it is reported that 'it's a job to get anyone to help, all clubs are the same - so many will do it'.

PERSONAL EFFECTS
Participants describe pigeon fancying as 'a cracking sport'. A number speak of pigeons 'as part of my life' and one reports that 'they are for some their whole life'. Most members, especially the retired, cannot imagine life without them. Wives of retired fanciers say, 'he is unlikely to take up another interest and what would he do?'

Through having pigeons members are active, they 'keep your mind active and your body responds'. Fanciers accept the daily discipline, they know 'the birds depend on them'. The retired say that they 'can't stay inside four walls', they want to be 'up and about'. For all, continuing to keep pigeons enables them to have a purpose in their life and maintain contact with friends.

Besides being an activity that gives members much to think about, it is also a relaxation. For those at work and for those who were at work pigeon fancying is a way of leaving behind pressures connected with work; 'pigeons help to forget worries at work, you go to work fresher'. Some respondents also report that looking after pigeons makes them feel content, for they witness their activities over a typical life span of 6-7 years.

It is often commented that with pigeons 'you only get out of them what you put into them'. One compares it with climbing a mountain to see the scenery 'but not for nothing because of the trouble and effort'. At least in preparing pigeons for races the value

188

of persistence is realised, they report that 'you've got to be stubborn'. The competitive spirit is always present for 'you are pitting your wits against the man down the road'. Good racing results mean that fanciers continue in buoyant mood at the same level of effort, but unsucessful ones often lead to intensified effort. There is no doubt when pigeons are entered for races that some members see their reputation at stake. With success it is they who receive congratulations and prizes, when their birds are not as successful as hoped they feel as though it is they who have failed. For these, prizes from pigeons they have 'bred and trained' demonstrate their skills and dedication. Some members speak of the great pleasure and satisfaction the hobby gives them, for example, 'I don't have pigeons just to win but to have the pleasure of seeing them grow up and race'.

Through their pigeon activities members gain in confidence and become proud of their achievements. A wife says that 'they gain skills and surprise themselves'. Members comment that the hobby 'has made me confident in meeting people' and 'I can talk to people about pigeons'. However, one member who has been involved with pigeons 'ever since I can remember' points out that he cannot say that keeping them has increased his confidence as he is not able to compare with a time when he did not have pigeons. A former president reports, 'as president I gained a lot from it, I felt good, people respected me'. The weekly excitement of the racing season and observing the birds' development impel them to improve their practice, to share their enthusiasm and to continue engrossed.

Most fanciers have looked after pigeons for many years and make constant reference to treating people and animals kindly and patiently; they express this feeling as a general principle, 'if you treat people, animals and birds well they will do well'. Many speak of their love of animals, particularly birds, and cruelty to animals is deplored. They enjoy seeing and talking about birds in the garden, the park and on the pond. A member says that 'you have to see pigeons as individuals, so at work I treat people in the same way, as individuals'. Fanciers observe their pigeons and see them as regards their temperaments as being no different from people. There are a few references to children. One member does his best 'with the pigeons and I've brought up my children to do their best; you've got to teach them from being babies, same with dogs, babies,

189

anything'. A fancier who has been involved with pigeons from childhood says that 'having pigeons is a bug, a disease. You think you can give it up, but early Spring you will want to be breeding young ones again'.

Feelings vary among fanciers. The 'decline in sportsmanship that doesn't give you the heart,' identified by some, has been mentioned. Others, including the retired who continue or even start up pigeon fancying with zest, find involvement in the activity at least as attractive as winning, although 'winnings make you feel good'.

EFFECTS ON FAMILY AND FRIENDS
Dealing with livestock has a substantial and enduring effect on members' families. In the majority of cases the lofts are on the doorstep, and so the members' activities are then at home. This makes contact easy for the family but of course the members' attention is with the pigeons. The effects tend to change as families have young children, who then grow up and develop their own interests. Where partners are already or become interested in pigeons, the hobby can bring them very close. Fanciers find it helpful to talk over their plans with partners. The conclusion of wives with whom the researcher spoke was positive; families generally accept the husbands' interest in pigeons, and they are certainly proud of their successes; trophies and cups are displayed to their best advantage.

When there are young children in the family members report that adjustments have to be made for pigeons 'have to suit your lifestyle'. Household budgets may also lead to financial adjustments as pigeons are money as well as time consuming. It is reported that friction can arise in young families as 'you can't go out just like that, the pigeons come first'. As children grow up some wives say that 'they resent not going on holiday'. The strong preference of fanciers to take holidays out of the racing season is said to be a bone of contention. To maintain harmony in the family members say that sometimes they have holidays at times selected by the family. Even on holiday it is said that a few fanciers 'worry about the pigeons'. In summer, where lofts are in allotments, families sometimes spend time there together.

As families grow up, members are generally able to attract the interest and help of the children. A few fanciers, however, say that

190

constantly cautioning their children to be careful when the birds were returning home from races and not to distract them may have been a factor in deterring the children's curiosity and interest in pigeons. With increasing independence and in some cases moving from the family home, most sons and daughters generally continue to help in looking after and training the pigeons, particularly in illness and holidays. Family sayings appear about pigeons: 'the silly season is here' and 'they can only talk about two things - pits and pigeons'. It was in only one instance that a fancier's wife discouraged her children from taking up pigeon fancying; while liking pigeons herself, she 'wouldn't want the children to have pigeons because too binding'.

Respondents acknowledge that they need help and understanding from their families and are grateful to them. They realise that they would not be as successful without the support of their wives. Clubs welcome wives as club secretaries. They know that the restrictions placed on the family through having pigeons are 'a bit hard'. In one family where father and son have their sets of pigeons the son says, 'we get on mum's nerves but she helps where it's needed'. Fanciers observe that the families share in the elation of success, but they have to be tactful when results are disappointing. When members leave work their wives often give them a hand in looking after the pigeons. Fanciers with grandchildren take great pleasure in showing them the pigeons as often as they can and in talking about them.

Members frequently talk to workmates and other friends about their hobby. Until a few years ago race results were published in the local paper and friends used to enquire or comment about the results. However, it is in the family that most experience about pigeons is gained. For most partners pigeons are part of the family circumstances, generally with pleasurable associations; the children are mainly interested and helpful but not many appear to follow in their footsteps if they leave the area, have responsible jobs or take up other interests.

WIDER EFFECTS

Pigeon fancying has some beneficial effect on the wider community through the charity activities organised at several pigeon shows. Many clubs organise fundraising events on behalf of local charities, and Sutton Central Club has run such events although not in the last year or so. At the regional and national shows fanciers and their families and friends are generous in supporting raffles and fundraising activities for a variety of charities including national ones. One of these is their 'own' British Fanciers Medical Research Fund which conducts research into pigeon lung. Fanciers also offer pigeons for auction and of course bid for them. At the Old Comrades Show at Birmingham in November 1992 £87,100 was distributed to 15 charities, about 80% of it to organisations concerned with the aged, spina bifida, heart trouble and pigeon lung. The charities are very grateful for this support and publicise its source. This will certainly make communities aware of pigeon fancying but probably does not directly inform people about the hobby or encourage them to take it up.   Neighbours who live or work near lofts are the most likely people in a community to be affected by pigeons. Fanciers are generally very considerate and tactful in dealing with neighbours, they 'try to be on good terms with them'. Some of the neighbours take an interest in the progress of the pigeons, and elderly ones like to watch them return after a race.   Gardeners on allotments where there are lofts have no objection to pigeons. They often talk to the fanciers about the races; they learn a little about pigeon fancying, seeing it as an activity taking place alongside their gardening. The local district council has no complaints about pigeons from the public. Pigeon fancying makes very little impact on the community; those who live or work near lofts may learn something of the hobby. For these and for fanciers the most lasting effect seems to be to reinforce attitudes of tolerance and understanding.

CONCLUSION
Pigeon fancying is an activity involving commitment, competition and co-operation. Apart from the large starting up costs, pigeons are small enough for the ordinary person to keep and breed; guinea pigs and greyhounds may be comparable but horses are in another league. Where the racing of livestock is concerned, pigeons are the smallest creatures to be raced and they are kept at or near home; numerically fanciers form the largest livestock racing group. The hobby keeps people active in mind and body, has a creative element and allows scope for insights to be brought into play. At the same

time it is a daily and time consuming commitment to care for them. Fanciers are of one mind, that to 'get anywhere with pigeons' takes a great deal of effort and persistence. They report that this leaves little time or indeed inclination to become deeply involved in other activities. The Club members, all with a minimum of formal education, readily take up highly complex learning, stimulated by a deep enjoyment of pigeons and the desire to have super birds and do well in competitions. For most, this learning started in childhood, but it goes at a fancier's individual pace, and develops through talking, reading and examining the results of changes they introduce. While much of a fancier's learning may be independent, talking to other fanciers enables members to clarify their ideas, think through implications and broaden their perspective on aspects of pigeon activities. The detailed discussions engaged in by fanciers serve to disseminate knowledge and are a form of group learning; such discussions appear to be an essential part of the learning process.

The great majority of members focus much of their leisure time on pigeons. Only one member reports involvement in another voluntary group - he and his wife run a social club for elderly people. Sutton Central is thus probably the most highly specialised of all our case study organisations, and its members are less involved with other interests and activities than any others.

This case study and that of the allotment society (No.24), both of which deal with living things, are examples in which children have been encouraged to take part. The two hobbies require repetitive tasks and planning; they can often be carried out by two or more people working together, and so form ideal conditions for children to actively acquire skills and background learning with parents and friends in an atmosphere of calmness and praise. Some of these features occur in other activities, for example fishing and first aid and, in our sample, football, judo and boxing (No.18). It appears that in pigeon fancying and gardening they are well developed. The daily commitment, sense of competition (with pigeons at least) and example of adult learning could well have a marked influence on children, and their taking up the activities in later life. Given the different social, leisure and employment circumstances in which young people are brought up nowadays, it is understandable that not as many of them take up pigeon fancying, but a few of the children of members have done so. However, in the competitive atmosphere of pigeon fancying, fanciers are persistent, singleminded and focused, and they keep up-to-date. These qualities are valuable to anyone let alone volunteers; it is difficult to believe that with such qualities fanciers will not find some way of keeping the pigeon flying.

Case Study 26

THE SUTTON CENTRE PARENT TEACHER ASSOCIATION

INTRODUCTION AND CONTEXT

Sutton-in-Ashfield has been briefly described elsewhere in this volume (cf. Case Study 24). Sutton Centre is a community school built in 1973 on a slum clearance site very close to the market place. The School, with about 800 pupils aged 11-18, is part of a complex containing a large sports centre, an adult education centre, a youth club and day care facilities, all of which were welcomed and continue to be heavily used. The School brought a new concept of education to the town, which is predominantly working class and at the time of its opening was steeped in the traditional values and loyalties of mining, hosiery and engineering. As regards the new kind of education provided, most people accepted it with open arms, but some were not so sure and decided to wait and see. A striking facility welcomed by the Parent Teacher Asociation (PTA) is that of providing pupils with opportunities in the evenings to continue their education and seek teachers' help and advice.

It was decided to include a parent teacher organisation in the Project as they generally involve mothers and fathers in their 30s and 40s whose principal concern is for their children. The PTA of Sutton Centre willingly agreed to take part, and the researcher is very grateful to its members for their help and co-operation. All the school's parents and teachers are, by definition, its members, but the great majority do not appear to have a sense of membership of the PTA. The Association continues because of the persistence and loyalty of a small number of parents and of teachers. Together they form the mainstay of the Committee, initiating and implementing the PTA programme. As one teacher said, 'the PTA is a minority group of positive parents.

PTAs have been regarded as harnessing and formalising the goodwill of parents, with teachers often playing a prominent part in them; this PTA, which started 15 years ago, was no exception. However, the turbulence in education during part of the 1980s not only led teachers but also parents to reconsider their attitudes to education. As part of its adjustment the Sutton Centre parents decided to abandon one of the PTA's long held roles of raising funds for extra equipment and facilities, as it was seen as too narrow and 'you become saturated by fund raising', and concentrate on educational issues.

The headteacher is the PTA's president and a parent is Chairwoman. Eight parents, the headteacher, who came in Autumn 1992, and six teachers were interviewed, two of the teachers briefly. Six of the parents are women. One parent was aged 31-40, six 41-50 and one 51-60. All left school at the minimum age apart from one who left at 17 and another at 22. Two parents are primary school teachers, one works in footwear manufacturing and three have part-time work. All are local to the area. The women are involved in other voluntary organisations: the cubs and scouts (3), Oxfam (2), yoga (1). Four were also members of primary school PTAs and another was a school governor and a Samaritan. One of the men has a long involvement in the Nottinghamshire Federation of PTAs, in a political party, and is a governor of the School. Those parents who are active in voluntary groups report that the experience in organising practical and social activities, as well as working with people from different backgrounds, has given them the skills and confidence to run Sutton Centre PTA.

Six members of staff are in the 41-50 age bracket and one is 51+. One is the secretary of the PTA, and four others attend the Committee meetings from time to time. Four have addressed PTA meetings and all attend parents' evenings where they are related to their work as teachers. Some attend the educational and social meetings initiated by the PTA, but report that few other teachers attend for 'they are too overburdened'.

The PTA and teachers are working together for the benefit of the pupils but they realise that their relationship has changed. The Committee is learning what it means to be independent: that planning, organisation and finance depend on them. The parents are in a majority and control the affairs of the Committee. The PTA aims to put parents' concerns to the staff and seek practical ways of dealing with them; it organises educational and social meetings but does not raise funds for the School.

Teachers report that they are having to cope with tremendous changes in main stream teaching, and also develop substantial post-16 courses. Yet in the midst of all this they 'have to convey a feeling of continuity to pupils and parents'. Parents and staff know that they contribute different perspectives to the work of the Committee; both recognise that informing each other of their concerns and discussing them 'is a two way process'. While parents are aware of their stronger position in choice of schools they also understand the delicacy of making complaints. For complaints are not about commodities but about the progress and treatment of their children. The attitudes and relationships of parents, pupils and staff are crucial, and parents seek solutions which maintain positive ones.

SOCIAL EFFECTS
The PTA organises a number of social and educational meetings each year. This academic year the social events, from which the small fund to run the PTA comes, include a cycle rally, a quiz, a fashion show, a carol concert, and a badminton tournament, for the last of which teachers' advice was sought. These events, carefully organised by Committee members and other parents, aim to 'provide a welcoming atmosphere'. They 'are quite well attended' by parents and teachers, with their families and friends. Fathers help, for example, by acting as stewards at the cycle rally. All these occasions are very much enjoyed, 'you have a bit of good fun and a laugh'.

Many parents already know each other as their children enter the secondary school either from the same primary school or because they live near each other. But as 'with secondary school you don't see parents regularly as you did in primary', there is less interchange of information and it is harder to remain close. The PTA social events and occasions such as meeting, for example,

197

when shopping enable parents to keep in touch and talk over school matters.

Most Committee members have helped or do help at social activities connected with the cubs and scouts and they make use of this experience in the PTA meetings.

The PTA Committee arranges breaks for light refreshments in small groups at the social and educational meetings it organises and also at the parents' evenings arranged by the School. This approach is adopted to encourage parents and teachers to come together in a relaxed way so that they 'feel able to talk'. Both parents and staff are aware that 'normally parents are willing to defer to the teachers, but social events mean we're partners and talk more freely'.

The PTA members welcome the opportunity to take up any spare places on School trips or theatre visits, for, besides the enjoyment of the occasion, it is another way for them to meet the staff informally. Parents report that on these occasions it is very easy to ask teachers for their views, for example, on balanced science, and 'talk about anything bothering you'. Where staff take pupils on extra-curricular activities such as sports matches and youth hostelling they welcome the help of PTA members with transport. This not only leads to good social relations, but teachers say that it is 'a bonding, we know we can trust them to help'.

The PTA's Chairwoman has also adopted an informal and friendly atmosphere at the Committee's meetings 'intended to put people at ease' and encourage them to 'say what they think without feeling foolish and to ask where they do not know'. Parents, particularly, and teachers report that in such a relaxed setting a constructive approach is evident.

The PTA's secretary, a teacher, notes that the Committee 'have very good social skills and put people at ease'. The Committee regard good organisation and informality as essential for the success of the social occasions, which help parents and teachers to get to know each other as people rather than in their professional or lay roles.

EDUCATIONAL EFFECTS

The PTA sees it as very important to help its members to learn about the educational issues which are affecting their children, and to 'work hand in hand' with the School. In working for better standards in education for their children the PTA looks for more understanding by teachers of how parents and pupils feel. At the same time the staff informs the PTA of its concerns and the pressures teachers feel.

Parents, aware that 'there is so much change in education and that people use abbreviations', are anxious to understand the National Curriculum and wider post-16 opportunities. They realise that present day education differs substantially from the more stable and traditional education of their own childhood, and are keen to help their children to gain good qualifications in a highly competitive job market. As a result the PTA is learning to focus on certain educational issues and 'target particular parent groups'. Committee members talk with as many parents as they can to find the issues they would like to learn about; members then feel in a good position to organise talks on matters of common concern. PTA members consider these meetings very useful, as they are 'helping us all to understand better'. Some teachers regretted the poor attendance at some of the educational meetings they have planned, but admit that those organised by the PTA are better attended.

PTA members are becoming aware that teachers have to adapt to a more demanding system and that at the same time schools have to organise their time and resources to prepare the most appropriate curricula for all students. Respondents say they are beginning to appreciate the effort required of staff to implement the changes.

Teachers are aware that the PTA has become more and more concerned with education. The long standing acceptance by parents of what teachers say without seeking elaboration has been replaced by a questioning and probing approach, which was at first seen by some teachers 'as encroaching on the professionalism of teachers'. PTA members are learning the value of a tactful and constructive approach and teachers learn to 'listen carefully'. Parents say that full discussion of complaints or uncertainty regarding their children broadens the understanding of both parties and makes for a more collaborative approach to overcome difficulties. Teachers report that everyone 'gains a lot' through this approach. PTA members thus gain a broader picture of secondary education, learn from other parents' experience and realise the need 'to always encourage your children'. They learn that other parents share their concerns and they value the discussions of common problems. The members 'become more aware of the broader range of behaviour of children and of the problems of some of them'. One thing the members are sure of is that 'we're always learning'.

The staff also obtain through Committee members and other parents contacts useful for work experience for pupils, and for sponsoring charitable events. The School has set up working parties on discipline and the PTA is very keen that its views should be taken into account, for it believes that children and parents are intimately involved. The School accepts this and will consider with the PTA how it can best be done. In these ways the PTA contributes to organisational learning on the part of the school.

OCCUPATIONAL EFFECTS

One interesting point that comes from the parents is the set of skills they bring to the work of the PTA. Seven of the parents interviewed are accustomed to working in voluntary groups. What they bring to the meetings are their committee skills and a willingness to work with others towards a common end. They 'bring people out and not inhibit them', they see the need for decisions after discussions. Their interpersonal skills enable them to work as a team on behalf of their children. Where members reflect on how changing conditions at work can affect their feelings and morale, they go on to think about how educational changes might affect teachers and eventually their children's education.

Just as they are adapting to changes in the School's curriculum and organisation, so teachers 'feel more flexible' and are also adapting to changing relationships with parents both at events organised by the School and by the PTA. The changed circumstances of schools, as regards, for example, the National Curriculum and attracting pupils to the School, make teachers consider the most appropriate responses to bodies and individuals having business with schools. Their experience with PTA members, especially over difficulties, helps to shape their response to others on school matters, and also encourages a 'diplomatic approach'. For her part the Chairwoman says that her jobs have made her 'well organised and systematic' and she brings a structured approach to the Committee's work.

200

POLITICAL EFFECTS

Besides broadening their educational knowledge and the work of the School, PTA members are becoming more aware that parents collectively can present their views to the School and try to influence its policy. This may include detailed matters such as the emergence of unsatisfactory situations or the working of the tutorial system. The Committee is very keen that its views relating to the School's provision of educational and social facilities, which could affect their children, are made known. The PTA discussed in detail the provision for and the siting of the youth club and also a proposal to house young ex-offenders near the School. The PTA's views will be made known to the Governors through one of the members who is on the Governing Body.

Parents have heard from sons and daughters and when meeting teachers that substantial changes are being planned for the School's post-16 programme. They believe that 'more time is necessary in years 10 and 11 (i.e. 15 and 16 year olds) on post-16'. The concern of Committee members to learn of the School's plans led to the PTA asking for and indicating the focus of a talk by the staff to parents of years 10 and 11. Preparation for the meeting took its tone from the Chairwoman's view that the post-16 opportunities 'are wider and more positive, they give pupils something to look forward to'. The headmaster, two staff and the PTA's Chairwoman spoke at the meeting, which was attended by 34 parents, some pupils and the researcher. The parents realise how important it is to their sons and daughters to have a well-structured, worthwhile course if they decide to stay on for another two years. They also became aware of the great investment of time and effort put in by the staff in developing the School's post-16 plans, and the uncertainties which affect planning. Handouts and opportunities to question and comment during the meeting and the refreshment interval were appreciated. This example illustrates how the PTA and staff work together to inform parents. When staff visit their feeder primary schools to speak to parents and pupils they always invite the PTA to send two parents. The PTA's ready acceptance provides primary school parents with an opportunity to ask PTA members about Sutton Centre.

Teachers report 'it is happening more and more' that parents are making suggestions. They 'have pushed quite hard', for example,

201

for earlier year 7 parents' meetings; the parents and their families 'would like to know after the first half term' how their children are settling down. As a result, the School has arranged an October evening meeting for parents of the new pupils and for prospective parents. The Chairwoman of the PTA speaks at this meeting and at the induction meeting of year 7 parents. The PTA has suggested to the School that 'you want to promote yourselves better'. This has led directly to a monthly newsletter in the local newspaper, which provides information about School events and describes important and distinctive features of the School's education. The PTA contributes to the School's twice termly news-sheet which helps to keep Governors, pupils and parents informed about what is happening at the Centre. Discussions are also taking place on providing a notice board for the PTA.

Through regular contact with staff respondents see 'what a committed group of people the teachers are'. They admire the School and the way it 'helps all the children including those in distress'; they learn to speak up for it and help to maintain the School's good name by, for instance, dispelling the myth that, because there is no playground, pupils need not go to lessons.

PERSONAL EFFECTS

Both parents and teachers report that through the PTA they are appreciating each others' point of view, and they realise how important good relationships are between teachers, parents and pupils. Some respondents speak of the 'good vibes' they had on first talking to their children's tutors.

PTA members realise the importance of people's emotions, for in their deliberations and learning they are ultimately wanting the best for their children. Their interactive and personal skills are used not only to 'smooth the waters', but to encourage members to talk about any worries concerning School, to question and express opinions.

All the Committee members feel that belonging to the PTA enables them to improve their understanding of education and help their children more effectively. They meet teachers on various occasions and 'are not intimidated about going into School'. Their wish to be 'involved in School for the children's sake' is constantly giving them satisfaction; they feel well informed in discussions with their sons and daughters, and are able to help other parents keep up-to-date. A noteworthy point from all but one of the parents on the Committee is that their experience in other voluntary organisations gives them confidence to join the PTA; typically 'because you're confident you'll go to an organisation'. The one who initially felt a lack of confidence, ('will people think I'm silly?'), says she is now contributing to the discussions. Committee members have children of different abilities and ages, and the work of the PTA heightens the awareness of both parents and teachers that educational decisions can have dramatic effects on pupils' future. Parents also realise more forcefully the value of family discussion and of being better prepared to help younger children as they reach particular stages of their education. As parents talk to teachers and other parents they are building up a network of people with whom they can discuss their uncertainities.

Parents are gaining a clearer understanding of the changes in education and the pressures on teachers' time, and the staff appreciate the feelings of parents who want to do the best for their children. Staff become very much aware of the fundamental matters of 'children's rights and entitlements of safety, respect and fairness' that parents are looking for. Committee members are deeply satisfied both as they 'get the feeling that teachers are interested in their children as people' and as they actively support their children's development.

INDIRECT EFFECTS ON FAMILIES AND FRIENDS

Committee members report that parents talk over school matters in the family, particularly after parents' evenings and meetings arranged by the PTA, when they feel well informed. Families regularly discuss their children's education, and more so when there are difficulties, choices of subjects to be made, or courses to be selected at 16. Committee members report that some children believe that parents do not understand the issues, and both parents and teachers say that children who attend parents' meetings show more confidence in discussions with parents. Parents want discussions with their children as they fear they will otherwise 'make the decisions themselves'. Members find that the experience of helping older children 'has helped the family' in the education of their younger ones. Some parents on the PTA Committee say that their children show an interest in the PTA and ask what they have talked about, but others are 'not keen on the idea'.

Those staff interviewed who are parents report that they feel just as keenly as Sutton Centre parents for the wellbeing of their children, and having experience 'on both sides of the fence' helps them to appreciate parents' concerns. A teacher says that a few spouses believe that their partners spend too much time at School.

Both parents and teachers say that they talk over with their partners issues arising from parents' meetings, and that they also discuss PTA and school matters with friends. This helps parents to see more clearly how they can best help their children; a few find, sadly, that some friends 'don't want to know'. A teacher who has set up courses on parenting finds his experience with the PTA 'sharpens his thinking'.

EFFECTS ON THE WIDER COMMUNITY

The PTA makes parents, teachers and their friends aware that there are people willing to work for close understanding between parents and the School to improve the quality of education. The pupils are the real beneficiaries even though they may be unaware of it. Developing a sense of trust between teachers and parents, appreciating each others' point of view and the limits of resources generate, albeit on a small scale, a glow and warmth of feeling that hearten adults' efforts to educate young people. The PTA Committee realise the lack of numbers, as 'a lot can't be bothered', seriously limits its efforts, but nevertheless it continues because of the successes it experiences - for example, the autumn meeting of new parents, a slot for the Chairwoman to speak at such meetings and also those of prospective parents, and the newsletter about the School's activities in the local paper.

The Library and local newspaper staff knew nothing about PTAs other than what they read locally; they feel they are worthwhile.

The Committee knows not only that its active numbers are small but also that it is not attracting 'the broad sprectrum of parents'. Some staff believe that this is partly due to a lack of confidence on the part of parents; on the other hand, a parent who is not on the Committee tells the researcher that she goes straight to the School when 'there is anything to sort out', and that she is unwilling to go to 'boring meetings'.

The teachers interviewed are aware that 'we are into market

forces and have to court the parents', but collectively recognise that their actual support of the PTA is not as strong or as consistent as ideally they would like it to be. The PTA actively supports the School's fundraising for charity and to help disadvantaged people; in this way local people and businesses hear of the PTA, but this is only one aspect of its work.

Very gradually the 'PTA is becoming advisory'. This is dawning on teachers and, regrettably, only on few parents. Nevertheless this voluntary group persists in its endeavours to secure as good an education as possible for the pupils. This belief buoys up the Committee to spread its message, and such leavening is to be welcomed in any community. The PTA knows that it has no power, but realises that it has the potential to influence the staff's thinking and works constructively to this end. As a Committee member put it, 'we're battling, but I think we're making an impression'.

Case Study 27

THE HOLBROOK PLAYGROUP

The inclusion of a pre-school playgroup in our case studies provides an example of a very familiar local voluntary organisation involving mainly women from a younger age range. A pre-school playgroup, as defined by the Pre-School Playgroups Association (PPA) is a local organisation 'offering sessional care for children, mainly aged three to five years of age, cared for with or without parents, no session lasting more than four hours'. The childen engage in supervised play activities suitable for their stage of development and in preparation for more formal education in school.

From its beginnings in 1961, the PPA has grown to 19,000 member groups in England alone, 6182 of which are located in villages. To be eligible for full membership of the PPA a group must adopt their approved constitution based on the democratic involvement of parents and other interested individuals. A network of local Branches gives support to groups and offers a range of training to parents, playgroup staff and volunteers.[1]

The playgroup selected for study is at Holbrook, a village of 2000 people seven miles north of Derby, attached by ribbon development along the high ridge between the Derwent and Amber valleys to the old mill town of Belper (population 16,500). Although contiguous with a sizeable town, Holbrook has the appearance of a self-contained village community. It has shops, several pubs, a petrol station and a post office, church and chapel, village hall and a village primary school with a steady 130 or so on the roll. Bus routes link it with local market towns and Derby. The village has become part of the commuter belt for Derby, Nottingham and the smaller industrial towns of the Erewash Valley. A 'new' estate was built 25 years ago and within the last five years a 'new, new' development has been added. Some of the tensions arising from the expansion of the village have affected the development of the playgroup.

THE PLAYGROUP

Holbrook playgroup was started 25 years ago, in the early years of playgroups, to cater for the needs of the families moving into the first phase of new housing. It was always a voluntary playgroup with a committee drawn from parents, but in the earlier years the supervisor seems to have been the dominant force, firmly keeping parents in what she believed was their place - on the other side of the playgroup door. The appointment of a new supervisor six years ago, following the retirement of the long-serving incumbent, changed its ethos to the delight of the parents. The new leader's welcoming attitude and openness has resulted in much greater involvement of the committee and members not only in the social and fund-raising activities but in every aspect of the organisation of the playgroup. Although the former regime was recollected by some members whose older children had then been going to the group, it is the impact and experience of the recent years which form the content of this study.

The playgroup meets five mornings and two afternoons per week in a smallish room in the Arkwright (village) Hall. Its cubic footage restricts attendance to thirteen children per session. Most children attend one or two sessions per week, so in all 35 children are catered for, representing 34 families. One morning session is reserved for Rising Fives, children who are shortly going to start school. There is no local nursery school or class; if nursery places are available at Belper, or at Kilburn, a larger village two miles away, a few Holbrook children may secure them. For most the playgroup offers their only pre-school experience.

As well as the supervisor, who is present at every session, two other paid helpers work half the sessions each and a rota of parents, in which all are expected to join, provides the third helper for each session. The management of the playgroup is the responsibilty of the committee of eleven members, elected at the Annual General

Meeting (AGM), joined by a co-opted representative of the Arkwright Hall Management Committee and three non-voting workers.

THE ENQUIRY

The methods of enquiry used were: a questionnaire, interviews and observation. All the members who wished, participated in interviews. Seventeen were interviewed of whom fifteen, just under 50% of the membership, were current members of the playgroup and two recent members were still very much in contact with the group. Eleven were interviewed on their own and the rest in two groups of three. All these interviews, which include those with two of the staff, are analysed together.

One of the ex-members is a parish councillor and some of her responses were from a parish council rather than a personal perspective. The headmaster of Holbrook primary school was also interviewed. The Social Services worker for under fives in Amber Valley, a local PPA tutor-organiser and the national PPA Information Assistant also provided helpful information.

A version of the individual supplementary questionnaires used for a number of our case studies (see Appendix B) was distributed by the kindness of the chairwoman to all the members. Only 13, roughly 40%, were completed and returned, despite reminders by the staff. The researcher attended a playgroup session and a committee meeting. She is most grateful to the committee for the welcome to a meeting, to all those who gave their time to talk to her, and especially to the chairwoman and the supervisor who helped in arranging the interviews and the distribution and collection of the questionnaires. She enjoyed her involvement initiated by the children on her visit to a playgroup session.

ANALYSIS OF THE QUESTIONNAIRES

The small number of completed questionnaires does little more than support and illustrate some of the points discussed in the more productive environment of the interviews. Because they were offered to all members and completed anonymously, the extent of the overlap between completed questionnaires and those interviewed is not ascertainable.

The questionnaire asks first about length of residence in

Holbrook. Eleven of the thirteen respondents were newcomers to the village; two had always lived there. Of the eleven, three had come from places no more than three miles away and another three from within ten miles. Two came from between 10 and 20 miles away and three from more distant parts of the country.

Of the newcomers, four had lived in Holbrook no longer than four years, five between five and ten years and two over ten years. The researcher's information was that about a third of the playgroup members were 'local' people as opposed to 'newcomers'. If the three who had moved to Holbrook from 'just down the road' are counted as 'local', then the balance of the sample was characeristic of the group as a whole.

Six respondents had been members of the playgroup up to one year, 2 for two years, one for three years and four for four years or more. Seven had sent one child to the group, four had sent two and one each three and four.

Three of the respondents were between 20 and 30, 9 between 31 and 40 years of age and one between 41 and 50.

In terms of age, length of membership and number of children, it seems, from observation, to be a representative sample of the membership as a whole. Playgroup involvement arises from having children in the 3 to 5 age range and passes as children grow older; the age of members and their number of years of involvement reflect this.

Terminal age of education fell into three bands:

15/16 - 5   18 - 4   22/23 - 4

A high proportion of the respondents work in an interesting spread of occupations, many of them part time:

1 housewife, formerly catering business owner
1 general practitioner - full time
1 teacher - full time
1 pub owner
1 solicitor's clerk
1 florist

The following were all part-time jobs:

1 secretary/bookkeeper
1 chambermaid/cleaner
1 merchandiser
1 sales consultant trainer

1 speech therapist
l teacher
1 playgroup assistant

The amount of information given about other involvements and activities confirms that work and looking after the family absorb most of the available time. Eight of the respondents did not belong to any other organisation. By the remainder, church was mentioned four times, professional organisation twice, a children's charitable organisation, a music society, a writers' workshop, the Parent Teacher Association and Cubs and Beavers all once each.

Seven said that they had or were attending no courses or classes; four had attended courses connected with their work; two went to French classes, one to first aid and one to computing.

Interests divided into three groups: sporting and physical activities - 15 mentions, the most popular being swimming (5) and aerobics/keep fit (4); domestic activities - 10 mentions, the most popular being dressmaking (3) and gardening (3); and broadly cultural activities - 10 mentions, the most often mentioned being reading (4).

In answer to the question: which of the organisations, activities and interests would you say grew from involvement with the playgroup (question 11), all respondents replied none, though one added the general comment: 'have become far more involved in Holbrook community life since being involved in playgroup'. It is difficult to understand why no link between membership of the playgroup and other activities was significant enough to spring to mind when answering the questionnaire while in interviews some respondents readily identified such links. This perhaps reflects the relative weakness of questionnaires as instruments used for this sort of research with groups unfamiliar with them.

THE INTERVIEWS - IMPACT ON MEMBERS

The interviews were an opportunity to probe more deeply into the impact that the playgroup made on members' lives than the schedule of the questionnaire. It is open to question how far the promptings of the researcher produced answers that she might wish to hear, or how far those being interviewed were anxious to give the 'right' answers and please the researcher. She can only say that when given the space to reflect on what the playgroup meant to

210

them and what they had learned and gained from involvement with it, the women gave full, spontaneous and often detailed answers as recorded in the following analysis. They were indeed anxious to be helpful, but this did not seem to lead them to relate experiences or feelings which were not genuine.

The prime intention of a playgroup is to benefit children, and the effects on them are outlined later. In the sections which follow, the impact on adult members, which in Holbrook means predominantly the mothers of the children, is recorded.

SOCIAL EFFECTS

All the respondents valued membership of the playgroup as a way of getting to know more people in and integrating into the village. Some felt that their socialising did not extend beyond the activities of the playgroup itself while for others playgroup friendships have become central to their social life.

The social value of the playgroup was felt equally by those who had lived in the village or its immediate area all their lives and those who were newcomers. The common factor for all the women was their motherhood, and many expressed their feeling that leaving the social milieu of the workplace to stay at home to care for babies and young children was a very isolating experience. The isolation led to loss of confidence and loneliness and a diffidence about mixing with adults outside the family. Such remarks as 'playgroup helped me come out of my shell', 'it brought me out of myself' and 'it helped me develop social skills, especially mixing with adults', illustrated the social benefits gained through membership. One Holbrook born-and-bred member, whose mother lives close by, found the playgroup a source of contact and social life with other young parents, while another who has no family roots in the area, spoke of being 'very reliant' on the playgroup for friends and support. One young mother who described herself as 'very shy' said that she had joined the playgroup for her daughter's sake but 'secretly for me as well'. Another said simply that 'it's nice to know there are people you can talk to.'

Social contact ranged from the pleasure of greeting people when out for a walk or at the village shop to nights-out at a disco in a neighbouring village and Christmas parties and outings. There was also clearly the easy popping into other member's houses for a chat

211

and a coffee which so vitally relieves the loneliness of the young mother.

EDUCATIONAL EFFECTS

Members identified two distinct areas of learning; the skills of running a voluntary organisation; and their knowledge and expertise as parents.

Three quarters of those interviewed were either past or present committee members and included vice-chairwoman, secretary, treasurer and past and present chairwomen. They spoke of acquiring organisational and decision-making skills and of learning how to deal with people, how to listen, how to communicate and how to work as a team. They had learned to discuss issues at meetings and to work out compromise positions, accepting the opinions of the majority. One said that she had 'learned to communicate with people more'; another is 'learning to deal with people, especially when they are being difficult'. Keeping the books, ways of fund raising including running a market stall, applying for grants and going to court for the licence for a bar were mentioned as particular pieces of learning.

The chairwoman reflected on her learning of the arts of leadership, delegation and persuasion. 'People expect me to tell them what to do but I am keen to share responsibilities and persuade people to get involved. I say in meetings "I'd like a volunteer to do this...or that"'. She is learning a lot 'about human nature - how different people react to circumstances, who will help and who won't'. She wished that she had been better prepared for her role and hoped that she would have the opportunity to pass on what she had learned to the next chairwoman. The treasurer valued her involvement as 'something separate which got my brain working again'. She learned how to do the books from a friend, is now using her bookkeeping skills to manage the family finances and is thinking of taking a bookkeeping course to gain a qualification.

For most respondents this was their first experience of working in a voluntary organisation and several spoke, with some surprise, of how much work is involved in running even a small local group. They had learned that an organisation needs a lot of continuing support and sustained contribution from members at a very detailed

212

level for it to run smoothly. One group of three said how much they enjoyed being on the committee, finding the meetings less formal than they had expected.

The researcher was able to observe much of this learning put into practice at a committee meeting. The atmosphere of the meeting, which took place in a member's sitting room, was warm and friendly. Participation was lively and relaxed and an amazing amount of business was dealt with. Organisation of both playgroup sessions and of social and fundraising activities involves commitment by each and every member to specific and often time-consuming tasks. The chairwoman showed skill in steering the meeting efficiently and briskly through the agenda. She made sure that all had their say and that the work was evenly shared out, using the strategies that she had outlined in her interview. One committee member commented that the chairman is forceful and controls the meeting well.

Learning about the behaviour and development of pre-school children was clearly an important benefit of involvement. Many respondents mentioned how helpful they found it to discover, through observation and discussion, that their children were not unique either in behaviour or in their rate of progress. 'Playgroup helps you to learn about children and to learn that your child isn't unique. You get a lot out of seeing children learn and understand your own child much better by observing others.' The playgroup is valued for the support it offers to parents concerned about their children and for the opportunity of sharing worries about their health and progress in an informal and non- threatening atmosphere: 'you don't feel as if you're on your own'. They valued their turns on the playgroup rota and said how they had learnt to communicate better both with children and with other adults through this experience. They found that children 'at different levels need different treatment' and learnt new ideas for activities and play for their children at home. One mother was able to compare her own children's rate of development with that of her much younger brother when he had been under five. She said that she 'didn't realise before how much children learned through play'.

Some respondents had pursued their interest to take up home study courses in nursery education 'to keep me ticking over', or to train for the 'Homestart' scheme which offers support to families

213

with young children. Another was thinking of taking the Open University course on the pre-school child. Several commented on how tough it is to get back into study after the break of having children: 'you vegetate, don't you?'

Respondents with older children realised clearly the value of playgroup as preparation for school. One mother who had been a teacher at the village school told how she 'used to see the difference in behaviour and in their ability to join in tasks between those who had been to playgroup and those who hadn't'. Such experienced parents share their learning with new parents who are less aware of what a playgroup offers.

The supervisors and members of the committee had learned how the provisions of the recent Children's Act would affect the playgroup. The supervisor-in-charge will need to study for the PPA playgroup diploma to qualify for her position. The requirements of registration draw attention to on-going training needs, health and safety requirements and the need to be aware of the signs of child abuse. A respondent who had recently spent some years in America where the risk of child abuse in privately run child care agencies is an issue of deep concern, valued particularly the safeguard ensured by parental participation in regular sessions at Holbrook playgroup.

OCCUPATIONAL EFFECTS

Half the respondents did not think that involvement with the playgroup had any significant impact on their occupation, taking that to mean their present or future employment. The others had a variety of experience to record.

For the supervisor and one of the part time paid helpers, involvement with playgroups as mothers of under fives had led directly to employment at the Holbrook playgroup. Their experience and learning as involved mothers had given them the skills, confidence and enthusiasm to work with under fives which they both found very rewarding (in terms of job satisfaction rather than financially!). For the supervisor, involvement as a volunteer when her child was of pre-school age led first to her becoming a registered childminder and then to applying for a job at a playgroup. She thought of training to be a nursery nurse or a teacher but felt that the amount of study required would put a strain on her family, so has opted for a career as playgroup supervisor. To date her learning has been more experiential than theoretical but now, as mentioned, she will have to study for the PPA diploma. A secondary school teacher found that involvement with the playgroup 'kept me occupied - filled the gap' until she returned to teaching on a job-share basis. Now she finds that her playgroup experience gives her confidence to speak up in discussions in staff meetings. A primary teacher has gained awareness of the needs of young children which will influence her when she returns to the classroom.

One respondent has found that the work on the committee kept up her office skills so that now she feels ready to apply for a post as a school secretary. Another is able to return to her hairdressing job part time while the playgroup and her mother look after her children. A lively discussion between three mothers may lead to the creation of a small business. One is doing homework making garments at exploitative rates of pay and has the idea of getting an Enterprise Allowance to set up her own garment making business. The second, who is doing secretarial work for the playgroup, offered to do the paper work for the new business while the third saw their contacts with local playgroups as the opportunity to sell in a captive market. Working together for the playgroup had given these three women the vision and confidence to plan a small business venture, and shows how enterprising members may take advantage of a busines opportunity generated by the voluntary organisation itself.

POLITICAL EFFECTS
Issues concerning resources for under fives, such as the choice of child care agencies and the availability of workplace nurseries, were of interest to respondents. Many said that they were now more aware of these issues, both through their own playgroup and through membership of the local branch of the PPA. Because lack of space restricts each child to two sessions a week at the playgroup, many were concerned about the lack of nursery places for Holbrook children. Parents, in their anxiety to 'do the right thing' for their children, value the playgroup for what it does, but would like to be able to have a choice. Some felt that by encouraging voluntary playgroups the government was getting

'nursery education on the cheap'. 'There is no government support or policy for under fives' was an expression of frustration about the patchy nature of provision.

Because the playgroup uses village hall premises, its members had been drawn into village politics. Several had served on the hall users' committee, which largely represents 'old' village interests and is often critical of the 'new' playgroup. One respondent described how she 'found myself in the line of fire of complaints' about alleged misuse of the premises. She fought and won a few battles on behalf of the playgroup and found the experience both exciting and stimulating.

A former chairwoman's involvement with the playgroup led directly to her standing for and being elected on to the Parish Council (PC). She has found the wider brief very different from involvement with the playgroup, 'lots of red tape, formality and very slow decision making processes'. She speaks on behalf of the playgroup and feels that she is beginning to change the attitude of the PC sub-committee which manages the hall.

For many respondents, membership of the playgroup was their first experience of participation in a voluntary organisation. For some it led to joining the local PPA branch and taking part in its training and fund-raising events. One respondent is treasurer of the branch and another on its committee. They commented that the branch at present has little support and neglects its local training role. This is partly because the few PPA development workers in Derbyshire concentrate on areas of greater need than Amber Valley and partly because members lack time rather than interest as they have jobs alongside family responsibilities.

Respondents described how, as their children grow and join other organisations, they find that they move into involvement with these groups. One explained that for her the playgroup has been 'the first step on the ladder' of increasing involvement with voluntary organisations which support her childen's development. Beavers, Cubs, Brownies and the Parent-Teacher Association of the village school, and, for those with older children, the local secondary school, were the most frequently mentioned. One respondent felt that the playgroup had started her interest in educational issues in general which she is expanding as a parent governor of the village school. By way of contrast, respondents felt they 'were not ready yet' to join the Women's Institute which they perceived as an activity for older women whose children have grown up and left home. Their responses indicated a slow widening of interests but their concerns remain centred on their own children.

One member represents under fives' interests on the local Community Education Council (CEC). From their contacts with the CEC and with Social Services, some members were aware of the Local Authority equal opportunities policies. Care was clearly taken to avoid gender stereotyping in children's activities, but the attempt to introduce 'ethnic' dressing up clothes, bought with CEC funding, was felt to be inappropriate because there are no black families in the neighbourhood.

Many respondents were worried about the difficulty of getting new people involved in the organisation of the playgroup; 'mums of today don't want to be involved'. They said that the same people always do the work, both in organising events and supporting them. It was difficult to get people to stay for AGMs because they feared that they would get put on the committee, a word which 'puts people off'. One commented that she 'was frightened when I first went on the committee. No one explains it, you don't realise what's involved until you're in it'. A former chairwoman felt that 'lots of people are frightened of being chairwoman, secretary or treasurer' and that it was always difficult to get people to take on these roles. Another commented that 'you've got to be dedicated to it - you wouldn't stick it if you weren't'.

The dilemma was clearly seen by the treasurer; 'if you keep on, others will just sit back and let you, but if you don't, no one will come forward. People feel put off because of the appearance of cliquiness'. A relative newcomer had been on a playgroup committee elsewhere where she had found that committee very cliquy and its meetings a waste of time; committee membership had been used as a mark of status in the community and 'the chairman was full of self importance'. This experience has 'thoroughly put her off' committees. She has observed that Holbrook is very different and she might wish to be on to the committee 'because of its friendly atmosphere'. Other respondents knew of playgroups which were 'cliquy' with 'secretive' committees and were glad that Holbrook was open and welcoming. However, one respondent felt

217

that 'people do not always speak their mind enough, because they don't want to offend each other'.

These experiences illustrate vividly the very detailed political education that participation in a voluntary organisation offers, and its limitations: the hard work and dedication required; the growing feeling of empowerment; the difficulty of attracting commitment; the hierarchies and the in-group that can quickly develop if either luck or good management do not prevent them; the importance of openness and the destructiveness of a bad experience. They also reflect how rare it is for people in organisations to possess the skills needed to involve new people in responsibility in non-threatening and acceptable ways.

PERSONAL EFFECTS

An increase in self confidence was the most frequently reported effect of involvement with the playgroup. Some felt that they had been confident before but that the playgroup had increased their capacity to be assertive and outgoing. One respondent, though always confident in the classroom, used to be embarrassed in adult groups. She felt that the playgroup has had 'a good effect on me as a person'. Another lost confidence while at home having babies and the playgroup 'brought my confidence back; the playgroup gave me a life outside the home. I became me again through it'.

Other respondents said that the playgroup had given them self confidence for the first time which 'is what people notice and comment on'. It enables them to 'go up to people and ask them what's wrong', 'have a go at more things', and speak up at meetings. One group had not gained enough confidence to return to formal learning, though they had thought of it; 'it's been such a long time'. Although looking for new opportunities, they were not ready to venture too far from home ground.

Some spoke of becoming more tolerant, more responsible and having a sense of personal commitment. Working for the playgroup gives them a sense of personal achievement and satisfaction and fills their need to feel that they are contributing usefully to the community. Some spoke of the personal benefit they felt from having the short but regular respite from child care; 'a period of sanity and a bit of private space'.

EFFECTS ON FAMILY AND LOCAL COMMUNITY

Children of members are an integral part and indeed the purpose of the playgroup, and the effect on them is immediate and, to adults involved, observable. All respondents valued the social benefits to their children. The playgroup gave their children a wider circle of friends in the village and established friendships which would be continued at infant school. Children develop social skills, mixing and learning ways of behaving in a larger group than the family. Different children respond in different ways; a shy little boy was helped to become more confident and outgoing while his boisterous sister became calmer and learnt to consider the feelings and wishes of other children.

The educational and cultural benefits of playgroup were spelt out by the parents. Children take the first steps towards socialisation into the culture of school in an atmosphere that is more relaxed and more like home than school can be. The Rising Fives session which introduces more formal activities is a valuable bridge between playgroup and school. The different play activities help the children to learn and develop skills of concentration, sharing and working co-operatively, communication and language both with each other and with adults outside the family.

Because of their observation and participation in playgroup sessions, parents offer a richer and more varied selection of play activities in the home. They feel more interested in what their children are doing and more confident and adventurous in ideas for their children and their friends. Other close family members and carers such as au pairs get involved in the playgroup too. At least one grandmother takes her place on the rota, and one father takes a turn when his work permits. Older children join in family sessions during school holidays. On the organisational side, one of the fathers is now the playgroup representative on the hall users' committee, and he has also acted as auditor for the playgroup accounts.

The main role of families is to support fund-raising events and to help in practical ways with maintenance and repairs. Most husbands of committee members are enlisted to help with preparations for the Christmas Fair. A group of them built the shed where the larger toys are stored. Some come along to social functions; others have to be 'dragged along' or rarely join in. The overall message conveyed by respondents was that families are supportive and value what the playgroup does, but essentially involvement is seen to remain in the female domain.

In terms of its impact on the village as a whole, members felt that the playgroup did not have much influence outside its membership. One member who is co-licensee of one of the village pubs and a relative newcomer to the village, feels that it is a good community with a lot of active small groups. Others who have lived in the village all their lives know that the many groups do not meet or mix. People polarise by age, sex and the length of time they have lived in the village. For example, younger women focus on the playgroup and village school, older ones on the Women's Institute.

The former chairwoman, speaking from her added insight as a parish councillor, said that a lot of the older Holbrook residents do not value the playgroup. They brought up their children without it and do not understand its purpose. She feels that it is not valued enough for the preventative social work it does; 'people don't appreciate the need for support for mums'. Several regretted that people not connected with the playgroup rarely attend its functions. A lot of effort and publicity went into a playgroup open night a year or two back but no one not already connected with the organisation attended. The experiences of the playgroup seem to reflect some latent antagonism between the 'old' village and the 'new', with the playgroup being associated, inaccurately, with 'newcomers'. Although some individuals are now building bridges between the PC, the hall committee and the playgroup, even after 25 years of continuous existence the playgroup committee still feels that their contribution to the community is undervalued.

A mother who is a G.P. in a neighbouring village has found Holbrook very difficult to break into. She and her husband went to the parish church but found little fellowship there and no new ideas. They left to join a church further away where the vicar is the same person but the people are very different. One respondent explained that 'it's the older people who do not like change and who rule what goes off'. From her professional perspective, the G.P. values the playgroup as a vehicle for childen to socialise and for young mothers to get together, to have a welcome rest from child care and for working mothers to have the opportunity to restart their careers.

The playgroup is seen by the Headmaster of the village school as a focal point in the community for families with young children. He values it for its preparation of the parent for school. Separation from the child can be traumatic for the parent; 'he just went; I felt empty'. The playgroup is a gentle way in for parents; 'it is a learning situation which many don't know they're in'. Through the links with Rising Fives, it enables parents to establish a relationship with school and to sort out problems before full-time education begins. It also provides the school with experienced parents who want to be involved with the Parent-Teacher Assocation to support the next stage of their child's education. All the eight parents who attended a recent AGM of the PTA had been or were still playgroup officers.

Playgroup is valued by the school as a preparatory step for children where they learn to get on with each other and with other adults. The Rising Fives link in with school playtime and assembly (which takes place in the village hall as there is no school hall) and children accept entry to full-time school as a natural progression. On a practical level, the playgroup gives the school reliable information about admissions for the following few years.

CONCLUSION

The nature of a playgroup as an organisation is governed by its membership and its purpose. The members are predominantly women under 40 years of age and children between 3 and 5 years of age. The life-span of membership is dependent on having childen of the right age and is thus limited. The purpose of a playgroup tends to place a number of inherent constraints upon external diffusion. It offers a practical service which demands no more involvement than a member chooses to give; the benefits of membership for the child can be gained from relatively limited commitment from the mother. The focal concern of the playgroup is its children, which tends to make it inward-looking. Often the playgroup appears to act as a 'first step' for younger women in bringing them into contact with wider associational life.

These features were observed in this case study. Holbrook playgroup responds to the needs of pre-school children in the village; the learning experienced by the children gives them a 'headstart'. The playgroup also has a substantial impact on its adult members, providing them with varied learning experiences at different levels. For some parents the playgroup is primarily a service for which they pay and which they value for their children. Some of these see playgroup as just a short stage in their child's development, a stage so short that 'it is not worth getting involved'. The researcher was told that most of those who declined to be interviewed came into this group. Some parents, anxious to give their children the best possible start in education, send them to the playgroup and a nursery, or two playgroups simultaneously, spreading their interest and financial commitment. This results in lack of any depth of involvement with any one playgroup and is a loss both to the organisation and to its learning potential for individuals.

Those who become regular helpers on the rota, who go on the committee and who take their turn at being one of the officers of the group recognise and value what they learn from the experience. They see their involvement as 'a whole learning exercise' and a beginning, sometimes of long term association with the playgroup movement, and sometimes of participation in a growing range of new activities. Some have already used that learning as the 'first step on the ladder' of activity in other organisations. As in other case studies, the benefit constantly stressed by members is the growth in their self-confidence. The discovery, within a friendly and non-threatening context, of the ability to form and express opinions, speak in public, make decisions and contribute in a team to the successful running of an event and a group, gives members the self-esteem, courage and inspiration to move onwards and outwards into other enterprises. A particular example of this growth in confidence has been observed in this case study, as well as in others such as West Kirby (Case Study 16). School teachers, competent and confident in the classroom amongst children, have spoken of their embarrassment and consequent withdrawal when faced with adult groups. Participation in a local voluntary organisation such as the playgroup has enabled them to develop assurance and ease in communicating and working with adults.

The impact of Holbrook playgroup both on its members and on the local community appears to be less rich and far reaching than, for example, that of Sibsey Women's Institute (Case Study 5) and Silverbridge National Women's Register Group (Case Study 1).

222

However, in the Silverbridge study it was noted that the effect of membership on the growth of interests 'is strongest on women who are beginning to emerge from heavy preoccupation with young children'. As the children of Holbrook playgroup grow in independence, their mothers will have more time to expand their own interests. Then they may recall the valuable learning gained from involvement with the playgroup and use it in fresh contexts.

Reference
[1] A useful survey of the work of the PPA and playgroups is presented in *Parents and Playgroups:* A study by the Pre-School Playgroup Association with foreword by Lady Plowden, 1981, Allen and Unwin, London.

Case Study 28

THE VOLUNTEER BUREAU'S CAR SCHEME, SUTTON-IN-ASHFIELD

INTRODUCTION

The Sutton-in-Ashfield Volunteer Bureau (SVB) is one of a network of such organisations set up and financed by the Nottinghamshire County Council with a contribution from the District Council, but governed independently by its own Management Committee. This includes 20% statutory representation, the rest being elected (mostly from voluntary organisations) at each AGM.

The Bureau supports voluntary organisations, particularly in their early days, involved in all aspects of community provision in Sutton-in-Ashfield. It interviews potential volunteers, about 80 a year, and places them with other voluntary groups. A women's group is supported, and also twenty play groups with the Bureau's mini-resources materials. Through an umbrella group it plays a large part in bringing together the statutory and voluntary sectors about six times a year. The Bureau is planning with the voluntary sector further consideration of support, training and insurance for volunteers. The staff, all part-time, consists of an organiser and five others, two of whom work on the mini-resources project and three on the car scheme.

SVB started the Voluntary Car Scheme (VCS) in 1988 as awareness of community car schemes grew, and in response to public demand. It is emphasised that the Bureau developed the scheme as an interim measure, and it expects the VCS soon to become independent. The VCS assists people with mobility problems, who need individual transport to particular places (for example hospital, shops or friends) which they cannot reach by any other means, to enable them to live as independent and active a life as possible. Those seeking to use the sevices of the VCS register with it. People requiring medical treatment are not taken as the drivers are not medically trained. The Social Services also use the VCS for helping families in distress. Drivers are reimbursed for the use of their cars by the Scheme at a standard mileage rate. The detailed organisation and running of the VCS has been in the hands of three staff since September 1992. Previously the receptionist did her work voluntarily. The three look after reception, bookings, allocation and accounts. The organiser and another member of staff are available for advice as required. Seven drivers are currently on the roster. They are volunteers, but they are not involved in the organisation or running of the Scheme; three of them, however, are members of the Management Committee. All decisions about whether or not to accept a request and allocating the driver are made by the receptionist.

Neither the SVB nor the VCS is thus a voluntary organisation in the strict sense in which the term is defined by our project. The SVB is what we have defined as a "volunteer employing agency" and the drivers - since they are in no way members of a coherent organisation nor responsible for managing their own activities - are its "agents", though unpaid. This case study would thus appear to be outside the remit of our project. It has been included and is recorded (though with deliberate brevity) for two reasons: in an area of gradual transitions it helps to define a place where a boundary has, as it were, been crossed, and it shows that some major benefits secured by local voluntary organisations as defined spill over into "agency" territory. Both giving and receiving of service by staff and volunteers result in personal learning and attitude change and make an impact which is transmitted to others and felt, however indirectly, in the community at large.

Six of the seven drivers, including Management Committee members, and 21 other respondents from SVB staff, the Management Committee, the District Council and various public services were interviewed, and the researcher is very grateful to all of them for their help.

Of the six drivers four are aged between 51 and 60, one between

225

61 and 70 and one is over 70. All had left school at the minimum age, 14 or 15. One used to run a family business and the others retired from or were made redundant by the mining industry. Two do other voluntary work in addition (as do several members of SVB staff); all had wanted to 'get out of the house' and had been recruited by the VCS through friends or advertisement.

SOCIAL EFFECTS

It is the SVB's policy to make its office a social and sociable centre for all who work there or visit, to make them feel both welcome and valued. Warm and good-humoured relationships are fostered and the atmosphere is entirely egalitarian. This is important for the drivers since both the contacts and the sense of being valued replace the social context of work they previously enjoyed. Both drivers and VCS staff find the Bureau 'provides friendship' beyond themselves, since senior staff, some Management Committee members and passengers or those calling on their behalf are included in this supportive network. For many of the passengers the Scheme is thus a 'lifeline' linking them to the outside world and enabling them to maintain social contacts. Those who make regular journeys tend to like having the same driver whenever possible, and friendships result. All the drivers report that users 'talk to us of their troubles' and 'like a laugh or a joke'.

EDUCATIONAL EFFECTS

Formal learning in the sense of support and training is organised by the staff 'to give confidence and achieve a sense of fulfilment'. It covers matters such as the eligibility criteria for users, finance, insurance and safety. Drivers quickly learn of the necessity to follow strictly the VCS procedures. However, the sociable and egalitarian ambience of the Bureau facilitates a very much wider range of informal learning based on open and constructive discussion and exchange of practical experience between drivers, senior staff, receptionists and Management Committee members. It should be borne in mind that some of the latter are able to contribute from their experience of work with the elderly. All those involved, however quiet to begin with, gradually find the confidence to take part.

The kind of informal and incidental learning which respondents

226

claim takes place includes especially a growing understanding of old people, their problems, their strengths and the difficulties which the behavioural characteristics of some of them can present. Drivers learn to recognise these, to be patient, but also resist the selfish or unreasonable demands of those who 'would keep you all day'. Typically, volunteers say 'now, I do listen to what people are saying' and one finds that 'you have to listen, then ask the right questions'. There is a growing understanding of the need to help the old to be as active as possible, to judge the degree of physical assistance they need in moving about or carrying loads, to give it sensitively as appropriate and, with equal tact, to withhold it.

OCCUPATIONAL EFFECTS

These were mainly found among the staff, but also to a growing extent among Management Committee members. All made substantial use of attendance at courses and conferences and the exchange of experience with other bureaux and schemes. They reported a variety of ways in which learning from work with the SVB and the VCS was developing their knowledge and skills in general, to the benefit of their other paid or voluntary activities in different contexts; 'I transfer to my voluntary activities what I have learned about evaluation'. This seemed to refer more particularly to the informal as well as formal inservice training for all concerned which is necessitated by rapid changes in legislation as it affects voluntary organisations concerned with personal and social service.

POLITICAL EFFECTS

The legislative changes, as well as the normal and inherent problems of personal service, have made all three constituent groups - Management Committee, staff and volunteer drivers - more aware of the political dimension of their activities. They have learned to question the status quo; why, for instance, is it assumed that it costs less to run a volunteer driver's car than that of a member or an employee of the County Council? One respondent spoke of having been 'politically naive, believing what one was told and accepting any financial help with gratitude'. In the face of new demands and complexities they have learned the need 'to question and negotiate', to collect and use statistics, write letters and generally campaign in support of their case for the funding needed to discharge growing tasks. Like so many others they find that all this takes a great deal of time which they feel ought to be spent on their real work. The Management Committee has learned to run a car scheme that is fair to staff, to the drivers and the users.

PERSONAL EFFECTS

Drivers and reception staff feel that working on the VCS has increased their self-esteem and confidence. 'Explaining things', 'discussing alternatives' and 'expressing my point of view' are now within their repertoire. One respondent who had 'not had confidence to learn anything' has found the courage now to attend evening classes and counselling courses. The drivers feel personally valued. Their services are appreciated and they are glad to be in a position 'to put something back into the community'. Being active and alert on a regular basis and carrying out useful work mean much to them. They claim changes in attitude and behaviour as a result of their work with the VCS and contact with their passengers. Thus they report that they show 'more patience with people, especially the elderly'. They are now more aware of the importance of communicating with 'the older generation', of 'giving them time to talk about their feelings'. They have become more patient with people, and listen constructively because 'when people want to talk about their troubles they will talk about something else first'.

Other Bureau staff and committee members confirmed what volunteer drivers said about themselves and they, too, report personal changes. One claims that voluntary work 'has changed me totally', for through it she has gained the confidence and skills to help the elderly. People have not only become more understanding of others but are convinced that they have grown in self-knowledge. They have also been strengthened in their convictions about the work of SVB and recognise the need to be 'persistent for what you believe in'.

EFFECTS ON OTHERS

Evidence about the transmission of learning was limited. Some drivers saw benefit in adopting in their domestic activities the disciplined approach to record keeping which the VCS requires of them. Families and friends of both drivers and committee members learn about the Scheme and the Bureau, and are at least tolerant and more often supportive. Drivers give their families and others an impression of what it means to have mobility problems, and how help can be given to those who are affected by them. They talk to their friends about the VCS and counter the lack of awareness of some 'who will be old themselves one day'. Friends and family attend social functions arranged by the SVB and they and a wider circle contribute regularly to fund-raising activities.

EFFECTS ON THE COMMUNITY

In the financial year 1992-3 approximately 8,600 journeys were made by the volunteer drivers and over 11,500 passengers were carried. In spite of this the VCS is not well known in the area generally except among the elderly, who pass on information about it by word of mouth. The Scheme is not advertised as the organiser believes there would be a surge in requests with which it could not cope. It does, however, contribute on a regular basis to the work of the statutory Social Services, who declare that they find it 'invaluable'. It develops the confidence and skills of drivers and other volunteers, and thus enables them to give a range of support to others who need it. In particular, the VCS helps those members of the community who have mobility problems to be active and remain as independent as possible. For them it delays or averts altogether the prospect of passive dependency and the closing of shutters. The users praise the friendliness, care and courtesy of the drivers; they are 'highly delighted' with the service and some say that 'they can't manage without it'. They contribute generously to fund-raising activities. If the Scheme is not well known as such, its effects are nevertheless widely transmitted because whatever it does for its immediate beneficiaries also benefits their families, their friends, and the services which would have to support them but for the maintainance of that mobility which the VCS provides.

Case Study 29

THE AEKTA CARERS' GROUP

Aekta is a word common to all the main Asian languages of the Indian sub-continent, meaning 'united' or 'oneness'. This name was chosen for the Asian Carers' Group in Derby to show that it aims to bring together people from all sections of the Asian community who care for relatives with a disability within the family home.[1] The need for such a group was perceived by the Development Worker for Asian People who, with the support of the Derbyshire Carers' Association, started Aekta about three years ago, and has been working with it ever since. She could see that Asian carers suffered isolation twice over; firstly because they had to stay at home for long periods of time with the disabled family member and secondly, partly arising from the initial isolation, because they were cut off by language and culture from many of the services and other voluntary groups which offer support to disabled people and their carers. The stereotypic view of the host community that 'the Asian community looks after its own' tended to confirm and intensify the isolation of Asian carers, who need support of the same range and quality as all carers.

By setting up this self-help group[2], the Development Worker was breaking new ground, at least in the Derby Asian community. Asian voluntary groups existed for political and religious purposes, but there was no tradition of self-help organisation for her to follow. For her, and for the recently appointed Community Worker for the group, this has been a learning process, and their experiences will be described alongside those of group members. The researcher is grateful to the Development Worker and the group's community worker for helpful interviews and especially to the five members who allowed her to visit them in their homes to talk about their experiences of group membership. Some of the interviews needed the services of an interpreter, and the researcher is grateful to the understanding and willingness of the young student who undertook this task. The views of the deputy head of the school where the group meets and some other related voluntary organisers were also sought. The researcher would like to thank all who contributed to this study.

THE GROUP AND ITS ACTIVITIES

Aekta currently has about 40 members on its books, but only a small number of these are able to attend meetings regularly. The fortnightly members' meeting is held in the community rooms of a centrally situated primary school. A weekly welfare rights surgery for members with individual problems is also held at the school, and since the appointment of a part-time Community Worker to the group, contact can be made for a few hours each weekday.

The group is run by a committee elected by its members which meets on a regular basis with the professional workers to plan for further expansion of the work of Aekta. The members define their needs and make decisions about the future direction of the group and the professionals assist them in finding the means to implement their schemes. For example, the members feel strongly that there is need for a respite care service to relieve them for short periods from their caring duties, and another voluntary group in Derby is undertaking a feasibility study for this. The members also brought forward the need for support to be available at weekends. In response to this, the Development Worker, the Community Worker and three or four other professionals are going to give up, on a voluntary basis, a weekend in rotation to be at the end of a telephone helpline.

The Community Worker is publicising information about Aekta on local radio and in hospitals, doctors' surgeries and Asian religious meeting places to try to make the self-help services offered by the group known to any Asian carer looking after anyone with any disability.

231

SOCIAL IMPACT

The importance of the group as a source of social contact was emphasised by all the respondents. Despite support from family and friends, carers feel that only other carers can really empathise with their problems; for then 'you feel better when you talk to each other'. They spoke of the value of sharing problems and difficulties with others in the same situation as themselves; 'you know you are not the only one'. One said that Aekta meetings help her to forget her worries, for a short time at least.

Members said how friendly the meetings are, and how willing people are to help each other in any way they can. Those who find difficulty in getting to meetings can be helped with transport, and those who can only rarely get to meetings telephone each other, or visit if they are near enough neighbours. They stressed how important it is to them that Aekta is an Asian self-help group. This means that language and culture are not barriers to be overcome. It is also significant to them that the group cuts across religions, and Hindus, Sikhs and Muslims work together to give each other mutual support and to improve the services available for carers. The experience of mixing together is an opportunity to extend social contact and especially to meet and work with people from different parts of the Asian community in Derby.

EDUCATIONAL IMPACT

The Development Worker explained that her initial aim had been to set up a social meeting point for carers, but very soon bigger problems were uncovered which demanded more work to solve. This became a learning experience both for her and for Aekta members and a further burden on the carers as they had to meet together to work out ways of solving their problems. This was a new experience within the Asian community which involved new structures and new kinds of meetings where decisions had to be made.

The chairman of the committee described how they had to decide whether to try to get their own base or their own worker first, and they made many applications to different funding bodies before they were successful in securing money to employ a worker. They then had to learn how to advertise the post and how to conduct interviews and choose the successful candidate. She explained that

232

they had chosen to appoint a male worker with the aim of encouraging more men to Join the group. She said that she had learnt what a lot of hard work is needed to run a voluntary organisation. The Community Worker has been in post since February 1993. It is his first Job, and his first months have been an intensive learning experience. He has been on courses organised by the local Council for Voluntary Service on Welfare Rights and on Assertiveness, and has learnt, with the support of the Development Worker, how to work with the Aekta members and how to support them and assist them to achieve their aims. He observes that the members are learning to articulate their needs more clearly and to expand their ideas now that they have the services of their own worker. The secretary confirmed this observation that Aekta is learning how to manage the new worker in order to make itself more effective. She has never been involved in any voluntary organisation before, but she feels that she is learning how to run the group better and how to make meetings more attractive to members. The chairman who has held that office since Aekta was formed feels that other members have expectations that she will be their leader. For this reason, and because her health is not good, she would like another member to take a turn at being chairperson.

All members have benefitted from the information which is collected and made available by the group about benefits and services to which disabled people and their carers are entitled. Speakers from the Department of Social Security have sometimes come to group meetings to answer questions, and the information is translated to members in their own language so that, perhaps for the first time, they can be fully aware of their rights. Members value the practical learning they gain from each other, sharing experiences of looking after someone with disabilities. One male member said that he wanted to learn how to look after his severely disabled son better, especially as he is himself growing older and finding it difficult to cope. He hopes that the group will be able to get funding for a 24 hour emergency and respite care service. He has found Aekta invaluable in enabling him to communicate with officialdom.

OCCUPATIONAL IMPACT
Being a carer is a full time occupation, so membership of Aekta can

233

have a substantial impact on all aspects of carers' lives. Aekta is already helping members to cope with their occupation, and as the group defines its needs and gets more experienced in finding ways of setting up responses to those needs, the burden of caring will be better shared.

For the Development Worker for Asian People, Aekta has been one of her major pieces of work over the past three years. She has found it a significant learning experience, which has been intensive and at times stressful. She is now supporting the new Community Worker in his learning, as he develops his skills of working with people in a voluntary group.

POLITICAL IMPACT

Involvement with Aekta raises the political awareness of both members and workers about the issues surrounding care in the community. The Development Worker feels that she, as a professional, as well as the public in general, have been misled about the Care in the Community policy. Contrary to expectations, there are no extra services or money available for improving care in the home. However, funding is channelled through community groups which means that the strength and activities of groups such as Aekta are now even more important. A carer group has to start an activity that is new and filling a gap in provision; it can then apply for money from Care in the Community to continue the new activitiy. Funding is not always available as Aekta found when its application for a substantial sum to provide respite care for members was not granted. It puts a great deal of responsibility on the group to be creative and to learn how to formulate strong bids.

The new system has involved both workers and members in learning about the strength and flexibiliity of a voluntary organisation and its freedom to campaign. Professionals often find their hands are tied, but a voluntary group can go public and can cut through some of the more bureaucratic procedures imposed on professionals. The Development Worker said that Asian self-help groups were having to learn 'British tactics' of canvassing support of people on committees and- getting publicity in local press and radio in order to get their voice heard. The chairman has learnt a great deal about the way self-help groups operate through her contact with other such groups in Derby. She has been to meetings

234

of representatives from different self-help groups and been asked to speak to them about Aekta's experiences. Another member also spoke of her growing awareness of the value of community action and the pressure that a voluntary group can exert.

The Community Worker said that until now he has not been politically active and working for even a short time with Aekta has made him much more politically aware. He has realised that minority groups suffer disadvantage because of the language barrier. Even when information is provided in Asian languages, it is often inadequate and bad translation distorts meaning. Asians who came to Britain as adults may, due to poor educational opportunities when they were young, be unable to read their mother tongue. He said that he is learning 'how hard it is for black groups to get started and to get funding' for their activities. The Community Worker who is a British born Asian has particularly valued the opportunity to help his own people. He feels that he is able to act as a bridge between the 'first generation' and younger Asians born in Britain. He is also learning more about his own cultural bacground and the culture and religion of Asian communities other than his own. He has experienced some problems, being a male Sikh, in establishing contact with Muslim women and remarked that he had learned how racial prejudice exists within the Asian community.

PERSONAL IMPACT

Members said how much they have grown in confidence through their membership of Aekta. The secretary said that being in the group has helped her to communicate better and to be able to put forward her point at meetings more forcefully. She feels she has become more assertive and more confident when insisting that she gets the help she needs. The chairman also said that she has gained enormously in confidence from being a member, and particularly from her position as chairman. Another member feels more self-assured when talking with her social worker and other professionals. She also feels better about herself and more confident that she can cope with her situation. The Development Worker has been in a good position to observe this growing confidence in members. She said that they became frustrated and discouraged in the early phases when there was little to show for all the meetings and discussion,but that they had persevered and now could see concrete results which they could demonstrate to other people. They have learnt to be assertive and to state their case forcefully. When one member recently went to a professional to state a problem and ask what could be done, the Development Worker was able to point out to her that she would not 'have had the confidence to do that a year previously. As well as self-confidence, Aekta has given its members self-esteem. They feel that now they are being listened to rather than just overlooked and forgotten. They are proud to be a self-sufficient Asian group, meeting their own needs. Their problems may not have gone away, but at least they are being recognised. The feeling that there is something that they can do together to bring about improvements makes their lives more bearable.

IMPACT ON FAMILIES AND FRIENDS

Membership of Aekta brings great benefit to the whole family of the carer. The disabled person, or people, in the family benefit from the increased access to services and the greater expertise and support that their carer gains from the group. It also brings the disabled person into more social contact if he or she is able to attend group meetings.

The whole family benefits from the support that Aekta gives to the main carer, because he or she feels better able to cope. This relieves the immediate family and other close relations of anxiety about where the carer can turn for advice and support and helps the whole family to feel that the burden of caring is shared. It is also a relief to friends to know that the carer is a member of a support group, as friends, however well intentioned, have their own families and problems to attend to.

WIDER IMPACT

Aekta is becoming better known within the Asian community and respected for its work. Members believe that there are still families who care for disabled elderly relatives in particular, who are isolated from help and do not know about the support that membership of Aekta can offer. They hope that more publicity will inform and bring in more members. They intend to build contacts with other Asian groups such as the Asian Women's Luncheon

Club, of which the chairman is a member. Aekta keeps in contact with the Derbyshire Carers Association (DCA) and its members are individual members of DCA. The executive director of DCA, with his experience of setting up 24 carers' groups all over Derbyshire, thinks that Aekta is an exceptionally good group with excellent aims which respect and address the particular needs of the Asian community. He feels that it is right that Aekta is a specialist group, now independent of DCA, as although language barriers can be overcome with good translations, cultural barriers are more difficult to cross within the very personal circumstances of caring situations. He confirmed that Aekta members had, in common with everyone organising a community group for the first time, learnt the skills of running a voluntary organisation. Aekta has built up contacts with other self-help groups and become part of the network of caring groups in Derby. Self-help groups that would like to extend their membership to include Asian sufferers of particular conditions have met and learnt from Aekta officers at Self-help conferences. In particular, links have been made with Umbrella, a self-help group which supports families with special needs children. Umbrella wants to improve its communication with the Asian community in Derby. Its co-ordinator said that at present the group do not feel that they are offering the same service to the Asian community as to others. Their translated leaflets have been criticised as inadequate and they feel that working alongside Aekta they could have more success in getting information to carers by word of mouth. Aekta's Community Worker is shortly starting a six month period of a weekly session of work at Umbrella's base in the Child Development Centre at Derby Royal Infirmary for the mutual learning of both groups. He said that he will value especially the experience of working alongside other workers rather than on his own. The staff of the Child Development Centre are looking forward to closer contact with an Asian group to whom they can make referrals of families who would benefit from the support of a self-help group.

At the school where Aekta meets and the Community Worker has his base, the group has earned respect for the work it does. The school has many Asian pupils and welcomes the opportunity to build links with the Asian community. One Aekta member who has some learning difficulties has been able to help the school by

237

working on a voluntary basis, with supervision, in the creche.

CONCLUSION
From the evidence of the interviews, Aekta has clearly involved learning at a number of levels. Its members have been supported and informed by its activities, have been given a sense of belonging which has alleviated their isolation, have learnt how to organise their group and make it effective and in so doing have gained confidence and self respect. The professionals working with the group have gained knowledge of how a self-help group can work within the Asian community and be a learning experience both for members and for those who support it. Within the Asian community, it is offering a model for other possible self-help groups, showing how a group organised by Asian people for Asian people can benefit its community.

As an Asian initiative, it has gained respect on the wider stage of self-help groups and voluntary organisations and is ready to share its expertise. It is contributing to greater understanding between Asian and white workers and volunteers in the voluntary sector. Working alongside Aekta is perceived by other groups and by professionals as one way of improving their communication and services to the Asian community.

References
[1] The term 'Asian' in the context of this case study refers to the communities whose countries of origin are India, Pakistan, Bangladesh and Sri Lanka. The Asian community in Derby is about 30,000 strong. Punjabis form the largest group; there are also significant communities of Pakistanis, Sikhs, and Kashmiris as well as smaller groups from other parts of the sub-continent. Although they speak many different mother tongues and dialects, Hindi is the lingua franca.

[2] There is a general note on the characteristics of self-help groups at the beginning of Case Study 8, page 97 of Vol 2 of these studies.

Case Study 30

THE LLANBERIS MOUNTAIN RESCUE TEAM

THE CASE STUDY AND THE CONTEXT

The Llanberis Mountain Rescue Team's area of responsibility covers the mountains on either side of that pass. These offer anything from simple walking to difficult and dangerous routes, and they expose those who explore even the simplest to the dangers of unexpected and sometimes severe weather conditions. In winter they can be deadly. Because these are the highest mountains within a weekend car journey's reach of anyone north of the Channel and south of the Border they attract numerous visitors of whom some are inexpert, ill equipped and irresponsible. Apart from these considerations of physical and social geography, the organisation was chosen to represent a number of varied factors in our typology. It is a public service group intended to deliver primarily individual assistance. It is an outdoor physical activity requiring considerable athleticism and a high level of competence. However, more perhaps than many such activities, it requires an array of intellectual and technical expertise; it makes considerable psychological and emotional demands upon its practitioners.

So far it might seem to have much in common with some other search and rescue services. Yet, in practice, the evidence suggests significant differences. Primarily these may spring from the fact that this is an autonomous and purely local organisation and in no way subject to external authority. Its discipline is real, but self-imposed. Another reason is, no doubt, that it draws upon a peculiarly individualistic group of people of which every single one must be capable of leading; it imposes upon them an ambiguous role which involves both great individual responsibilities and a willingness to entrust the task and their own lives to a team.

Since mountaineers are said to be individualists - indeed a law unto themselves - rescue teams differ greatly from each other in organisation and approach, and the Llanberis Team should not be regarded as representative. Rightly or wrongly, some of their comments could be interpreted as suggesting that they take some pleasure in regarding themselves as untypical. This appears to cause mixed feelings among some outside observers from co-operating services and organisations.

Members are not only busy and subject to the emergencies for the sake of which the Team exists; they are engaged in such a wide variety of duties, activities, expeditions and courses that getting hold of them for interview was - despite their own goodwill and their Secretary's patient energy - rather like counting chickens. A first trip to North Wales produced seven interviews with nine individuals of whom one was a non-climbing wife. Only one of the others was not in some way professionally involved in mountaineering. A representative of the RAF helicopter squadron which serves the area could only be interviewed by telephone. A second visit was arranged in order, more particularly, to interview some of the more recent team members, including people who make their living off the mountain and maybe representatives of the small proportion of women members. In the event two interviews resulted, one with with five members and one individual. All six were men and although they had full-time jobs in activities other than mountaineering they, too, were long-term members. It seems that there has been very little turnover in the team's personnel for some time, though recruitment of new members is now accelerating. The second visit also yielded interviews with co-operating public services (the police and the accident hospital) and, subsequently, a telephone interview with a senior officer of the regional and national mountain rescue bodies.

There was thus a total of 12 interviews. Seven of them involved altogether 13 team members (out of a total of about 45), and 5 were with a variety of observers. A questionnaire was distributed and 13 were returned. Findings from them will be discussed at appropriate points. The researcher is most grateful for the efforts which were made to set up interviews and for the generosity with which everyone who could do so responded.

THE GROUP

Informal rescue arrangements had existed locally for some time but, following a number of fatalities, the present formally constituted organisation was founded 25 years ago. The founding members were, and the Team remains, a mixture of competent local mountaineers from a variety of backgrounds and "professionals" such as National Park Wardens, centre wardens and mountaineering instructors from various outdoor pursuits centres. The team is linked to the North Wales regional and the national mountain rescue organisations but, like all others, remains strictly independent and self-governing through its officers and committee. However, it collaborates with the local police force who have overall responsibility for search and rescue and who help at base; with the ambulance service, and with the Royal Air Force whose own rescue organisation and especially its rescue helicopter are increasingly involved. Air Force personnel involved in mountain rescue volunteer for these duties and there is indeed fierce competition for them. Helicopters are used increasingly whenever practicable and rapid transport to hospital has transformed the prospects of accident victims. The effects upon the Team will be discussed later.

The radio communications equipment used by the Team is provided by the police; they, the ambulance service, the National Park and sometimes the RAF provide various forms of help in kind. At the outset, however, the Team had to raise its own funds and members still meet all their own travel costs and personal outgoings. Donations from victims and their families are the main source of funding for specialist equipment. Mountain rescue teams work formally on behalf of the police and members are insured by them. Fit members who wish to continue beyond the insurance age limit do so at their own risk.

The current membership of about 45 is organised in four "lists". Three of these contain active members with, between them, a balanced range of skills. The fourth consists of probationer members and of established ones who prefer to be kept in reserve. Alarms, whatever their source, are relayed to the police, who contact the "head of list" or in his absence the next in line. Actual call-out teams have often to be drawn from several lists in order to mobilise those who are most immediately available. Not surprisingly these often include professional mountaineers such as wardens and instructors who happen already to be on the mountain concerned. They and all Team members carry radios when out on the hills during potentially "busy" times and seasons, and some heads of lists carry bleepers.

The number of call-outs varies greatly not just over the calendar year but with climatic conditions. Recent mild winters have reduced the overall number of emergencies and the use of helicopters has reduced the number of occasions when the Team needed to be called out in addition to any members already on the mountain. A member who is in charge of one of the Team's bases reckoned that there had been about 60 rescues during the preceding twelve months, and that he had been personally involved in about 40 of these. Other members who might be less easily accessible score less heavily.

Unlike some other teams which provide such training, being a competent and fit mountaineer is a primary condition of membership in the Llanberis Team. Would-be members apply and are invited to join if they meet this basic criterion. They are then placed on the reserve list as probationers until they have acquired the necessary first aid, rescue and radio skills and established their personal suitability, after which they join an active list. Their backgrounds are very mixed; a scan of the records produced, apart from the professional mountaineers, ambulance personnel, teachers, plumbers, TV presenters, engineers, carpenters, civil servants, National Grid engineers, solicitors, butchers, GPO staff, a doctor, Countryside Commission staff and unemployed and retired people. Five are women.

The interpretation of both the interview evidence and that from the questionnaires is problematic because the researcher was unable to ascertain the degree to which the respondents were adequately representative of the membership. The information which was obtained from members and from their returns does seem to match comment from external observers, but on the other hand some of the questionnaire returns were very incomplete or even contradictory. Any general or numerical conclusions that may be drawn should therefore be regarded as tentative.

One closely involved external observer distinguished three groups among members: the National Park Wardens, who have their own hierarchical structure to which they pay a primary allegiance, with consequences he regarded as negative. His second group were local people with an interest in the work as such, and a third "expatriates" such as instructors and other mountain professionals who are immigrants to the area. The 13 questionnaire returns paint a slightly different picture. Eight (77%) are from natives of North Wales and 3 (23%) from English immigrants, only one of whom happens to be a mountain professional. Their age distribution is unexpected and probably significant:

-40: 0; 41-45: 3; 46-50: 4; 51-55: 4; 56-60: 1; 61-65: 1.

Nine of them (69%) have been members for 20 or more years (including 4 founder members) and 3 have been in the Team for 10, 15 and 18 years respectively.

Five (38%) were mountain professionals (four National Park Wardens and one centre warden); the other eight respondents included one small businessman, a civil servant, four in skilled manual or technician jobs and two graduate professionals. Only 11 terminal education ages were returned or could be reliably deduced. Four (31%) were minimal at 15, two left at 17, one each at 19 and 20 and 3 at 21 or later.

The amount of commitment was impossible to determine reliably from the replies. During the last, exceptionally quiet, year they had varied from 5 to 10 call-outs for 4 members, 10-20 for 3, and 25 to 60 for 6 of them. A call-out can, of course, be very brief or might last all night or longer, and attempts to arrive at a year's total of hours for call-outs, training sessions and other meetings failed. The range may well be in the region of about 100 to 250 hours in a quiet year.

Asked what previous experience had led them to join, members unanimously mentioned their mountaineering experience, whether acquired as an end in itself, a job, or in army service. Just one answered directly (the desire to provide help he hoped would be his if needed), though respondents to the interviews were more forthcoming.

A question about what they had had to learn as *members* produced nil returns from 3 of the professionals and it seemed significant that it was those who subsequently disclosed a wider variety of interests and leisure pursuits who admitted not just technical needs but personal skills such as co-operating with others under pressure, modern search techniques (2 only), looking after oneself and coping with distress and trauma in others. The question about which of these learnings in the Team had been passed on and to which other persons, found even more notable replies: none from 6 (46%) including 3 of the 5 mountain professionals, and communication skills were mentioned but once, all others being technical.

The usual attempt was made to obtain 'histories of participation' from the questionnaire returns, but the manner of completion of some at least made this difficult. It is clear, however, that all members were active mountaineers before founding, or joining, the Team. Most of them were, and continue to be, engaged in a variety of other physical outdoor activities in addition. It seems that the team and the learning experiences it provided invariably *followed from* these pre-existing commitments. Seven (54%) of the respondents had next to no other interests or activities, and these limited to outdoor and other physical pursuits. These included all 5 mountain professionals and 2 of those in skilled manual jobs. The other 6 (46%) followed a range of physical, craft and intellectual pursuits and public service activities, involving modest to extremely heavy commitments. These included the civil servant, the two professionals, the skilled technician, but also two members with minimum TEAs.

Members had started or were engaged in almost all the interests and activities which they listed quite separately from the Team. As a source of development or stimulus beyond itself the Llanberis Mountain Rescue Team thus seems to be among the least active of the organisations the Project has studied. Meeting people, ambulance work and industrial archaeology are mentioned once each, and becoming a voluntary Warden in the National Park twice. Members are, however, persistent. Very little has been given up as a result of joining the Team, and the few instances reflect age rather than waning interest.

As far as may be judged from the returns it seems that the Team is profoundly self-sufficient. It is an important part of its members' lives, but largely separate from the rest of their concerns and activities. For most of them it appears to be an end in itself, and such enthusiasm as there may be for a continuous development of their mountain search and rescue skills is often somewhat muted. Where a willingness to go on learning and to up-date skills is declared, it seems to go along with a variety of other, quite unrelated, interests and activities. It is most likely to be found among those team members who are not professional mountaineers, and are therefore called out less often. In this small and possibly unrepresentative sample there is no reliable correlation between willingness to learn and TEA. Finally, the age structure of the team as judged by their returns is significantly skewed towards the upper end; none came from members who were young or in early middle age, or from recent recruits, and the interview sample included just one such individual.

It must be stressed again that the degree to which the returns are representative is unknown. However, the individual histories and the group image they appear to project mesh remarkably with the outcome of the interviews. This follows, but it should be remembered that it covers almost exactly the same group of individuals, with the important difference that it includes the responses of outside observers.

PERSONALITIES, MOTIVES AND SOCIAL EFFECTS

Neither its own members nor outside observers regard Llanberis as "a typical team". The reasons given by the respondents differ less in their substance than in the values which *they* attach to them. Thus a number, when questioned about the part the team plays in their social lives, described themselves as 'outsiders, individualists or introverted'. An observer said the team 'has become a kind of anchor for many of these' and for some 'their sense of the team is so great, if you took it away they'd become virtually shells'. Given predominant personalities, this observer thought it might be their strong sense of autonomy which bred 'a reputation of being isolationist or even parochial'. The awareness expressed by most members that the frequency of helicopter rescues has reduced their own involvement and practice is echoed from the viewpoint of co-operating services as a claim that not all team members co-operate as readily with the helicopters as the primacy of the casualty's interests would suggest.

Attitudes differ widely, however, because of the great variety of personalities within the Team, which is a source of its strength. Naturally social lives are disrupted, especially at busy times, but the Team has the primacy: 'Every mountaineer is a very selfish person (says one with numerous other interests and a record of public service!) ... we *become* a team' and, in the process, learn perhaps grudgingly a certain amount of social flexibility, 'get used to mixing with each other.' However, 'you get to know people very well if you're on the end of a rope.' As a mixed group of local people it is the shared and not uncommonly testing experiences over many years which are the major factor in forging these close relationships with a deep, perhaps almost physical, sense of mutual reliance at their centre. In its early days there was more of a Team social life, but this seems now to be confined to an annual Christmas party with spouses and the occasional drink at the end of a call-out in the pub next door to the Team's headquarters. However, the friendships forged in the early days continue as a network of relationships which pervades the whole group and binds it together. Some regret the loss. 'We were a lot on the hill together ... a camaraderie developed ... nobody likes accidents but we had a lot of fun together.' With a reduced number of call-outs there is less of this social satisfaction and one respondent is 'a little bit sad that a bit of our social lives has fallen apart.'

Having established the sense of mutual knowledge and reliance upon each other as mountaineers which gives the Team its strength, their relationships to-day are primarily *not* social. The fact that "professional mountaineers" with their own hierarchy and allegiance form such a high proportion of the most active team members affects the pattern as well as individual motives. Most of the professionals and some other old-established members see rescue work simply as part of their mountaineering. On the other hand a group consisting of "non-professional" members were unanimous in seeing the Team's work as a separate activity whose purpose was 'putting something back into your pastime ... putting something into people's minds when you're on the hill'. For one at least it started from the experience of 'being lost and found'. It is interesting that the agreed statement contains two separate objectives: to give a service to one's interest community, and to teach people about mountaineering and the life of the hills.

EDUCATIONAL EFFECTS

The outside observers summed up both the strengths in the Team's educative functioning and the learning problems it now faces. Unlike some other teams (which provide such training as may be needed) it insists on mountaineering competence as a precondition of membership, but all the search and rescue skills have to be developed in service. Expectations, especially in search methods, first aid and interpersonal skills, are rising. They emphasise the need for training, but participation in it is said not to follow invariably. Because of the lower accident rate and the short-circuiting of rescues by the use of helicopters there is less opportunity to develop and maintain proficiency through field practice, and initial and inservice training are all the more important.

The region is fortunate since a systematic and well articulated scheme of specialised mountain first aid courses is available locally. It was originally developed here but is now nationally and internationally recognised. Since the courses are attended by doctors, nurses and ambulance personnel as well as members of all teams from the region, they are an opportunity to learn from each other and forge close relationships between services. They have resulted in a number of changes of occupation, including two course members (from other teams) who were inspired to become mature students and are now fully fledged doctors working elsewhere. The number of Llanberis Team members who have attended the standard course is unknown; only two or possibly three were said to have been to the advanced one.

Regional courses of internationally recognised standard are also available on modern methods of conducting searches, and there are similar high level courses on interpersonal skills, including interviewing and communications - areas of learning with which the sponsors find 'introverts need a lot of help'.

What members themselves say they have learned varies in range and balance as one would expect from such individualists. It seems best to start with a full but abbreviated account of one response. In his view the Team's training functions and exercises are now substantial and make up a structured training programme for everybody, probationers and inservice. The call-out lists have been reorganised in accordance with this. First aid courses are being

247

provided for the Team and some others. Specific training in rescue skills includes stretcher work, cliff rescue, helicopter practice, work with the Team's two search dogs and radio communications. In this process people acquire greater self-knowledge: they become acquainted with their limitations as well as their strengths. They learn how to judge conditions, practicalities, priorities. They come to understand the risks which arise from peer group pressure, for instance to press on regardless when conditions are such that they should not. They learn to judge and, where necessary, to try and modify the motivations of team members and to develop the actual composition of the call-out lists and of rescue teams accordingly. They learn to judge each other's individual potential and to plan, lead and co-operate accordingly. They come to accept unusual individuals and develop mutual trust. They have come to realise that team members need to be psychologically prepared for the stress of coping with injury, death, bereavement, and for giving support to fellow Team members dealing with them, as well as to those directly affected.

All this implies a great deal of organisational learning, not just that of the individual, in the sense that the Team becomes the repository of a continuously developing stock of experience and skill. As an instance of highly developed individual skill and judgment, as well as continuous organisational learning for performance development, it compares closely with Case Study No. 14, the Newstead Abbey Singers. The distinction is that here there is no equivalent to a professional conductor since all are by definition professional amateurs; it is a group of highly individualistic performers without any "expert" individual in charge, learning to act and sometimes to learn together.

Others add their individual details to the general account. Apart from the obvious technical content which all mention and the development of improved mountaineering skills to which a very few admit, they include team work and team decision making and the confidence to rely upon each other. Members learn to think about their experience as it is acquired, to understand its implications, remember it as part of the Team's own accumulated store, and above all to make constructive use of it. They learn to cope with their and other people's traumas in face of injury, pain and distress. 'It's coping skills; coping with the sort of conditions people shouldn't be out in, coping with pain, with the shock of victims, with supporting the victim's companions. One gets hardened but what I can't get over is when it's kiddies.' No team member can escape learning to 'make very hard life and death decisions ... to look at real human suffering ... and to match the situation.'

The skill of leadership and the ability to deploy it is important in all this. As with Case Study 5 (Sibsey Women's Institute) there is a three-year limit on tenure of the chair. On actual rescues it is the head of list who leads the team, but there is always an initial discussion of how a particular problem is to be tackled, and consensus is achieved. This means people have to learn to discuss systematically but also quickly, to recognise and home in on essentials. Heads of list will therefore consult or even hand over leadership if someone more experienced turns up, and authority shifts according to what is required in the particular instance or process, such as skills on rock, or in first aid. Because they are a team of equals of whom all possess recognised expertise, all have to learn to be capable of leading, and this means all have to learn to work with people, however crusty they may be. All of this feeds gradually into the historic experience of the Team as a whole. A few of the respondents were very conscious of this, and of the need to ensure that all members have such completely unobstructed access to it that organisational learning becomes intuitive skill available to all, as well as sensitivity to its expression, from whatever source.

Only one respondent (one of the "professionals" as it happened) expressed strongly positive feelings about the value of course provision from outside and particularly regional courses and co-operation with other teams in both known and new techniques. Nevertheless 'first and foremost you're a mountaineer; mountain rescue is secondary'. This is because, in his opinion, a rescue team has to 'be very low profile (if the) wrong ethos isn't to creep in'.

'Working on the team has made me very safety-conscious' and has caused this and a few other members of the team to use not just any formal training function they may carry but informal contact on the hill to give preventive advice. There is probably much more of this than became evident in the interviews, when members seemed intent upon keeping up the introverted and stiff-upper-lipped mountaineer's image. The practice of seeing oneself hardly as a teacher but more as a leaven in the lump of all those who frequent these hills, trying to help people to enjoy them in safety as well as finding, caring for, or rescuing them when necessary, is likely to be far more common among the respondents than their traditions allowed them to admit.

OCCUPATIONAL EFFECTS

One of the observers found that what these effects are depends very much on the work people do, but whatever they have learned by way of 'interpersonal skills, confidence, self-discipline is bound to spill over' into it. In the case of the "professional mountaineers" the transfer of learning from the work of the Team to their jobs was as clear as that from mountaineering to rescue skills, which were regarded quite simply as an extension of the job. 'Any mountaineer', as one of them rightly said, 'would always help', but may not often be a skilled rescuer. Though it was not stated it must therefore be assumed that knowledge, skill and understanding acquired as Team members also improve the occupational competence of those who make their living on the mountain. It may be 'a small part of the job, but it colours my attitude to it ... makes it much more interesting. Some of my fondest memories are of rescues.'

At the simplest level some of the team members become first aiders at work. Knowledge of injuries and first aid to an advanced level assists another member directly in his work in Health Service administration. However, experience of team work and team decision making and consequent mutual reliance is even more important in administrative processes. This effect was more fully expressed by a small group. Their first reaction was to stress that their professional performance in their jobs could, but must not, be affected 'if one happens to have been out all night'. They are conscious of their professional competence being raised by their team experience of rushed decision making, of management under stress, where the quality of the decision can nevertheless be a matter of life or death. All these crisis experiences expand understanding and affect the value of any advice they might give in their very responsible work. They also feel they have become better organisers and managers because they have learned both to shoulder and to share or indeed hand over responsibility and choice to others, to develop co-operative groups which are greater than the sum of their individual parts. Another member finds that 'the translation of experience into example' is fundamental to good leadership wherever it is performed. So is the 'conducting relationships on a personal rather than a bureaucratic level, the building of rapport with people (which) tends to getting things done'. In all this 'empathy is crucial' and this informal element in leadership is the most important contributor to success in team building which he has translated from team experience to his practice at the head of a large institution.

POLITICAL EFFECTS
Some interviews produced a nil response under this heading, even when prompts were used. An outside observer thought most members' service was conceived by them as being to the Team, and inward-looking, rather than consciously based on wider social concepts. One small group seemed not greatly concerned about linking the Team with the idea of active citizenship. These responses may, of course be part of the severely minimalist and understated ethos typical of this organisation. 'To help other people' as a social or civic objective, or 'to put something back into the community' are admitted to after some prompting. If anything, however, it is more a sense of gratitude for one's own experience of the mountains that causes rescue work to be seen as a grudgingly admitted categorical imperative: 'people feel they've got something to contribute' and, therefore, 'why shouldn't they?' rather than an unadmitted but deeply felt 'they ought to'. On the other hand these and others were concerned about public or governmental decisions which affect their work or the quality of the service they are able to deliver, such as a change of helicopter type, the imposition of VAT on rescue equipment, and the spectre of litigation conjured up by recent EEC draft regulations. The extreme position was illustrated by one member, something of a conscientious anarchist, whose main concern, beyond dislike of all 'rules and regulations', was any risk of a paid rescue service being imposed and 'the undermining of the quality of the social fabric' by handing over voluntary work, or its control, 'to paid people'.

The turnover in the chair of the Team is thought by some

251

members to secure a significant degree of democratic movement. 'At the end you do feel you're doing *some* good ... but people do it because they want to, they *enjoy* doing it. It's fun and you're bound to laugh about something, especially if X is with you.'

There was a significant number of exceptions to these cautious responses. One member quite firmly stated that membership of the Team was his first experience of public service, that it triggered off his active interest in it, and this led into committee service, youth work and local politics. One of the outside observers thought Team members were more likely to be active in their local communities than the average. A solely "non-professional" interview group firmly if modestly admitted to a public service motive, and most of these were also church wardens, local councillors, volunteer wardens, members of committees, involved with environmental issues and quite used to 'picking a fight with local government when necessary'. But, unlike the one individual whose response has been mentioned, they saw no one-way causal relationship between mountain rescue and these interests. They were, like everyone else, very independent, not to say isolationist, and proud of it. Members may be quietly conscious of being engaged in an important and demanding voluntary public service operation, but most would be embarrassed to admit it.

PERSONAL EFFECTS
The stiff upper lip and the habit of hard-boiled understatement extend to many of the responses under this heading. Indeed, one external observer's response fell into the same category. He was 'unaware of any problems arising in members. They're very tough sort of people.' Other observers did note personal developments. Referring to the great responsibilities borne by members, one of them said that 'people either are or become good in all sorts of crises. So they tend to be called on for other difficult or critical tasks ... in their communities.' Another spoke of notable growth in self-confidence and in personal authority and self-sufficiency. Members become more articulate because of 'the constant discussion about techniques'. Even quiet people are gradually brought out by this process: 'the activity itself forces them to participate in the discussions and stand up for their own opinion'.

Among members who felt able to speak of changes in themselves

252

there was a wide range. One argued himself gradually into admitting to himself that he had needed to get 'hardened' because his perception of pain and suffering had become more acute. This, he thought, was the reason why 'you develop an in- built safety device' in the form of grim humour and jokes when dealing with fatalities. Two spoke of their much wider and deeper awareness of the causes of accidents in general, and of their attempts to teach people about them - including, of course, the Team's own useful safety leaflet addressed to all who come to their area. However, 'I think that life is a dangerous business and we should all be prepared to take a reasonable risk with it'. For this member this means taking the risk of human contact through team membership, using it as his 'bridge to humanity'.

In one of the groups the possibility of personal change was firmly denied in the first instance. There was a complete reversal later as they came to talk about the effect of their experience of deaths, and especially those of children, and of supporting relatives or companions. They felt they had developed qualities such as understanding, tact, patience, empathy, especially for victims' families or companions. In short, they had learned to 'deal with tragedy'. They, too, spoke of acquiring a grim humour, and described it as a veneer to make their own pain bearable. At a quite different level they pointed out that they had learned to sink their own personalities to the extent of being able to work in a team regardless of who was leading, and with other services regardless of who would earn kudos.

This deeply personal change of attitude may well arise in part from change to a more mature form of motivation. 'My attitudes have changed. In the past it was my own adventure. It's a buzz, the adrenalin was going. But now, I think more about the person that's injured. It isn't the adventure now, it's coping with fear, exhaustion. It makes you think more about things.' Another respondent went into some detail about the actual process of learning and change. Service with the Team has taken him 'into extreme situations and these experiences are subsequently a source of 'a sense of well-being' because 'you've done it and got home'. What follows is that 'I can reflect on situations and coping in them' and this, in turn, becomes a means of both self-discovery and inter-personal understanding: 'it's strengthened and deepened my understanding of myself and others ... I've felt fear and I still go on the hill ... it gives me an inner searching.' In practice 'it's prepared one for all sorts of difficult situations, from meeting media, coroner, comforting families ... It's widened my experience of life ... and the difficult experiences certainly strengthened me ... Every time you place yourself in unique situations, and you discover that because you have to, you can ... It played quite an important part in my growing up and possibly it's satisfied some sort of desire to help.'

This abbreviated personal account of what must have been a process which took years found a curious echo in one of the group interviews. When these respondents were first presented with the question whether they were aware of any personal learning or change in themselves that had resulted from their service with the Team they began with the usual understatements in masterly form. They claimed to be at least as egotistical as most climbers; 'I was there' was the important thing about rescue work. What was interesting was the way this discussion developed from that point, without any further intervention from the researcher. Yes, what had been said was true as far as it went. But should it not be considered in relation to the effort, adaptation and quite possibly self-sacrifice that goes into team building at this level? They also accept and learn to deal with the emotional stress that is part of rescues. True, there is satisfaction in saving the injured, but 'it's grim that nothing's gained when they're dead'. This is why the strain has to be relieved by humour.

All these accounts, and others reported in earlier sections, recall much recent discussion of post-traumatic stress experienced by members of other rescue services and their need for counselling to relieve it. Neither of these currently chic terms happened to be used by any of the respondents. It seems that the Llanberis Team has evolved its own ways of recognising and dealing with this syndrome by means of the group's own recognition of the experience, and the mutual support of its members. It *may* be that a small, informal and autonomous group enjoys certain advatages over a disciplined service in this regard, possibly because the latter isolates individuals from each other to the extent that it focuses them on the service rather than each other.

But 'dealing with people - death, serious injury - focuses the mind on things - life, the world.' 'Dealing with dead people has forced

254

me to think out my position about God, the existence of a human spirit' or, in the case of other respondents in this group, to abandon and cope without religious belief. They were quite clear that they were learning 'to talk things out' even at this level, to be sensitive to the need of both team members and the injured and those with them, readier to listen. Maturity is being developed all the time but is also continually required of them. In any case rescue work, with its built-in demands and extremes has 'the attraction of dealing with the unknown; you're more alert ... stretched mentally and emotionally.' Respondents felt that the work forces them to grow, to get closer to their potential, to be 'more intensely alive'.

EFFECTS ON FAMILY AND OTHERS

Both the modesty of members and difficulties in making arrangements mean that evidence under this head is very scanty indeed. Here especially the idea (perhaps the pretence?) that rescue work is no more than common-and-garden mountaineeering came into its own. Wives were said to be fellow-mountaineers anyway and therefore unaffected and uninfluenced. The one mountaineering wife of a member whom the researcher met by chance and managed to interview briefly fitted this image perfectly and came out pat with the standard hard-boiled reactions.

Mountaineering does indeed very largely run in families, and several members took proper pride in the achievements of their sons; one respondent's son-in-law had followed him into the Team. Daughters, maybe by chance, got no mention. One or two members had passed on to family and friends some of their interest and skills in first aid and some taught it formally. In some respects it was again the outside observers who were either more aware of some of the true situation or at any rate willing to discuss it. According to them team members are frequently using their first aid skills in the home and the neighbourhood. They also tend to be called in to deal with local accidents on the roads, farms, and diving accidents in the lakes. Within the village there is some degree of open hostility to the idea of people 'wasting their time and money' on irresponsible strangers. 'Why don't you just leave them up there?' Nevertheless members tend to become the first port of call when there is a crisis or a problem to be solved in the village, whether it happens to be a lost dog, or sheep, or first aid to a neighbour.

A surprisingly high proportion of team members (other than the National Park wardens) are self- employed and single-handed. Those who are in jobs with other people *are* seen differently, though rarely with much understanding except by fellow mountaineers. However, people turn to them for first aid, and they are usually asked about the outcome when the media report a rescue.

However much the effects beyond themselves may be played down by the members, skilled long-term observers do see them. 'I see people developing over the years and it's bound to feed into their work. It also results in their being seen differently, gives them "kudos"; people know that they're in the Team.' The same respondent also suggested that the changes - personal growth and maturity, ability to discuss and tolerate disagreement, ability to take and to hand over responsibility - would inevitably affect the lives at least of members' families and their eventual behaviour and contribution.

In so far as it was mountaineering experience that had affected members' behaviour and impact on others it clearly could not be claimed - nor was it - that rescue experience was responsible. Nevertheless one of the interview groups felt that, given the very great changes which that experience had worked in them, 'it's bound to have an effect on how I deal with other people' and, therefore, what may be transmitted through them. One of this group, at least, claimed that the depth and quality of the learning he had done as a team member had had 'a notable effect' on the depth and quality of his management teaching.

Only one group admitted that family support was essential to them in rescue work, and not only because by definition it is bound to disrupt routine, and does so most of all at holiday times and weekends. The one non-mountaineering wife of a long- term member whom the researcher was able to ask about her experience made it only too clear. She had learned to cope, after a fashion, with the fear when he is called out. 'It doesn't get less but I know now that if I can be on my own and get on with some work I can cope with it. But I'm very angry and bad- tempered with him when he comes home. It all comes out then.'

EFFECTS ON THE COMMUNITY
One interview group thought that theirs was mostly a service

256

required by visitors to the area. In providing it they are an asset to the police and may co-operate with others, but they could not see how this might be regarded as a contribution to the quality of life of the area. They seemed intensely embarrassed and tongue-tied on the topic. This understated attitude seemed to be general. Yes, they do educate the public in groups and individually in matters of safety and responsible mountaineering, respecting and loving mountains rather than trying to arrogantly battle with them. (Why was it this respondent had refrained from disclosing that information when asked about any teaching they do?) Yes, they do co-operate with the relevant public bodies. But none of this seemed to involve any awareness (or admission?) on the part of this respondent and others who reacted like him that these were services to the public and a positive contribution to the quality of their lives. 'I could be next. It's the attitude of people doing the same thing. You do what you wish they'd do for you.'

Others were prepared to admit the public service element while defending themselves staunchly against any imputation of that being their motive: 'I look at it as something I'm lucky to be able to do and enjoy doing' and he certainly does not regard himself as an active citizen. It was observers again, and a minority of members who were prepared to break through their own defences. 'There must be some impact from the fact that we display a sense of duty and put something back into climbing, don't just take the fun.' But this respondent certainly did not feel that this gives the team 'a high profile' in the local community. It was a skilled outside observer who was aware of both local criticism and local need: 'the community looks to them as a source of help and confidence, someone to turn to in a time of trouble or a minor crisis.'

A member with opportunities to take a wide view thought that the village was very much aware of the Team and of the fact that its service is voluntary, but he saw no evidence of it changing the quality of local life. On the contrary, he was very much aware that local people are critical of the Team because they object to climbers who are "foreigners" and who are a nuisance when they have accidents. However critical, they nevertheless turn to team members when they have a crisis of their own. Farmers do so regularly for animal rescues. It means that in so far as the team contributes to the quality of life it does so mostly by saving those

257

of visitors (on whom the local economy depends!), and only incidentally and without acknowledgment or their own admission, for locals.

All this ignores the influence, albeit modest, which the experience of individual members exerts directly or indirectly upon their own contributions to public life, and which was recorded in the appropriate section of this study. Given the extreme modesty of the respondents, the researcher was lucky to witness two significant events. When he arrived at one team member's home he had just been called out and was standing in his kitchen, rapidly eating bread and cheese and drinking a mug of coffee to prepare for an expedition of unknown duration, while rehearsing in his mind the precise territory of the accident and the condition of the rock as he had investigated it that very morning, thinking there might be trouble in that area later in the day. - While the researcher was interviewing another member at one of the Team's bases, another called in briefly. He was taking himself and his dog for a Sunday afternoon stroll on the hill but, as a matter of course, picked up a radio set in case he should be wanted.

It is in the nature of mountaineering that even experienced and responsible practitioners may have accidents, or simply fall ill. Of the difference it makes to all in the area that there is, at all times, a substantial number of experts ready to leap into action when needed, there can be no doubt. Neither should their impact in teaching more sensible mountaineering be under-estimated. The Welsh Tourist Board has given the Team a medal for service to the community - evidence if any were needed that here is as direct and immediate an instance of an area's quality of life being improved by the action of a local voluntary organisation. But it was pure chance that the researcher learned of it.

APPENDIX A

AIDE MEMOIRE FOR GROUP INTERVIEWS (COMPRESSED)

BACKGROUND (collect separately as far as possible and supplement in interview)
1. Factual information about the catchment population, brief description of the town and its services as relevant to the survey.
2. Group pogrammes, activities, initiatives, membership over the years.

B. IMPACT ON MEMBERS
1. Sociable (e.g. company, friendship, something to do together with others, a new range of activities, relief from other social circumstances, etc.
2. Educational and Cultural (eg learning about things or ideas, undertaking new activities, appreciating new things or activities, learning to learn, learning to co-operate, learning to discuss, to tolerate and value other opinions, learning to take responsibility, learning to organise, etc.
3. Occupational (eg have any of the educational, social or personal learnings affected the ways in which members conduct their occupational activities inside / outside home? Have they affected the ways in which members are perceived by other people in these contexts? Have they affected the nature and scope of these activities? etc.
4. Political (eg has members' awareness of social / civic / political issues at any level changed? Has their level of participation changed? etc.
5. Personal (are members aware of any changes in themselves that would be due partly or wholly to the experience of membership, eg in their tastes, interests, use of time, competencies, confidence, self-knowledge?)

C. INDIRECT IMPACTS ON MEMBERS' FAMILIES / PERSONAL CONTACTS
As for B.:
1. Social
2. Educational
3. Occupational
4. Political
5. Personal

D. INDIRECT IMPACTS ON MEMBERS' OCCUPATIONAL CONTEXTS
1. In home as an occupational base }
                       } (using same headings as appropriate)
2. On people at work outside home }
3. On the organisation / structure of work (a) at home and (b) job

E. ANY WIDER ORGANISATIONAL / CULTURAL / CIVIC / POLITICAL IMPACTS
1. as an organised group
2. as individuals

APPENDIX B

SUPPLEMENTARY INDIVIDUAL QUESTIONNAIRE
(compressed)

1 Have you always lived in Holbrook (or near Holbrook)? Yes/No
2 If your answer was 'No', how long have you lived here? .....years
3 From where did you move to or near Holbrook?
4 How long have you been a member of the Playgroup?
5 How many of your children have been members of the Playgroup?
6 Please ring your age group: 20-30, 31-40, 41-50
   and the age at which your formal education (school, college etc) ended: 15 16 17 18 19 20 21 22 23 24+
7 What is your present occupation (please indicate full or part time), or what was your last paid employment?
8 Do you belong to any other organisations (including clubs, groups, professional, religious or political organisations) as well as the Playgroup? Please list all of them.
9 Have you attended any classes, courses or conferences as an adult? Yes/No - Please list briefly any you attended in the last 5 years and underline those which were arranged by the playgroup or the PPA.
10 Please list any other interests and leisure activities you have.
11 Please look again at your answers to 8, 9 and 10. Which of the organisations, activities and interests would you say grew from involvement with the Playgroup?
12 Please feel free to add any comments or information you think might be helpful.